Current
Directions
in
BIOPSYCHOLOGY

READINGS FROM THE
ASSOCIATION FOR
PSYCHOLOGICAL SCIENCE

Current
Directions
in
BIOPSYCHOLOGY

EDITED BY
A. Courtney DeVries and Randy J. Nelson
The Ohio State University

Boston • New York • San Francisco
Mexico City • Montreal • Toronto • London • Madrid • Munich • Paris
Hong Kong • Singapore • Tokyo • Cape Town • Sydney

Acquisitions Editor: Michelle Limoges
Editorial Assistant: Christina Manfroni
Marketing Manager: Kate Mitchell
Production Editor: Patty Bergin
Editorial Production Service: TexTech International
Composition Buyer: Linda Cox
Manufacturing Buyer: JoAnne Sweeney
Electronic Composition: TexTech International
Cover Administrator: Linda Knowles

For related titles and support materials, visit our online catalog at www.ablongman.com.

Between the time website information is gathered and then published, it is not unusual for some sites to have closed. Also, the transcription of URLs can result in typographical errors. The publisher would appreciate notification where these errors occur so that they may be corrected in subsequent editions.

Library of Congress Cataloging-in-Publication Data

Current directions in biopsychology : readings from the Association for Psychological Science / edited by A. Courtney DeVries and Randy J. Nelson.

   p. ; cm.

   "Reprinted as [they] originally appeared in Current directions in psychological science."

   Includes bibliographical references.

   ISBN-13: 978-0-205-59748-2
   ISBN-10:   0-205-59748-3

1. Psychobiology.
   [DNLM: 1. Psychophysiology—methods—Collected Works. 2. Behavior—physiology—Collected Works. 3. Brain—physiology—Collected Works.
4. Mental Processes—physiology—Collected Works. WL 103 C976 2009]
I. DeVries, A. Courtney. II. Nelson, Randy Joe. III. Association for Psychological Science. IV. Current directions in psychological science.
   QP360.C87 2009
   612.8—dc22

                    2007051145

Printed in the United States of America

10 9 8 7 6 5 4 3 2 1   11 10 09 08

Contents

Current Directions
Directions
in
BIOPSYCHOLOGY

Introduction

Biopsychology emphasizes the interaction between biology and behavior. One major goal of this subdiscipline of psychology is to understand the biological bases of cognition, affect, and behavior. This has taken two broad approaches: (1) the comparative approach, which examines the evolutionary and adaptive relationships among species, and (2) the neuroscience approach, which examines the molecular and neural mechanisms underlying brain function and structure. Biopsychology represents the area of psychology that morphs from a social science into a life science. Increasingly, however, other subdisciplines of psychology have successfully adopted biological approaches to the study of behavior. Indeed, biological influences have seeped into studies of virtually all aspects of psychology. For instance, social and personality psychologists have become conversant with evolutionary concepts in their studies of traits, prejudice, and even physical attraction. Many cognitive psychologists have forsaken black boxes in favor of fMRI brain scans, and clinical psychologists have adopted behavioral pharmacology in detail to facilitate the mental and physical health care of their clients. Some psychologists, with interests in biological influences on behavior, have coalesced into a new subdiscipline, evolutionary psychology.

We have divided the papers included in this reader into five sections. The first section, "Genes, Evolution, and Behavior," contains papers that examine the genes and evolutionary processes underlying behavior. These changes in behavior require long periods of time and many generations. In contrast, Section 2, entitled "Plasticity," is comprised of papers about plasticity, or changes in behavior within the course of an individual's life. This topic is usually considered in the context of learning and memory, although other psychological processes, such as stress adaptation or depression, may involve brain plasticity.

Section 3 contains papers that explore plasticity in the context of "Resilience," or the ability to recover or adapt physiologically and behaviorally to stressors. This capacity to cope with stress is critical to survival. Indeed, stress-induced anxiety and depression are associated with a myriad of life-threatening health conditions. Non-resilient individuals are likely to die prematurely and leave fewer offspring than individuals with good stress coping abilities. The selected readings emphasize that both genes and environment contribute to resilience.

Whereas the articles in the Sections 2 and 3, addressing plasticity and resilience in the brain, highlight how experiences throughout life can alter brain structure and function, the articles in Section 4, entitled, Drugs, highlight that ingestion of substances also can induce persistent changes in the brain, in turn affecting behavior long after the drug use has ceased.

Indeed, sometimes individuals abuse drugs, such as cocaine, amphetamine, opiates, nicotine, and alcohol to cope with stressors, anxiety, or depression (i.e., self-medication). In addition to the well-described pharmacological influences of drugs, there are strong environmental and psychological factors modulating their effects on the brain and behavior. Placebo effect studies clearly demonstrate the potential for the mind to alter physiological states, and emphasize the importance of understanding the psychological components of drug effects on the body.

In the final section of this reader, entitled, "Health," papers are included that explore the interactions among the nervous, endocrine, and immune system to influence well-being and optimal functioning. Traditionally, theses physiological systems were studied as independent entities, but we now know that behavior can be influenced by the immune system, and importantly, that the immune system can be influenced by the brain. The papers selected for this final section provide insights into how these interactions occur as well as their functional consequences.

Taken together, these 26 articles were chosen to augment courses in Behavioral Neuroscience or Biopsychology. We trust they will impart a taste of the exciting and rapidly progressing field of Biopsychology.

Section 1: Genes, Evolution, and Behavior

The first section provides an overview of the building blocks (genes) and dynamic processes (evolution) that shape brain and behavior. In the first paper, Danielle Dick and Richard Rose review the current state of behavior genetics and predict new directions of this field. Traditionally, behavioral genetics aimed to discover the genes contributing to specific behaviors or traits. Studies of twins have indicated that many behavioral domains are linked to genetic variation; Dick and Rose propose that behavior genetics will move beyond verification of genetic variation contributing to individual differences to reveal specific genes and environmental conditions that affect behavioral and cognitive development. The authors rightly emphasize that "genes confer dispositions, not destinies." Behavioral phenotype is the result of both genes and environment. Psychologists can contribute to this exciting expansion of human genomics by providing the tools to assess the environmental contributions to behavioral development, as well as leading the way in addressing the ethical, legal, and social issues associated with identification of genes discovered to contribute to human disorders.

Within the past 15 years a novel intellectual bridge has been formed between psychology and molecular biology. Molecular biologists have mapped large segments of the mouse genome as part of the ambitious Human Genome Project. As genes have been identified and sequenced, molecular biologists have begun the difficult task of identifying the physiological function of these genes, often while partnering with psychologists to examine the behavioral, cognitive, and affective influences of specific genes. The second paper by Thomas Bouchard emphasizes that all psychological traits are influenced by genetic factors. An important goal of current behavior genetics is to determine the amount of variation in a trait that is due to genes, environment, and the genes by environment interactions. Bouchard notes several important psychological traits including personality, intelligence, psychiatric disorders, and social attitudes are significantly influenced by genes and he suggests that any comprehensive theory of human psychological traits must incorporate these genetic factors underlying individual differences. Bouchard also notes that most psychological traits are moderately, rather than variably, inherited suggesting a general biological phenomenon consistent with physical traits observed in humans and other animals.

The next paper by Danielle Posthuma and Eco de Geus reports on the progress in the molecular and genetic studies of intelligence. This topic has been highly controversial because of its historical association with eugenics. The fear of genetic determinism in human behavior mainly reflects confusion that genes determine, rather than guide, behavioral outcomes. Intelligence is likely influenced by several genes that affect several cognitive functions including reading ability, working memory, attention, as well as brain size or neurotransmitter numbers. Although blocks of genes may correlate with intelligence, single genes each contribute modest, often indirect, effects upon this trait. Posthuma and de Geus review several whole-genome linkage scan studies that converge on the importance of Chromosomes 2 and 6 for intelligence. They also examine the results of several studies that examined variation in candidate genes (i.e., genes selected based on previous evidence) associated with intelligence, most of which have not been replicated. A promising approach requires examination of candidate genes only in regions of the chromosomes revealed by linkage studies to be involved in intelligence, such as the gene for cholinergic muscarinic receptor subtype 2 (CHRM2).

Not all genes are equal. During the process of evolution through natural selection, genes that fail to promote survival and reproductive success are weeded out. One might consider such genes, "bad genes." Thus, "good genes" promote survival and reproductive success. During courtship, potential mates want to choose mates with "good genes," but cannot directly observe and assess DNA (at least not yet). Thus, individuals assess various traits dependent on "good genes" that may be important for survival and reproductive success, and choose to mate with those individuals. The article by Steven Gangestad, Randy Thornhill, and Christine Garver-Apgar take an evolutionary approach to the psychological adaptations that may have evolved around a reproductively salient event, viz., human ovulation. In most species, males compete for access to females in peak reproductive condition, and females choose among them for mating. However, unlike most other primates, ovulation is hidden in women, and they will copulate even when they are not fertile. Although women mate through out their menstrual cycles, they shift in what they consider attractive according to their fertility. Around the time of ovulation, women report more attraction to masculine traits (both physical and behavioral) and increased attraction to non-partners compared to when they are not ovulating. The cues being used to make these determinations are reviewed by Gangestad and colleagues.

A central problem in comparative biology and psychology is to determine the evolutionary mechanisms underlying similarity between species. Studies of altruism in human and nonhuman animals have diverged in that evolutionary mechanisms are rarely evoked in the study of human altruism. Altruism is often studied in humans by social psychologists who study situational factors associated with altruism or who address motives for altruism, such as empathy. Rarely are the origins or ultimate functions of behavior addressed. How did altruism arise? How is it maintained? Altruism was also a difficult problem for evolutionary theory. If success in life is measured by reproductive success, then why do some individuals sacrifice to help other individuals succeed? A theoretical framework for understanding altruism was provided by W.D. Hamilton in the mid-1960s with his concept of inclusive fitness. He noted that helpful behavior only made sense through inclusive fitness; i.e., for closely related kin to help one another. A mother might sacrifice herself to a predator if she saved offspring with whom she shared genes. Although such an act would be phenotypically altruistic, such a sacrifice might be genetically selfish. Inclusive fitness is also called "kin selection." However, kin selection could not easily explain why strangers might sacrifice themselves or, less dramatically, why strangers might help. At the ultimate level, one might think they did it for the "good of the species," but this requires a naïve view of group selection. The concept of reciprocal altruism was developed by Robert Trivers—a theoretical and evolutionary basis for "I'll scratch your back if you scratch mine." Reciprocal altruism requires moderate social relationships among individuals who have good memories so that helpful acts could be reciprocated and cheaters could be shunned in the future. Francis McAndrew examines these perspectives on altruism in humans. He also evokes a multilevel-selection theory to account for the evolution of altruism, which resuscitates group-selection explanations. McAndrew also uses costly-signaling theory to help explain charity that is unlikely to be reciprocated.

In the final article of this section, Frans de Waal extols the virtues and vices of evolutionary psychology. The goal of evolutionary psychology is to provide "an evolutionary account of human behavior." He notes that psychology, with one foot in the life sciences, is among the first of the Social Sciences to flirt with evolutionary theory and concepts to explain behavior. De Waal advocates strongly for psychology to embrace evolutionary theory as the central unifying concept to understand behavior at all levels, and to liberate itself from the old dualisms between human and animal, nature versus nurture, and mind and body. He questions certain assumptions that comprise the field of evolutionary psychology. Although de Waal also suggests how the ideas of evolutionary psychology can be employed in the development of specific, testable hypotheses, about human brain and behavior. Certainly, one of the most crucial tasks for evolutionary psychologists in the coming decades will be the identification and elucidation of psychological adaptations. The most of the obvious and plausible psychological adaptations have already been catalogued, but many more remain undiscovered or inadequately characterized. Because adaptations are the product of natural selection operating in ancestral environments, and because psychological traits such as jealousy, language, and self-esteem, are not easily reconstructed from material evidence such as fossils and artifacts, direct evidence for behavioral adaptations may be difficult to obtain. One of the challenges for evolutionary psychology will be to develop increasingly more rigorous and systematic methods for inferring the evolutionary history of psychological characteristics, as well as determine how best to characterize psychological adaptations. de Waal warns against the imprecise use of adaptations to explain human behavior—it leads to tautological thinking. Why does a certain trait exist? Because it is adaptive. Why is it adaptive? Because it exists. It would be erroneous to believe that each and every trait is adaptive as it exists today. Biopsychologists must lead their psychology colleagues to examine human brain and behavior in the context of evolution through natural selection.

Behavior Genetics: What's New? What's Next?

Danielle M. Dick and Richard J. Rose[1]

Department of Psychology, Indiana University, Bloomington, Indiana

Abstract

What's new in behavior genetics? With widespread acceptance that nearly all behavioral variation reflects some genetic influence, current studies are investigating developmental changes in the nature and magnitude of genetic and environmental effects, the extent to which different behaviors are influenced by common genes, and different forms of gene-environment correlation and interaction. New designs, focused on assessment of unrelated children in the same households or neighborhood environments, and use of measured environmental variables within genetically informative designs, are yielding more incisive evidence of common environmental effects on behavior. What will be next? Behavior genetic techniques and analyses will be used to inform efforts to find genes altering susceptibility for disorder and dispositional genes affecting behavioral variation. The developing integration of behavioral and molecular genetics will identify genes influencing specific behavioral variation and enhance understanding of how they do so. Psychologists will play a pivotal role in communicating that understanding to the public and in facilitating consideration of the inevitable ethical issues then to be confronted.

Keywords

behavior genetics; molecular genetics; development; gene–environment interaction

Through most of its brief history, behavior genetics had a single and simple goal: to demonstrate that some of the variation in behavior is attributable to genetic variance. Now, a diverse array of behaviors has been investigated with twin and adoption designs, yielding evidence that genetic variation contributes to individual differences in virtually all behavioral domains (McGuffin, Riley, & Plomin, 2001). Is behavior genetics, then, a thing of the past, a field whose success makes it obsolete? Not at all: Never has behavior genetic research held more promise. Investigators now possess analytic tools to move from estimating latent, unmeasured sources of variance to specifying the genes and environments involved in behavioral development, and the ways in which they interact. Our modest aim in this essay is to describe the questions now asked by behavior geneticists and to sketch the role that the field will assume in the emerging era of behavioral genomics.

A DEVELOPMENTAL PERSPECTIVE

Traditional behavior genetic analyses divide observed behavioral variance into three unobserved (latent) sources: variance attributable to genetic effects, that due to environmental influences shared by siblings (e.g., family structure and status), and that arising in unshared environmental experience that makes siblings differ from one another. Estimates of the magnitude of these genetic and environmental effects are usually obtained from statistical path models that compare identical twins, who share all their genes, with fraternal twins, who like ordinary siblings, on average, share one half their genes. Behavior genetic research now identifies developmental changes in the importance of genetic dispositions and environmental contexts in accounting for individual differences in behavior. Such changes can be dramatic and rapid. For example, we assessed substance use in a sample of adolescent Finnish twins on three occasions from ages 16 to $18\frac{1}{2}$; we found that genetic contributions to individual differences in drinking frequency increased over time, accounting for only a third of the variation at age 16, but half of it just 30 months later (Rose, Dick, Viken, & Kaprio, 2001). Concurrently, the effects of sharing a common environment decreased in importance. Interestingly, parallel analyses of smoking found little change in the importance of genetic and environmental effects, illustrating the trait-specificity of gene-environment dynamics: Some effects are stable across a developmental period; others change.

DIFFERENT BEHAVIORS, SAME GENES?

It is well known that certain behaviors tend to co-occur, as do certain disorders, but the causes of such covariance are much less understood. Behavior genetic models assess the degree to which covariation of different disorders or behaviors is due to common genetic influences, common environmental influences, or both. An example can be found in the significant, albeit modest, correlations observed between perceptual speed (the minimum time required to make a perceptual discrimination, as assessed with computer display methods) and standard IQ test scores (Posthuma, de Geus, & Boomsma, in press); those correlations were found to be due entirely to a common genetic factor, hypothesized to reflect genetic influences on neural transmission. Another example is found in our study of behavioral covariance between smoking and drinking during adolescence. Genes contributing to the age when teens started smoking and drinking correlated nearly 1.0 (suggesting that the same genes influence an adolescent's decision to begin smoking and to begin drinking), but once smoking or drinking was initiated, genes influencing the frequency with which an adolescent smoked or drank were quite substance-specific, correlating only about .25.

GENE-ENVIRONMENT INTERACTION AND CORRELATION

The interaction of genes and environments has been difficult to demonstrate in human behavioral data, despite consensus that interaction must be ubiquitous. New behavior genetic methods are demonstrating what was long assumed. These methods use information from twins who vary in specified environmental exposure to test directly for the differential expression of genes across different environments. For example, genetic effects played a larger role in the use of alcohol among twin women who had been reared in nonreligious households than among those who had been reared in religious households (Koopmans, Slutske, van Baal, & Boomsma, 1999). Similarly, we found greater genetic effects on adolescent alcohol use among Finnish twins living in urban environments than among those living in rural environments (Rose, Dick, et al., 2001).

These demonstrations of gene–environment interaction used simple dichotomies of environmental measures. But subsequently, we explored underlying processes in the interaction effect of urban versus rural environments by employing new statistical techniques to accommodate more continuous measures of the characteristics of the municipalities in which the Finnish twins resided. We hypothesized that communities spending relatively more money on alcohol allow for greater access to it, and communities with proportionately more young adults offer more role models for adolescent twins, and that either kind of community enhances expression of individual differences in genetic predispositions. And that is what we found: up to a 5-fold difference in the importance of genetic effects among twins residing in communities at these environmental extremes (Dick, Rose, Viken, Kaprio, & Koskenvuo, 2001), suggesting that the influence of genetic dispositions can be altered dramatically by environmental variation across communities.

Analysis of gene-environment interaction is complemented by tests of gene-environment correlation. Individuals' genomes interact with the environmental contexts in which the individuals live their lives, but this process is not a passive one, for genetic dispositions lead a person to select, and indeed create, his or her environments. Perhaps the most salient environment for an adolescent is found in the adolescent's peer relationships. In a study of 1,150 sixth-grade Finnish twins, we (Rose, in press) obtained evidence that they actively selected their friends from among their classmates. This result is consistent with the inference that people's genetic dispositions play some role in their selection of friends. People like other people who are like themselves, and genetically identical co-twins make highly similar friendship selections among their classmates.

MEASURING EFFECTS OF THE ENVIRONMENT IN GENETICALLY INFORMATIVE DESIGNS

In traditional behavior genetic designs, environmental influences were modeled, but not measured. Environmental effects were inferred from latent models fit to data. Such designs understandably received much criticism. Now, behavior geneticists can incorporate specific environmental measures into genetically informative designs and, by doing so, are demonstrating environmental effects that latent models failed to detect. Thus, we have studied effects of parental monitoring and home atmosphere on behavior problems in 11- to 12-year-old Finnish twins; both parental monitoring and home atmosphere contributed significantly to the development of the children's behavior problems, accounting for 2 to 5% of the total variation, and as much as 15% of the total common environmental effect. Recent research in the United Kingdom found neighborhood deprivation influenced behavior problems, too, accounting for about 5% of the effect of shared environment. Incorporation of specific, measured environments into genetically informative designs offers a powerful technique to study and specify environmental effects.

In other work, new research designs have been used to directly assess environmental effects in studies of unrelated children reared in a common neighborhood or within the same home. We have investigated neighborhood environmental effects on behavior in a large sample of 11- to 12-year-old same-sex Finnish twins. For each twin, we included a control classmate of the same gender and similar age, thus enabling us to compare three kinds of dyads: co-twins, each twin and his or her control classmate, and the two control classmates for each pair of co-twins. These twin-classmate dyads were sampled from more than 500 classrooms throughout Finland. The members of each dyad shared the same neighborhood, school, and classroom, but only the co-twin dyads shared genes and common household experience. For some behaviors, including early onset of smoking and drinking, we found significant correlations for both control-twin and control-control dyads; fitting models to the double-dyads formed by twins and their controls documented significant contributions to behavioral variation from nonfamilial environments—schools, neighborhoods, and communities (Rose, Viken, Dick, Pulkkinen, & Kaprio, 2001).

A complementary study examined genetically unrelated siblings who were no more than 9 months apart in age and who had been reared together from infancy in the same household. An IQ correlation of .29 was reported for 50 such dyads, and in another analysis, 40 of these dyads were only slightly less alike than fraternal co-twins on a variety of parent-rated behaviors (Segal, 1999). Clearly, appropriate research designs can demonstrate effects of familial and extrafamilial environmental variation for some behavioral outcomes at specific ages of development.

INTEGRATING BEHAVIOR AND MOLECULAR GENETICS[2]

Where do the statistical path models of behavior geneticists fit into the emerging era of behavioral genomics (the application of molecular genetics to behavior)? In the same way that specific, measured environments can be incorporated into behavior genetic models, specific information about genotypes can be included, as well, to test the importance of individual genes on behavior. Additionally, the kinds of behavior genetic analyses we have described can be informative in designing studies that maximize the power to detect susceptibility genes. Many efforts to replicate studies identifying genes that influence clinically defined diagnoses have failed. Those failures have stimulated the study of alternatives to diagnoses. When several traits are influenced by the same gene (or genes), that information can be used to redefine (or refine) alternatives to study, to enhance gene detection. For example, because heavy smoking and drinking frequently co-occurred in the Collaborative Study of the Genetics of Alcoholism sample, combined smoking and alcohol dependence was studied (Beirut et al., 2000). The combined dependency yielded greater evidence of linkage with a chromosomal region than did either tobacco dependence or alcohol dependence alone.

This approach is not limited to co-occurring behavioral disorders. It applies to normative behavioral differences, as well: A multidisciplinary international collaboration (Wright et al., 2001) has initiated a study of covariation among traditional and experimental measures of cognitive ability and will employ the correlated measures, once found, in subsequent molecular genetic analyses. And in a complementary way, behavior genetic methods can be useful to identify behavioral outcomes that are highly heritable, because these outcomes are most likely informative for genetic studies: When the definition of major depression was broadened, genetic factors assumed a larger role in women's susceptibility to this disorder (Kendler, Gardner, Neale, & Prescott, 2001), and, interestingly, this broader definition of depression suggested that somewhat different genes may influence depression in men and women.

A second strategy to enhance the power of molecular genetic analyses is to more accurately characterize trait-relevant environmental factors and also incorporate them more accurately in the analyses. In searching for genes, traditional genetic research effectively ignored the interplay of genetic and environmental influences in behavioral and psychiatric traits. Now, new analytic methods are being developed to incorporate environmental information better (Mosley, Conti, Elston, & Witte, 2000). But which specific environmental information is pertinent to a particular disorder? And how does a specific risk-relevant environment interact with genetic dispositions? Behavioral scientists trained in the methods of behavior genetics will play a key role in answering these questions.

BEYOND FINDING GENES

The traditional endpoint for geneticists is finding the gene (or genes) involved in a behavior or disorder. At that point, psychologists should become instrumental in using this genetic information. Applying genetic research on complex disorders to clinical practice will be complicated, because gene-behavior correlations will be modest and nonspecific, altering risk, but rarely determining outcome. Genes confer dispositions, not destinies. Research examining how risk and protective factors interact with genetic predispositions is critical for understanding the development of disorders and for providing information to vulnerable individuals and their family members. Far from ousting traditional psychological intervention, advances in genetics offer opportunities to develop interventions tailored to individual risks in the context of individual lifestyles. Enhanced understanding of the interactions between genetic vulnerabilities and environmental variables may dispel public misconceptions about the nature of genetics and correct erroneous beliefs about genetic determinism. Informed psychologists can play a vital role in disseminating the benefits of genetic research to families whose members experience behavioral and psychiatric disorders, and to the public in general.

CONCLUSIONS

Research questions now addressed by behavior geneticists have grown dramatically in scope: The questions have expanded into developmental psychology and sociology, as researchers have employed measures of the home and community, and utilized longitudinal designs. And behavior geneticists now study the effect of measured genotypes, a study traditionally left to geneticists. These developments create new and compelling research questions and raise new challenges. One such challenge is in addressing the complexity of behavioral development despite current reliance on methods that largely assume additive, linear effects. People who appreciate the complex, interactive, and unsystematic effects underlying behavioral development may be skeptical that the genomic era will profoundly advance understanding of behavior. But there is a preliminary illustration that advance will occur, even within the constraints of additive models: the identification of a gene (ApoE) that increases risk for Alzheimer's disease, and the interaction of that gene with head trauma (Mayeux et al., 1995). Further, new analytic techniques are being developed to analyze simultaneously hundreds of genes and environments in attempts to understand how gene–gene and gene-environment interactions contribute to outcome (Moore & Hahn, 2000). These techniques are beginning to capture the systems-theory approach long advocated by many researchers as an alternative to linear additive models.

This is not to deny that unresolved problems remain. For example, we are enthusiastic about including measured environmental information in genetic research designs, but we note, with disappointment, that the magnitude of shared environmental effects detected to date has been modest. Equally disappointing are the results of recent research efforts to specify nonshared environmental effects (Turkheimer & Waldron, 2000). Such findings underscore a problem acutely evident in contemporary behavior genetics: an imperative need for better measures of trait-relevant environments. Now that researchers have tools to search for measured environmental effects, what aspects of the environment should they measure—and with what yardsticks? These are questions that psychologists are uniquely positioned to address.

Another set of challenging questions will arise from the ethical, legal, and social issues to be confronted once genes conferring susceptibility to disorders are identified. How should information about the nature and meaning of susceptibility genes be conveyed to the media, the public, and the courts? How can erroneous beliefs about genetic determinism be dispelled effectively? Such issues will be even more salient once dispositional genes for normal behavioral variation are identified: Ethical issues surrounding prevention of behavioral disorders are undeniably complex, but surely they are less so than the ethical issues surrounding enhancement of selected behavioral traits.

Results from the first phase of behavior genetics research convincingly demonstrated that genes influence behavioral development. In the next phase, that of behavioral genomics, psychologists will begin to identify specific genes that exert such influence, seek understanding of how they do so, and accept the challenge to interpret that understanding to the public.

Recommended Reading

The Human Genome [Special issue]. (2001, February 16). *Science, 291.*
Rutter, M., Pickles, A., Murray, R., & Eaves, L. (2001). Testing hypotheses on specific environmental causal effects on behavior. *Psychological Bulletin, 127*, 291–324.
Turkheimer, E. (1998). Heritability and biological explanation. *Psychological Review, 105*, 782–791.

Acknowledgments—We gratefully acknowledge the contributions of Lea Pulkkinen, Jaakko Kaprio, Markku Koskenvuo, and Rick Viken to FinnTwin research, and support from the National Institute on Alcohol Abuse and Alcoholism (AA00145, AA09203, and AA08315) awarded to R.J.R. Manuscript preparation was supported by the Indiana Alcohol Research Center (AA07611) and by a National Science Foundation Pre-Doctoral Fellowship awarded to D.M.D.

Notes

1. Address correspondence to Richard Rose, Indiana University, Department of Psychology, 1101 East 10th St., Bloomington, IN 47405.

2. We use the term molecular genetics broadly to include statistical genetic techniques that test for gene-behavior associations.

References

Beirut, L., Rice, J., Goate, A., Foroud, T., Edenberg, H., Crowe, R., Hesselbrock, V., Li, T.K., Nurnberger, J., Porjesz, B., Schuckit, M., Begleiter, H., & Reich, T. (2000). Common and specific factors in the familial transmission of substance dependence. *American Journal of Medical Genetics, 96,* 459.

Dick, D.M., Rose, R.J., Viken, R.J., Kaprio, J., & Koskenvuo, M. (2001). Exploring gene-environment interactions: Socio-regional moderation of alcohol use. *Journal of Abnormal Psychology, 110,* 625–632.

Kendler, K.S., Gardner, C.O., Neale, M.C., & Prescott, C.A. (2001). Genetic risk factors for major depression in men and women: Similar or different heritabilities and same or partly distinct genes? *Psychological Medicine, 31,* 605–616.

Koopmans, J.R., Slutske, W.S., van Baal, G.C.M., & Boomsma, D.I. (1999). The influence of religion on alcohol use initiation: Evidence for genotype × environment interaction. *Behavior Genetics, 29,* 445–453.

Mayeux, R., Ottman, R., Maestre, G., Ngai, C., Tang, M.X., Ginsberg, H., Chun, M., Tycko, B., & Shelanski, M. (1995). Synergistic effects of traumatic head injury and apolipoprotein-E4 in patients with Alzheimer's disease. *Neurology, 45,* 555–557.

McGuffin, P., Riley, B., & Plomin, R. (2001). Toward behavioral genomics. *Science, 291,* 1232–1249.

Moore, J.H., & Hahn, L.W. (2000). A cellular automata approach to identifying gene-gene and gene-environment interactions. *American Journal of Medical Genetics, 96,* 486–487.

Mosley, J., Conti, D.V., Elston, R.C., & Witte, J.S. (2000). Impact of preadjusting a quantitative phenotype prior to sib-pair linkage analysis when gene-environment interaction exists. *Genetic Epidemiology, 21*(Suppl. 1), S837–S842.

Posthuma, D., de Geus, E.J.C., & Boomsma, D.I. (in press). Perceptual speed and IQ are associated through common genetic factors. *Behavior Genetics.*

Rose, R.J. (in press). How do adolescents select their friends? A behavior-genetic perspective. In L. Pulkkinen & A. Caspi (Eds.), *Paths to successful development.* Cambridge, England: Cambridge University Press.

Rose, R.J., Dick, D.M., Viken, R.J., & Kaprio, J. (2001). Gene-environment interaction in patterns of adolescent drinking: Regional residency moderates longitudinal influences on alcohol use. *Alcoholism: Clinical and Experimental Research, 25,* 637–643.

Rose, R.J., Viken, R.J., Dick, D.M., Pulkkinen, L., & Kaprio, J. (2001, July). *Shared environmental effects on behavior: Distinguishing familial from non-familial sources with data from twins and their classmate controls.* Paper presented at the annual meeting of the Behavior Genetics Association, Cambridge, England.

Segal, N.L. (1999). *Entwined lives.* New York: Penguin Putnam.

Turkheimer, E., & Waldron, M. (2000). Nonshared environment: A theoretical, methodological, and quantitative review. *Psychological Bulletin, 126,* 78–108.

Wright, M., de Geus, E., Ando, J., Luciano, M., Posthuma, D., Ono, Y., Hansell, N., Van Baal, C., Hiraishi, K., Hasegawa, T., Smith, G., Geffen, G., Geffen, L., Kanba, S., Miyake, A., Martin, N., & Boomsma, D. (2001). Genetics of cognition: Outline of a collaborative twin study. *Twin Research, 4,* 48–56.

Genetic Influence on Human Psychological Traits: A Survey

Thomas J. Bouchard, Jr.[1]
University of Minnesota, Minneapolis

Abstract

There is now a large body of evidence that supports the conclusion that individual differences in most, if not all, reliably measured psychological traits, normal and abnormal, are substantively influenced by genetic factors. This fact has important implications for research and theory building in psychology, as evidence of genetic influence unleashes a cascade of questions regarding the sources of variance in such traits. A brief list of those questions is provided, and representative findings regarding genetic and environmental influences are presented for the domains of personality, intelligence, psychological interests, psychiatric illnesses, and social attitudes. These findings are consistent with those reported for the traits of other species and for many human physical traits, suggesting that they may represent a general biological phenomenon.

Keywords

behavior genetics; heritability; individual differences

Among knowledgeable researchers, discussions regarding genetic influences on psychological traits are not about whether there is genetic influence, but rather about how much influence there is, and how genes work to shape the mind. As Rutter (2002) noted, "Any dispassionate reading of the evidence leads to the inescapable conclusion that genetic factors play a substantial role in the origins of individual differences with respect to all psychological traits, both normal and abnormal" (p. 2). Put concisely, all psychological traits are heritable. Heritability (h^2) is a descriptive statistic that indexes the degree of population variation in a trait that is due to genetic differences. The complement of heritability ($1 - h^2$) indexes variation contributed by the environment (plus error of measurement) to population variation in the trait. Studies of human twins and adoptees, often called behavior genetic studies, allow us to estimate the heritability of various traits. The name behavior genetic studies is an unfortunate misnomer, however, as such studies are neutral regarding both environmental and genetic influences. That they repeatedly and reliably reveal significant heritability for psychological traits is an empirical fact and one not unique to humans. Lynch and Walsh (1998) pointed out that genetic influence on most traits, as indexed by estimates of heritability, is found for all species and observed that "the interesting questions remaining are, How does the magnitude of h^2 differ among characters and species and why?" (p. 175).

WHY STUDY GENETIC INFLUENCES ON HUMAN BEHAVIORAL TRAITS?

A simple answer to the question of why scientists study genetic influences on human behavior is that they want a better understanding of how things work, that is, better theories. Not too many years ago, Meehl (1978) argued that "most so-called 'theories' in the soft areas of psychology (clinical, counseling, social, personality, community, and school psychology) are scientifically unimpressive and technologically worthless" (p. 806). He listed 20 fundamental difficulties faced by researchers in the social sciences. Two are relevant to the current discussion: heritability and nuisance variables. The two are closely related. Nuisance variables are variables assumed to be causes of group or individual differences irrelevant to the theory of an investigator. Investigators seldom provide a full theoretical rationale in support of their choice of nuisance variables to control. As Meehl pointed out, removing the influence of parental socioeconomic status (SES; i.e., treating it as a nuisance variable) on children's IQ, when studying the causes of individual differences in IQ, makes the assumption that parental SES is exclusively a source of environmental variance, as opposed to being confounded with genetic influence.[2] Meehl argued that this example "is perhaps the most dramatic one, but other less emotion-laden examples can be found on all sides in the behavioral sciences" (p. 810). His point was that knowledge of how genetic factors influence any given measure (e.g., SES) or trait (e.g., IQ) will allow scientists to develop more scientifically impressive and worthwhile theories about the sources of individual differences in psychological traits.

Evidence of genetic influence on a psychological trait raises a series of new questions regarding the sources of population variance for that trait. All the questions addressed in quantitative genetics (Lynch & Walsh, 1998) and genetic epidemiology (Khoury, 1998) become relevant. What kind of gene action is involved? Is it a simple additive influence, with the effects of genes simply adding up so that more genes cause greater expression of the trait, or is the mode of action more complex? Are the effects of genes for a particular trait more pronounced in men or women? Are there interactions between genes and the environment? For example, it has been known for a long time that stressful life events lead to depression in some people but not others. There is now evidence for an interaction. Individuals who carry a specific genetic variant are more susceptible to depression when exposed to stressful life events than individuals who do not carry the genetic variant (Caspi et al., 2003). Are there gene-environment correlations? That is, do individuals with certain genetic constitutions seek out specific environments? People who score high on measures of sensation seeking certainly, on average, tend to find themselves in more dangerous environments than people who score low for this trait. McGue and I have provided an extended list of such questions (Bouchard & McGue, 2003).

ESTIMATES OF THE MAGNITUDE OF GENETIC INFLUENCE ON PSYCHOLOGICAL TRAITS

Table 1 reports typical behavior genetic findings drawn from studies of broad and relatively representative samples from affluent Western societies. In most, but not all, of these studies, estimates of genetic and environmental influences were obtained from studies of twins. Because the studies probably undersampled people who live in the most deprived segment of Western societies, the findings should not be considered as generalizable to such populations. (Documentation for most of the findings can be found in Bouchard & McGue, 2003.)

Personality

Psychologists have developed two major schemes for organizing specific personality traits into a higher-order structure, the Big Five and the Big Three. As Table 1 shows, the findings using the two schemes are much the same. Genetic influence is in the range of 40 to 50%, and heritability is approximately the same for different traits. There is evidence of nonadditive genetic variance. That is, genes for personality, in addition to simply adding or subtracting from the expression of a trait, work in a more complex manner, the expression of a relevant gene depending to some extent on the gene with which it is paired on a chromosome or on genes located on other chromosomes. Research has yielded little evidence for significant shared environmental influence, that is, similarity due to having trait-relevant environmental influences in common. Some large studies have investigated whether

Table 1. *Estimates of broad heritability and shared environmental influence and indications of nonadditive genetic effects and sex differences in heritability for representative psychological traits*

Trait	Heritability	Nonadditive genetic effect	Shared environmental effect	Sex differences in heritability
Personality (adult samples)				
Big Five				
Extraversion	.54	Yes	No	Perhaps
Agreeableness (aggression)	.42	Yes	No	Probably not
Conscientiousness	.49	Yes	No	Probably not
Neuroticism	.48	Yes	No	No
Openness	.57	Yes	No	Probably not
Big Three				
Positive emotionality	.50	Yes	No	No
Negative emotionality	.44	Yes	No	No
Constraint	.52	Yes	No	No
Intelligence				
By age in Dutch cross-sectional twin data				
Age 5	.22	No	.54	No
Age 7	.40	No	.29	No
Age 10	.54	No	.26	No
Age 12	.85	No	No	No
Age 16	.62	No	No	No
Age 18	.82	No	No	No
Age 26	.88	No	No	No
Age 50	.85	No	No	No
In old age (>75 years old)	.54–.62	Not tested	No	No
Psychological interests				
Realistic	.36	Yes	.12	NA
Investigative	.36	Yes	.10	NA
Artistic	.39	Yes	.12	NA
Social	.37	Yes	.08	NA
Enterprising	.31	Yes	.11	NA
Conventional	.38	Yes	.11	NA

Trait	Heritability	Nonadditive genetic effect	Shared environmental effect	Sex differences in heritability
Psychiatric illnesses (liability estimates)				
Schizophrenia	.80	No	No	No
Major depression	.37	No	No	Mixed findings
Panic disorder	.30–.40	No	No	No
Generalized anxiety disorder	.30	No	Small female only	No
Phobias	.20–.40	No	No	No
Alcoholism	.50–.60	No	Yes	Mixed findings
Antisocial behavior				
Children	.46	No	.20	No
Adolescents	.43	No	.16	No
Adults	.41	No	.09	No
Social attitudes				
Conservatism				
Under age 20 years	.00	NR	Yes	NR
Over age 20 years	.45–.65	Yes	Yes in females	Yes
Right-wing authoritarianism (adults)	.50–.64	No	.00–.16	NA
Religiousness				
16-year-olds	.11–.22	No	.45–.60	Yes
Adults	.30–.45	No	.20–.40	Not clear
Specific religion	Near zero	NR	NA	NR

Note. NA = not available; NR = not relevant.

the genes that influence personality traits differ in the two sexes (sex limitation). The answer is no. However, sometimes there are sex differences in heritability.

Mental Ability

Early in life, shared environmental factors are the dominant influence on IQ, but gradually genetic influence increases, with the effects of shared environment dropping to near zero (see the twin studies in Table 1). Although not reported here, adoption studies of (a) unrelated individuals reared together and (b) adoptive parents and their adopted offspring have reported similar results—increasing genetic influence on IQ with age and decreasing shared environmental influence. Results from two twin studies of IQ in old age (over 75) are reported in Table 1. Both studies found a substantial level of genetic influence and little shared environmental influence. The results do, however, suggest some decline in heritability when compared with results for earlier ages. There is no evidence for sex differences in heritability for IQ at any age.

Psychological Interests

Heritabilities for psychological interests, also called vocational or occupational interests, are also reported in Table 1. These heritabilities were estimated using data gathered in a single large study that made use of a variety of samples (twins, siblings, parents and their children, etc.) gathered over many years. All respondents completed one form or another of a standard vocational interest questionnaire. There is little variation in heritability for the six scales, with an average of .36. As with personality traits, there is evidence for nonadditive genetic influence. Unlike personality, psychological interests show evidence for shared environmental influence, although this influence is modest, about 10% for each trait.

Psychiatric Illnesses

Schizophrenia is the most extensively studied psychiatric illness, and the findings consistently suggest a very high degree of genetic influence (heritability of about .80), mostly additive genetic influence, with no shared environmental influence. There do not appear to be gender differences in the heritability of schizophrenia. Major depression is less heritable (about .40) than schizophrenia. Men and women share most, but not all, genetic influences for depression. Panic disorder, generalized anxiety disorder, and phobias are moderately heritable, and the effect is largely additive, with few if any sex differences. The heritability of alcoholism is in the range of .50 to .60, mostly because of additive genetic effects. Findings regarding the possibility of sex differences in the heritability of alcoholism are mixed.

Antisocial behavior has long been thought to be more heritable in adulthood than childhood. The results of a recent analysis do not support that conclusion. The genetic influence is additive and in the range of .41 to .46. Shared environmental influences decrease from childhood to adulthood, but do not entirely disappear in adulthood. There are no sex differences in heritability.

Social Attitudes

Twin studies reveal only environmental influence on conservatism up to age 19; only after this age do genetic influences manifest themselves. A large study (30,000 adults, including twins and most of their first-degree relatives) yielded heritabilities of .65 for males and .45 for females. Some of the genetic influence on conservatism is nonadditive. Recent work with twins reared apart has independently replicated these heritability findings. Conservatism correlates highly, about .72, with right-wing authoritarianism, and that trait is also moderately heritable.

Religiousness is only slightly heritable in 16-year-olds (.11 for girls and .22 for boys in a large Finnish twin study) and strongly influenced by shared environment (.60 in girls and .45 in boys). Religiousness is moderately heritable in adults (.30 to .45) and also shows some shared environmental influence. Good data on sex differences in heritability of religiousness in adults are not available. Membership in a specific religious denomination is largely due to environmental factors.

A Note on Multivariate Genetic Analysis

In this review, I have addressed only the behavior genetic analysis of traits taken one at a time (univariate analysis). It is important to recognize that it is possible to carry out complex genetic analyses of the correlations among traits and compute genetic correlations. These correlations tell us the degree to which genetic effects on one score (trait measure) are correlated with genetic effects on a second score, at one or at many points in time. The genetic correlation between two traits can be quite high regardless of whether the heritability of either trait is high or low, or whether the correlation between the traits is high or low. Consider the well-known positive correlation between tests of mental ability, the evidentiary base for the general intelligence factor. This value is typically about .30. The genetic correlation between such tests is, however, much higher, typically closer to .80. Co-occurrence of two disorders, a common finding in psychiatric research, is often due to common genes. The genetic correlation between anxiety and depression, for example, is estimated to be very high. Multivariate genetic analysis of behavioral traits is a very active domain of research.

CONCLUDING REMARKS

One unspoken assumption among early behavior geneticists, an assumption that was shared by most for many years, was that some psychological traits were likely to be significantly influenced by genetic factors, whereas others were likely to be primarily influenced by shared environmental influences. Most behavior geneticists assumed that social attitudes, for example, were influenced entirely by shared environmental influences, and so social attitudes remained largely unstudied until relatively recently. The evidence now shows how wrong these assumptions were. Nearly every reliably measured psychological phenotype (normal and abnormal) is significantly influenced by genetic factors. Heritabilities also differ far less from trait to trait than anyone initially imagined. Shared environmental influences are often, but not always, of less importance than genetic factors, and often decrease to near zero after adolescence. Genetic influence on psychological traits is ubiquitous, and psychological researchers must incorporate this fact into their research programs else their theories will be "scientifically unimpressive and technologically worthless," to quote Meehl again.

At a fundamental level, a scientifically impressive theory must describe the specific molecular mechanism that explicates how genes transact with the environment to produce behavior. The rudiments of such theories are in place. Circadian behavior in humans is under genetic influence (Hur, Bouchard, & Lykken, 1998), and some of the molecular mechanisms in mammals are now being revealed (Lowrey & Takahashi, 2000). Ridley (2003) and Marcus (2004) have provided additional examples of molecular mechanisms that help shape behavior. Nevertheless, the examples are few, the details are sparse, and major mysteries remain. For example, many behavioral traits are influenced by nonadditive genetic processes. These processes remain a puzzle for geneticists and evolutionists, as well as psychologists, because simple additive effects are thought to be the norm (Wolf, Brodie, & Wade, 2000). We also do not understand why most psychological traits are moderately heritable, rather than, as some psychologists expected, variable in heritability, with some traits being highly heritable and others being largely under the influence of the environment. It seems reasonable to suspect that moderate heritability may be a general biological phenomenon rather than one specific to human psychological traits, as the profile of genetic and environmental influences on psychological traits is not that different from the profile of these influences on similarly complex physical traits (Boomsma, Busjahn, & Peltonen, 2002) and similar findings apply to most organisms.

Recommended Reading

Bouchard, T.J., Jr., & McGue, M. (2003). (See References)
Carey, G. (2003). *Human genetics for the social sciences.* Thousand Oaks, CA: Sage.
Plomin, R., DeFries, J.C., Craig, I.W., & McGuffin, P. (Eds.). (2003). *Behavioral genetics in the post genomic era.* Washington, DC: American Psychological Association.
Rutter, M., Pickels, A., Murray, R., & Eaves, L.J. (2001). Testing hypotheses on specific environmental causal effects on behavior. *Psychological Bulletin, 127,* 291–324.

Notes

1. Address correspondence to Thomas J. Bouchard, Jr., Psychology Depaartment, University of Minnesota, 75 East River Rd., Minneapolis, MN 55455-0344; e-mail: bouch001@ umn.edu.
2. See Evans (2004, Fig. 1) for a recent commission of this error.

References

Boomsma, D.I., Busjahn, A., & Peltonen, L. (2002). Classical twin studies and beyond. *Nature Reviews: Genetics, 3,* 872–882.
Bouchard, T.J., Jr., & McGue, M. (2003). Genetic and environmental influences on human psychological differences. *Journal of Neurobiology, 54,* 4–45.
Caspi, A., Sugden, K., Moffitt, T.E., Taylor, A., Craig, I.W., Harrington, H., McClay, J., Mill, J., Martin, J., Braiwaite, A., & Poulton, R. (2003). Influence of life stress on depression: Moderation by a polymorphism in the 5-HTT gene. *Science, 301,* 386–389.
Evans, G.W. (2004). The environment of childhood poverty. *American Psychologist, 59,* 77–92.
Hur, Y.M., Bouchard, T.J., Jr., & Lykken, D.T. (1998). Genetic and environmental influence on morningness-eveningness. *Personality and Individual Differences, 25,* 917–925.
Khoury, M.J. (1998). Genetic epidemiology. In K.J. Rothman & S. Greenland (Eds.), *Modern epidemiology* (pp. 609–622). Philadelphia: Lippincott-Raven.
Lowrey, P.L., & Takahashi, J.S. (2000). Genetics of the mammalian circadian system: Photic entrainment, circadian pacemaker mechanisms, and postranslational regulation. *Annual Review of Genetics, 34,* 533–562.
Lynch, M., & Walsh, B. (1998). *Genetics and analysis of quantitative traits.* Sunderland, MA: Sinauer.
Marcus, G. (2004). *The birth of the mind: How a tiny number of genes creates the complexities of human thought.* New York: Basic Books.
Meehl, P.E. (1978). Theoretical risks and tabular asterisks: Sir Karl, Sir Ronald, and the slow progress of soft psychology. *Journal of Consulting and Clinical Psychology, 46,* 806–834.
Ridley, M. (2003). *Nature via nurture: Genes, experience and what makes us human.* New York: HarperCollins.
Rutter, M. (2002). Nature, nurture, and development: From evangelism through science toward policy and practice. *Child Development, 73,* 1–21.
Wolf, J.B., Brodie, E.D.I., & Wade, M.J. (Eds.). (2000). *Epistasis and the evolutionary process.* New York: Oxford University Press.

This article has been reprinted as it originally appeared in *Current Directions in Psychological Science*. Citation information for this article as originally published appears above.

Progress in the Molecular-Genetic Study of Intelligence

Danielle Posthuma[1] and Eco J.C. de Geus

Department of Biological Psychology and Center for Neurogenomics and Cognitive Research, Vrije Universiteit, Amsterdam, The Netherlands

Abstract

The past decade has seen a major shift in the genetic study of human intelligence; where classic studies aimed to quantify the heritability of intelligence, current studies aim to dissect this heritability into its molecular-genetic components. Five whole-genome linkage scans have been published in the past year, converging on several chromosomal (or genomic) regions important to intelligence. A handful of candidate genes, some of which lie in these genomic regions, have shown significant association to intelligence and the associations have been replicated in independent samples. Finding genes brings us closer to an understanding of the neurophysiological basis of human cognition. Furthermore, when genes are no longer latent factors in our models but can actually be measured, it becomes feasible to identify those environmental factors that interact and correlate with genetic makeup. This will supplant the long nature–nurture debate with actual understanding.

Keywords

cognition; quantitative trait locus; gene–environment interaction; gene–environment correlation

Individual performance on a single aspect of cognitive ability is highly predictive of performance on other aspects of cognitive ability. About 40% of the variance in multiple aspects of cognitive ability can be accounted for by a single general-intelligence factor. Genetic analyses of data obtained from monozygotic (from a single egg) and dizygotic (from different eggs) twin pairs indicate that this general-intelligence factor is highly heritable. Estimates range from 40% in childhood to 80% in late adulthood.[2] In keeping with the postulate of a general-intelligence factor, substantial genetic overlap is found not only between different aspects of cognitive ability (such as reading ability, working memory, and attention) but also between different biological levels of cognitive ability, such as brain size or protein levels. This observation has led to the recent formulation of the "generalist genes" hypothesis, which states that the same genes affect multiple cognitive abilities (Plomin & Kovas, 2005).

In recent years, molecular-genetic studies have indeed started to identify these genes, with the full awareness that they are "polygenes"—i.e., they may each explain only a very small part of the variation in one or more cognitive abilities. The generalist-genes hypothesis also implies that cognitive disabilities are the extremes of normally distributed dimensions of cognitive abilities. Therefore, exactly those genes that have been associated with normal cognitive abilities could provide important clues to underlying mechanisms of milder but more prevalent forms of impaired cognitive functioning, like reading disorder, dyslexia, and attention deficit hyperactivity disorder, or even the severe cognitive deficits seen in autism and schizophrenia.

GENE-FINDING STRATEGIES

To identify genes underlying genetic variation in intelligence, two main strategies are available: linkage analysis and candidate-gene association studies. In linkage analysis, a number of DNA markers of known location, evenly dispersed throughout the entire set of chromosomes (the genome), are measured in genetically related individuals. DNA markers can be mutations in a single base pair (the smallest unit of the DNA helix; such mutations are called single nucleotide polymorphisms, SNPs) or a variable number of repeats of two or more base pairs (micro-satellites). They need not be part of a functional gene—they are merely landmarks in the genome. For each DNA marker, evidence for linkage to a particular trait, like cognitive ability, is obtained through statistical procedures that trace how often the trait and the DNA marker are jointly passed along in familial lineages (cosegregation). If such a cosegregation of a DNA marker and a trait can be established with sufficient statistical confidence, then one or more genes in the vicinity of the marker are possibly involved in trait similarity among individuals, because genetic material on chromosomes is passed on in chunks. Linkage analysis thus serves to detect the regions (called quantitative trait loci) of the genome where genetic variants with a quantitative effect on the trait must be located.

The first whole-genome linkage scan for intelligence was published in 2005 (Posthuma et al., 2005), and four more studies have been published since (Buyske et al., 2006; Dick et al., 2006; Luciano et al., 2006; Wainwright et al., 2006). The sample used in the first study consisted of a Dutch sample (159 sibling pairs) and an Australian sample (475 sibling pairs). Results indicated two areas of significant linkage to general intelligence—one on the long arm (denoted as q) of chromosome 2 (i.e., 2q) and one on the short arm (denoted as p) of chromosome 6 (i.e., 6p)—and several areas of suggestive linkage (an additional site on 2q, as well as areas on 4p, 7q, 20p, and 21p). The chromosome-2 area has been implicated in linkage scans for autism and dyslexia, while the chromosome-6 area is the main linkage area for reading ability and dyslexia.

Two studies with a partly overlapping sample confirmed the importance of the areas on chromosomes 2 and 6 for specific aspects of intelligence (Luciano et al. 2006) as well as for academic achievement, which is different from IQ score but predicts IQ very well (correlation around 0.6; Wainwright et al., 2006). The Luciano et al. (2006) study additionally showed that both word recognition and IQ were linked to chromosome 2, confirming the notion of the same genes influencing different aspects of cognitive ability (Plomin & Kovas, 2005). A completely independent study by Dick et al. (2006) using data collected as part of the Collaborative Study on the Genetics of Alcoholism (COGA) also confirmed linkage of intelligence to the chromosome-6 area. A second scan based on that dataset (Buyske et al., 2006) found strong evidence for linkage of specific cognitive abilities to chromosome 14, an area that showed suggestive evidence for linkage in three of the five linkage studies (see Fig. 1). Although the COGA dataset has been selected for alcohol dependence and may thus not be representative of the

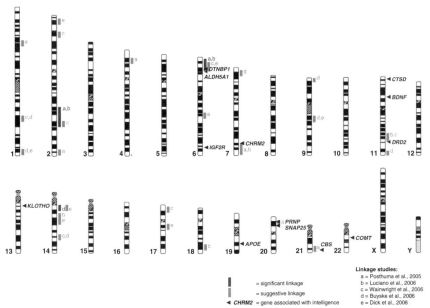

Fig. 1. Ideogram (chromosome map) of the human genome, showing which regions of chromosomes are likely to contain genes for intelligence (marked in red), as based on the five linkage studies for intelligence that have been conducted to date. It also shows the chromosomal regions of all the genes that have been associated with intelligence so far (marked in orange).

general population, Dick et al. (2006) showed that alcohol dependence explained less than 1% of the variance in IQ scores. Moreover, a correction for the selection strategy used (i.e., alcohol dependency) did not change the results significantly.

In association analysis, candidate genes are selected based on existing neuroscientific evidence. Variation in these genes (i.e., alleles) is measured and tested for association with intelligence. These measured allelic variants can either be functional variants that change the gene's effect on intelligence or variants that do not alter the gene effect but are in close vicinity to the true (but unmeasured) functional variant. Case-control association studies—in which, for example, a sample of subjects with high IQ scores (cases) is compared with a sample of subjects with lower IQ (controls)—have the highest statistical power but may provide spurious associations as a result of the use of stratified samples. If many alleles show a different distribution across cases and controls for reasons unrelated to IQ (e.g., due to unbalanced ethnicity in the cases and controls or due to nonrandom or assortative mating in which mate selection is based on resemblance for IQ), all of these alleles will show a spurious statistical association to IQ. Family-based association studies are statistically less powerful than case-control studies but control for these effects of population stratification, as allelic association is tested exclusively within members of the same family.

In association analysis, the choice of candidate genes is crucial. It is usually based on prior knowledge of the gene's involvement in biological functions relevant to intelligence, such as neurophysiological systems known to influence human memory and cognition. Candidate genes can also be selected based on results from animal studies in which the genes have been shown to influence performance on tests of learning and memory. Finally, a large number of genes have been associated with mental retardation (Inlow & Restifo, 2004). Although most mental retardation is monogenetic—i.e., caused by a severe mutation in a single gene only—subtler variation in these genes might influence normal variation in intelligence.

In 1998, Chorney et al. published the first genetic association for normal variation in intelligence, effectively marking the advent of the current era of molecular genetics. They tested 37 markers on the long arm of chromosome 6 for association with IQ in young children. Chromosome 6 was chosen basically because it was the first large chromosome expected to be sequenced by the Human Genome Project, but also because it contained the insulin-like growth factor-2 receptor (IGF2R) gene, which was previously found to be active in brain regions involved in learning and memory. The IGF2R gene was indeed shown to be associated with high IQ in children (Chorney et al., 1998). Four years later, however, this gene was not found to be associated with IQ in an enlarged sample (Hill, Chorney, Lubinski, Thompson, & Plomin, 2002). The same group of researchers continued with a major effort to identify further genetic variants using a whole-genome association approach. This approach resembles linkage more than it resembles the candidate-gene approach in that it aims to identify quantitative trait loci throughout the entire genome, although based on association of the trait to DNA markers rather than cosegregation of the trait and the markers within families. The only association with intelligence in young children that survived rigorous adjustment for multiple testing was a significant association of a functional variant in the aldehyde dehydrogenase 5 family, member A1 (ALDH5A1) gene that causes increased activity of the aldehyde dehydrogenase enzyme (Plomin et al., 2004).

Because heritability increases from 40% in childhood to 80% in adulthood, young children may not be the optimal population for gene finding. At the same time, samples including the elderly may inadvertently confound genetic effects on intelligence with genetic effects on the speed of cognitive aging. The ε4 variant of the apolipoprotein-E (APOE) gene, for instance, has been associated with cognitive deterioration in old age but does not seem to be unambiguously related to cognitive ability or intelligence in children or adults (Deary et al., 2002). Its effect on cognitive ability in the elderly may well derive entirely from the role of this gene in the development of Alzheimer's dementia.

As summarised in Figure 1, various other genes have shown significant association to intelligence.[3] These include the CTSD gene, the PRNP gene, the DRD2 gene, the CBS gene, the BDNF gene, and the COMT gene. These genes have been associated not only with intelligence but with a wide range of cognitive abilities, mostly related to attention (DRD2) and working memory (COMT, BDNF), or to pathological brain states like Alzheimer's dementia (CTSD, BDNF, APOE, PRNP, CBS, COMT), aphasia (APOE, PRNP), and mental retardation (APOE, CBS). To understand the underlying mechanisms linking individual differences in specific cognitive abilities to intelligence or to brain pathology we should adopt a multivariate approach in which we test, for example, whether the same set of genes influences both the specific cognitive ability and an index of brain pathology. This multivariate approach has the added advantage of increasing the power of gene-finding studies.

It is important to note that most of the associations in Figure 1 have proven difficult to replicate. Poor replication of an initially promising association or linkage result is a common concern in the molecular-genetic study of complex brain functioning. Ideally, associations with candidate genes are replicated in independent samples and these candidate genes should also surface in whole-genome searches. To date, only one such genetic association is known for intelligence. In 2003, Comings et al. reported that a variant of the cholinergic muscarinic receptor 2 (CHRM2) gene explained 1% of the variance in full-scale IQ. Two years later, suggestive linkage for intelligence was found on the long arm of chromosome 7 (7q), right above the CHRM2 gene (Posthuma et al., 2005). Subsequently, Gosso et al. (2006) replicated the association between the CHRM2 gene and intelligence in a combined sample of Dutch 12-year-olds and Dutch adults. Here the gene explained 2% of the total variance in full-scale IQ. Although both Comings et al. (2003) and Gosso et al. (2006) did not include functional variants of the CHRM2 gene, the variants they tested were in the same region of this gene, suggesting that functional variants within that region are important to intelligence.

In summary, the last decade has started to see the now well-established heritability of cognitive ability being dissected into its molecular-genetic elements. Association studies have yielded a handful of polygenes of small effect, of which only one has shown replicated association with intelligence. Recent linkage studies for intelligence will refocus association studies to those genes that lie in areas of genetic linkage, a strategy that has proven successful for the CHRM2 gene. These polygenes bring us one step closer to understanding the biological basis of intelligence, although we still face the daunting task of charting the exact route from genetic variation to variation in brain function and on to individual differences in intelligence.

GENE–ENVIRONMENT INTERACTION AND CORRELATION

Complex traits such as intelligence are expected to be influenced at least partly by interactions between genes and environmental factors, and genetic variation may not be evenly distributed across all environments. The gene-finding strategies reviewed earlier completely ignore gene–environment interaction and gene–environment correlation. This may prove a costly oversimplification, and a main improvement in future gene-finding strategies would be to bring the environment into the equation.

Crucial to the estimation of the heritability of intelligence is the observation that monozygotic twins, who are effectively genetically identical, correlate about .60 to .80 on tests of intelligence, whereas dizygotic twins, who share only half of their genetic material, correlate around half of that. Under the assumption that such a pattern of twin correlations is explained by a simple addition of the separate effects of genes and shared and nonshared environmental factors, this yields a heritability of intelligence in adulthood of 60 to 80%. However, the same pattern of twin correlations may also partly result from interactions between genetic and shared environmental effects, or by correlations between genetic variation and environmental factors.

The interaction between genes and shared environment will mimic genetic effects in statistical models. It comes about when a favorable—e.g., intellectually stimulating—family environment has more impact on individuals with a particular genetic make-up than it does on others ("fertile ground"). Environmental mediation of genetic effects for intelligence has for example been shown for socioeconomic status (SES) and parental education, in the sense that the heritability of intelligence is lower for subjects with low SES or when their parents have received less years of education, and higher for persons with high SES or when parents received many years of education.

Gene–environment correlation may occur when parents transmit not only their genes but also their environment, a mechanism known as cultural transmission. For example, parents who are at the high end of the intelligence scale may transmit both the genetic variants associated with higher intelligence and a home environment that provides easy access to intellectual knowledge (such as the availability of books, intellectual discussions at the dinner table, and focus on obtaining high grades at school). Such gene–environment correlation tends to increase the DZ correlation, while the MZ correlation remains the same. Another form of gene–environment correlation occurs when a genetic makeup that favors high intelligence will also more often result in the selection of a societal niche that is conducive to the development of intelligence (such as smarter kids being admitted to the more advanced forms of schooling). Even more complex models allow reciprocal causation between intelligence and environmental factors, resulting in strong correlations between genetic endowment and favorable environmental conditions (Dickens & Flynn, 2001).

A final well-known form of actively induced gene–environment correlation is assortative mating, which not only affects the presence of environmental factors in a given person but also affects resemblance in traits among that person and his or her offspring. Assortative mating is reflected in a spousal correlation greater than zero, and is known to indeed exist for intelligence, where spousal correlations range around 0.30. When smart mothers more often elect smart fathers as mates (and vice versa), this will increase the resemblance between parents and offspring as well as that between siblings and that between dizygotic twins. In twin studies, this may conceal the presence of non-additive genetic effects (gene–gene interactions or genetic dominance) and overestimate the influence of additive genetic factors.

If we assume that the high heritability of intelligence is at least partly explained by complex mechanisms such as gene–gene interaction, gene–environment interaction, and gene–environment correlation, gene finding without taking these complex mechanisms into account will prove very difficult (as is already proving to be the case). Fortunately, as genes are no longer "latent factors" in our models but can actually be measured, investigating genetic effects while allowing for the interplay between genes and environmental factors has now become a realistic goal. Measured candidate genes, such as the CHRM2 gene, allow testing the effects of genes under different "experimental" environmental conditions, using simple designs such as comparing the effect of variation in the gene in groups of children with high- or low-educated parents.

By identifying, replicating, and functionally describing more polygenes like CHRM2, the next era of molecular-genetic research on intelligence will be better enabled to consider the complex interplay of genes and environmental influences. Ultimately, we may be able to supplant the long nature–nurture debate on intelligence with actual understanding of the biological processes in brain development that lead to individual differences in cognitive abilities and disabilities alike. Such understanding will have clear practical benefits for education and learning theories. Genes influencing psychometric IQ are just tiny pieces in this very complex puzzle. However, they are edge pieces. As with any complex puzzle, it may be a good idea to start laying it from the edges.

Recommended Reading

Dickens, W.T., & Flynn, J.R. (2001). (See References)
Goldberg, T.E., & Weinberger, D.R. (2004). Genes and the parsing of cognitive processes. *Trends in Cognitive Sciences, 8*, 325–335.
Gray, J.R., & Thompson, P.M. (2004). Neurobiology of intelligence: Science and ethics. *Nature Reviews Neuroscience, 5*, 471–482.
Kovas, Y., & Plomin, R. (2006). Generalist genes: Implications for the cognitive sciences. *Trends in Cognitive Sciences, 10*, 198–203.
Plomin, R., & DeFries, J.C. (1998). The genetics of cognitive abilities and disabilities. *Scientific American, 278*(5), 62–69.

Acknowledgments—Supported by the Human Frontiers of Science Program (grant number RG0154/ 1998-B), and the Netherlands Organization for Scientific Research (NWO/ MaGWVernieuwingsimpuls 016-065-318).

Notes

1. Address correspondence to Danielle Posthuma, Vrije Universiteit Amsterdam, Department of Biological Psychology, van der Boechorststraat 1, 1081 BT Amsterdam, The Netherlands; e-mail: danielle@psy.vu.nl.

2. The heritability of a trait is a ratio of the genetic variance to the total variance of that trait, so changes in heritability can be the result of changes in environmental variation or in genetic variation. The latter in turn may be caused by the same genes having differential effects across different ages (gene amplification) or by genes turning on and off at certain points in development (gene emergence).

3. Although many X-linked genes have been related to mental retardation, most of these genes are monogenetic genes as detailed earlier. These genes are extensively reviewed in Inlow and Restifo, 2004, but are not included in Figure 1.

References

Buyske, S., Bates, M.E., Gharani, N., Matise, T.C., Tischfield, J.A., & Manowitz, P. (2006). Cognitive traits link to human chromosomal regions. *Behavioral Genetics, 36*, 65–76.
Chorney, M.J., Chorney, K., Seese, N., Owen, M.J., McGuffin, P., Daniels, J., Thompson, L.A., Detterman, D.K., Benbow, C.P., Lubinski, D., Eley, T.C., & Plomin, R. (1998). A quantitative trait locus associated with cognitive ability in children. *Psychological Science, 9*, 159–166.
Comings, D.E., Wu, S., Rostamkhani, M., McGue, M., Lacono, W.G., Cheng, L.S., & MacMurray, J.P. (2003). Role of the cholinergic muscarinic 2 receptor (*CHRM2*) gene in cognition. *Molecular Psychiatry, 8*, 10–11.

Deary, I.J., Whiteman, M.C., Pattie, A., Starr, J.M., Hayward, C., Wright, A.F., Carothers, A., & Whalley, L.J. (2002). Cognitive change and the APOE epsilon 4 allele. *Nature, 418,* 932.

Dick, D.M., Aliev, F., Bierut, L., Goate, A., Rice, J., Hinrichs, A., Bertelsen, S., Wang, J.C., Dunn, G., Kuperman, S., Schuckit, M., Nurnberger, J., Jr., Porjesz, B., Begleiter, H., Kramer, J., & Hesselbrock, V. (2006). Linkage Analyses of IQ in the Collaborative Study on the Genetics of Alcoholism (COGA) Sample. *Behavioral Genetics, 36,* 77–86.

Dickens, W.T., & Flynn, J.R. (2001). Heritability estimates versus large environmental effects: The IQ paradox resolved. *Psychological Review, 108,* 346–369.

Gosso, M.F., van Belzen, M., de Geus, E.J.C., Polderman, J.C., Heutink, P., Boomsma, D.I., & Posthuma, D. (2006). Association between the CHRM2 gene and intelligence in a sample of 304 Dutch families. *Genes, Brain and Behavior.* Retrieved July 3, 2006, from http://www.blackwell-synergy.com/doi/pdf/10.1111/j.1601-183x. 2006.00211.x

Hill, L., Chorney, M.J., Lubinski, D., Thompson, L.A., & Plomin, R. (2002). A quantitative trait locus not associated with cognitive ability in children: A failure to replicate. *Psychological Science, 13,* 561–562.

Inlow, J.K., & Restifo, L.L. (2004). Molecular and comparative genetics of mental retardation. *Genetics, 166,* 835–881.

Luciano, M., Wright, M.J., Duffy, D.L., Wainwright, M.A., Zhu, G., Evans, D.M., Geffen, G.M., Montgomery, G.W., & Martin, N.G. (2006). Genome-wide Scan of IQ Finds Significant Linkage to a Quantitative Trait Locus on 2q. *Behavioral Genetics, 36,* 45–55.

Plomin, R., & Kovas, Y. (2005). Generalist genes and learning disabilities. *Psychological Bulletin, 131,* 592–617.

Plomin, R., Turic, D.M., Hill, L., Turic, D.E., Stephens, M., Williams, J., Owen, M.J., & O'Donovan, M.C. (2004). A functional polymorphism in the succinate-semialdehyde dehydrogenase (aldehyde dehydrogenase 5 family member A1) gene is associated with cognitive ability. *Molecular Psychiatry, 9,* 582–586.

Posthuma, D., Luciano, M., de Geus, E.J.C., Wright, M.J., Slagboom, P.E., Montgomery, G.W., Boomsma, D.I., & Martin, N.G. (2005). A genome-wide scan for intelligence identifies quantitative trait loci on 2q and 6p. *American Journal of Human Genetics, 77,* 318–326.

Wainwright, M.A., Wright, M.J., Luciano, M., Montgomery, G.W., Geffen, G.M., & Martin, N.G. (2006). A linkage study of academic skills defined by the Queensland Core Skills Test. *Behavioral Genetics, 36,* 56–64.

This article has been reprinted as it originally appeared in *Current Directions in Psychological Science.* Citation information for this article as originally published appears above.

Adaptations to Ovulation: Implications for Sexual and Social Behavior

Steven W. Gangestad[1] and Christine E. Garver-Apgar
Department of Psychology, University of New Mexico
Randy Thornhill
Department of Biology, University of New Mexico

Abstract

In socially monogamous species in which males heavily invest in offspring, there arises an inevitable genetic conflict between partners over whether investing males become biological fathers of their partners' offspring. Humans are such a species. The ovulatory-shift hypothesis proposes that changes in women's mate preferences and sexual interests across the cycle are footprints of this conflict. When fertile (mid-cycle), women find masculine bodily and behavioral features particularly sexy and report increased attraction to men other than current partners. Men are more vigilant of partners when the latter are fertile, which may reflect evolved counteradaptations. This adaptationist hypothesis has already generated several fruitful research programs, but many questions remain.

Keywords

mating; evolutionary psychology; attraction

Human sex can result in conception only about 20% of the time: from 5 days before ovulation to the day of ovulation. Yet unlike in humans' close primate relatives, human females lack conspicuous sexual swellings that vary across the cycle, and people have sex throughout the cycle. Continuous receptivity, however, need not imply that women's sexual interests or preferences remain constant. Indeed, it would be surprising if selection had not forged psychological adaptations in one or both sexes to be sensitive to conception risk—and recent research confirms this expectation. The ways people are sensitive to it provide keys to understanding how selection shaped human sexual relations. In short, romantic relationships take shape out of people's adaptive design for cooperating with partners—often lovingly—in pursuit of shared interests, in conjunction with each sex's adaptive design for pursuing its own interests (or those of same-sex ancestors) that conflict with those of partners.

EVOLUTIONARY BACKGROUND: MATE CHOICE FOR GENES

Over evolutionary time, natural selection sifts through available genetic variants, saving those that promote success within a species' niche and discarding others. Our genes are typically "good genes" that have passed a test of time. But some aren't. Genes mutate. Though each gene is copied correctly 99.99+% of the time, sperm or eggs commonly contain one or more new copying errors. Because mutations typically have minor effects (much as slight impurities in a tank of

29

gas subtly compromise car performance), most survive multiple generations before being eliminated. On average, an individual probably has several tens if not hundreds of mutations. Additionally, although the world to which humans must adapt is constant in many ways (e.g., its gravitational fields), in other subtle-but-profound ways it is not. Pathogens constantly evolve to better thrive in the human body, and humans must change merely to keep pace. Despite selection on thousands of ancestral generations to resist pathogens, humans do not possess sure-fire defenses against them.

The ubiquity of maladapted genes may explain why sex evolved. A gene mutated in an asexual, cloning organism persists in all descendants. Sexual organisms pass on just half of their genes to offspring, and what may make sex worthwhile is that offspring need not get all maladapted genes; some offspring get fewer than either parent.

Through good fortune and bad, not everyone has the same number of maladapted genes. The best way to minimize maladapted genes in offspring is to mate with someone lacking them. While mate choosers cannot directly compare DNA copying errors in suitors, they can do so indirectly—for precisely the reason that choosing mates with good genes is important: Genes affect their bearers' performance. Selection ensures that mate choosers evolve to be attuned and attracted to elements of performance that are sensitive to poorly adapted genes within the species—whether it be growth, the ability to physically dominate or outwit others, or possessing "good looks."

TRADE-OFFS BETWEEN MATERIAL AND GENETIC BENEFITS

In relatively few species do both females and males intensively nurture offspring. Humans may be one. While questions remain about how and to what extent men nurture their own offspring in foraging societies, in most societies men and women typically form socially monogamous pairs and men attempt to direct resources (meat, protection, direct care, money) to mates and offspring. Chimpanzees, bonobos, and gorillas don't share this pattern and are probably poor models of human sexual relations. As many bird species form social pairs, however, theories about their mating may offer insight into how selection shaped human sexual psychologies.

Many socially monogamous birds are not sexually monogamous. On average across species, 10 to 15% of offspring are fathered by males other than social partners—so-called "extra-pair" males. Multiple reasons that females seek extra-pair mates are being investigated, but one is that male assistance in raising offspring doesn't eliminate selection pressure on females to obtain good genes. Not all females can pair up with males with high genetic fitness. Those who don't could potentially benefit from getting social partners' cooperation in raising offspring but getting other males' genes. This pattern has been elegantly demonstrated in the collared flycatcher. A large male forehead patch advertises good genes. Females don't prefer large-patched males as social partners, as they work less hard at the nest. Small-patched males, however, are more likely to be cuckolded and large-patched males the biological fathers. Indeed, females time extra-pair copulations to occur during peak fertility, favoring paternity by extra-pair partners.

More generally, in socially monogamous species in which pairs have males as close neighbors, an inevitable conflict between the sexes arises. All else being equal, females mated to males not possessing the best genes could benefit by getting genes from someone else. At the same time, selection operates on investing males to prevent cuckoldry (e.g., by mate guarding or being able to recognize offspring not their own). Selection hence operates on each sex against the interests of the other sex; thus "sexually antagonistic adaptations" evolve. Depending on which sex evolves more effective adaptations (which may depend on ecological factors affecting the ease with which males guard their mates, the relative value of good genes, the amount of assistance males give females, etc.), the actual extra-pair sex rate may be high (20% or more) or low (5% or less). Even when it is low, however, the genetic conflict exists and sexually antagonistic adaptations may evolve.

THE OVULATORY-SHIFT HYPOTHESIS

We (Gangestad & Thornhill, 1998) proposed to look for human adaptations that are footprints of these selection forces, based on the fact we began with: Women are fertile during a brief window of their cycles. If ancestral females benefited from multiple mating to obtain genetic benefits but at some potential cost of losing social mates, selection may have shaped preferences for indicators of those benefits to depend on fertility status: maximal at peak fertility and less pronounced outside the fertile period. Cycle shifts should furthermore be specific to when women evaluate men as short-term sex partners (i.e., their "sexiness") rather than as long-term, investing mates (Penton-Voak et al., 1999). The logic is that costs do not pay when benefits cannot be reaped.

Over a dozen recent studies show that female preferences clearly do shift. At mid-cycle, normally ovulating, non-pill-using women particularly prefer physical symmetry, masculine facial and vocal qualities, intrasexual competitiveness, and various forms of talent.

The *scent of symmetrical men*. Asymmetry on bilateral traits that are symmetrical at the population level (e.g., finger lengths, ear dimensions, wrist width) reflects developmental instability, perturbations due to mutations, pathogens, toxins, and other stresses. Developmental instability, in turn, could affect numerous other features of men, including their scent. In four studies, men wore tee-shirts for two nights and women rated the attractiveness of the shirts' scents. All studies found that, when they were fertile, women particularly preferred the scent of symmetrical men (see Fig. 1). When women were not fertile, they had no preference for symmetrical men's scents. Although the chemical mediating this effect has not been identified, data and theory suggest the existence of androgen-derived substances, the scent of which women evaluate more positively when fertile.

Masculine faces. Male and female faces differ in various ways. Most notably, men have broader chins and narrower eyes (due to development of the brow ridge). Men vary, however, in the extent to which they possess masculine facial features. Women's preference for more masculine faces is more pronounced when they are fertile than when they are infertile, particularly when they rate men's sexiness, not their attractiveness as long-term mates (e.g, Penton-Voak et al., 1999; Johnston, Hagel, Franklin, Fink, & Grammer, 2001).

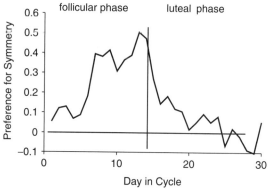

Fig. 1. Women's preference for the scent of symmetrical men as a function of their day in the cycle (*N* = 141). The vertical line corresponds to women's average day of ovulation. The follicular and luteal phases precede and follow ovulation, respectively. Each woman's ratings of scent attractiveness (a sum of ratings of pleasantness and sexiness) were measured against men's physical symmetry. Data are compiled from three separate studies: Gangestad & Thornhill (1998), Thornhill & Gangestad (1999), and Thornhill et al. (2003).

Behavioral displays of social presence and intrasexual competitiveness. We (Gangestad, Simpson, Cousins, Garver-Apgar, & Christensen, 2004) had women view videotapes of men being interviewed for a potential lunch date. Men independently rated as confident and who acted toward their male competitors in condescending ways were found more sexy by women when the women were fertile than they were when the women were not fertile (see Fig. 2).

Vocal masculinity. When rating men's short-term attractiveness, women find masculine (deep) voices more attractive at mid-cycle than they do at other times (Puts, 2005).

Talent versus wealth. Haselton and Miller (in press) found that, when faced with trade-offs between talent (e.g., creativity) and wealth, women choose talent

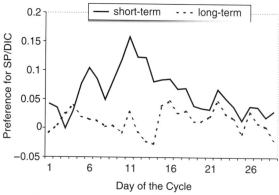

Fig. 2. Women's preference for men who display social presence (SP) and direct intrasexual competitiveness (DIC) as short-term partners (solid line) and as long-term partners (dotted line), as a function of day of their cycle (*N* = 238). From Gangestad et al. (2004).

more often when fertile than they do when nonfertile, but only when evaluating men's short-term mating attractiveness.

All of these characteristics may well have been indicators of good genes ancestrally. Not all positive traits are sexier mid-cycle, however. Traits particularly valued in long-term mates (e.g., promising material benefits) do not appear to be especially attractive to fertile women. For instance, follow-up analyses showed that while the women in the Gangestad et al. (2004) study found arrogant, confrontative, and physically attractive men particularly sexy mid-cycle, their attraction to men perceived to be kind, intelligent, good fathers, and likely to be financially successful—traits particularly valued in long-term mates—didn't change across the cycle. And men judged to be faithful were rated as less sexy mid-cycle than at other times (see also Thornhill et al., 2003).

SHIFTS IN WOMEN'S SEXUAL INTERESTS

Patterns of women's sexual interests also shift across the cycle. In one study, normally ovulating women reported thoughts and feelings over the previous 2 days twice: once when fertile (as confirmed by a luteinizing hormone surge, 1–2 days before ovulation) and once when infertile. When fertile, women reported greater sexual attraction to and fantasy about men other than their primary partners than they did at other times—but their level of attraction to primary partners at this time was no greater than it was when they were infertile (Gangestad, Thornhill, & Garver, 2002; cf. Pillsworth, Haselton, & Buss, 2004).

In fact, however, the ovulatory-shift hypothesis expects a more finely textured pattern. On average, ancestral women could have garnered genetic benefits through extra-pair mating, but those whose primary partners had good genes could not. Selection thus should have shaped interest in extra-pair men mid-cycle to itself depend on partner features; only women with men who, relatively speaking, lack purported indicators of genetic benefits should be particularly attracted to extra-pair men when fertile. We (Gangestad, Thornhill, & Garver-Apgar, 2005) tested this prediction in a replication and extension of Gangestad et al. (2002). Romantically involved couples participated. Again, individuals privately filled out questionnaires twice, once when the female was fertile and once during her luteal phase. Men's symmetry was measured. Once again, women reported greater attraction to extra-pair men and not their primary partners when fertile. Effects, however, were moderated by the symmetry of women's partners. At high fertility, women with relatively asymmetrical partners were more attracted to extra-pair men—and less attracted to their own partners—than when they were infertile. No such effects were found during the luteal phase. Controlling for relationship satisfaction, another important predictor of women's attraction to extra-pair men, did not diminish the effect of partner symmetry. (See also Haselton & Gangestad, in press.)

MALE COUNTERSTRATEGIES ACROSS THE CYCLE

If women have been under selection to seek good genes mid-cycle, men should have been under selection to take additional steps to prevent them from seeking extra-pair sex at this time. Multiple studies indicate that they do so by being more vigilant, proprietary, or monopolizing of mates' time during those times (e.g., Gangestad et al., 2002; Haselton & Gangestad, in press).

There are several candidate cues of fertility status men might use. Three studies found that men find the scent of ovulating women particularly attractive (e.g., Thornhill et al., 2003) and one found that men judge women's faces more attractive mid-cycle. If women's interests change across the cycle, their behavior might too. Whatever the cues, women are unlikely to have been designed through selection to send them. As noted at the outset, women do not have obvious sexual swellings mid-cycle, and they have sex throughout the cycle. These features may well be due to selection on women to suppress signs of fertility status. Men, nonetheless, should be selected to detect byproducts of fertility status not fully suppressed. Consistent with this idea, we (Gangestad et al., 2002) found that enhanced male vigilance of partners mid-cycle (as reported by women) was predicted by enhanced female interest in extra-pair men and not their partners. Men may be particularly vigilant of their partners mid-cycle, when their partners least want them to be.

ADDITIONAL OVULATORY ADAPTATIONS AND BYPRODUCTS

Women's preferences and biases may shift not only toward certain men, but away from clearly undesirable mating options (e.g., incest, rape; e.g., Chavanne & Gallup, 1998). Fessler and Navarrete (2003) assessed women's disgust in several domains: maladaptive sex such as incest and bestiality, food aversiveness, and filth. Only disgust to maladaptive sex rose with fertility.

Women can identify male faces as male more quickly when fertile (e.g., Macrae, Alnwick, Milne, & Schloerscheidt, 2002). This effect is perhaps a byproduct of greater salience of masculine features in male faces associated with their preference when women are fertile. Adaptive ovulatory shifts in preferences, sexual interests, and biases may produce a variety of other byproducts.

CONCLUSION

In any socially monogamous species in which males heavily invest in offspring, there is an inevitable genetic conflict between partners over where the female obtains genes for her offspring. Changes across the ovulatory cycle in women's and men's behavior may contain telltale signs of this conflict.

Many questions remain unanswered. Which female mate preferences strengthen mid-cycle; which don't? Is the pattern consistent with the good-genes hypothesis? Some preferences may be for compatible genes, ones that complement those of the mate chooser (e.g., dissimilar major histocompatibility complex [MHC] genes). Are preferences for compatibility maximal mid-cycle (see Thornhill et al., 2003)? How do male-partner features (e.g., symmetry, MHC dissimilarity) or relationship characteristics (e.g., satisfaction) affect female sexual interest mid-cycle? Do cycle shifts endure across women's reproductive lifespan? Are they robust across human populations? How, precisely, do men behave differently toward fertile partners and what cues mediate changes? Do women resist partners' proprietary actions more mid-cycle? What proximate mechanisms (e.g., hormones) mediate cycle shifts? (Changes in female preferences for the scent of symmetrical men are best predicted by corresponding changes in women's testosterone [positively] and progesterone [negatively], but other candidates [e.g., estrogen, luteinizing hormone] are possible.) Do men's hormones (e.g., testosterone) fluctuate in response to female partners' ovulatory status?

An evolutionary approach uniquely views ovulation as a highly important event around which psychological adaptations might evolve. Alternative nonevolutionary approaches could not have predicted a priori or accounted for these findings. More generally, then, the ovulatory-shift hypothesis illustrates the heuristic value of an adaptationist perspective, guiding researchers to explore domains otherwise unexplored and generating fruitful predictions not offered by other approaches.

Recommended Reading

Gangestad, S.W., Thornhill, R., & Garver-Apgar, C.E. (in press). Adaptations to ovulation. In D.M. Buss (Ed.), *Evolutionary Psychology Handbook*. Boston: Allyn-Bacon.

Jennions, M.D., & Petrie, M. (2000). Why do females mate multiply?: A review of the genetic benefits. *Biological Reviews, 75*, 21–64.

Kappeler, P.M., & van Schaik, C.P. (Eds.) (2004). *Sexual selection in primates: New and comparative perspectives*. Cambridge, U.K.: Cambridge University Press.

Rice, W.R., & Holland, B. (1997). The enemies within: Intragenomic conflict, interlocus contest evolution (ICE), and the intraspecific Red Queen. *Behavioral Ecology and Sociobiology, 41*, 1–10.

Note

1. Address correspondence to Steve Gangestad, Department of Psychology, University of New Mexico, Albuquerque, NM 87111; email: sgangest@unm.edu.

References

Chavanne, T.J., & Gallup, G.G. (1998). Variation in risk taking behavior among female college students as a function of the menstrual cycle. *Evolution and Human Behavior, 19*, 27–32.

Fessler, D.M.T., & Navarrete, C.D. (2003). Domain-specific variation in disgust sensitivity across the menstrual cycle. *Evolution and Human Behavior, 324*, 406–417.

Gangestad, S.W., Simpson, J.A., Cousins, A.J., Garver-Apgar, C.E., & Christensen, P.N. (2004). Women's preferences for male behavioral displays change across the menstrual cycle. *Psychological Science, 15*, 203–207.

Gangestad, S.W., & Thornhill, R. (1998). Menstrual cycle variation in women's preference for the scent of symmetrical men. *Proceedings of the Royal Society of London, B, 262*, 727–733.

Gangestad, S.W., Thornhill, R., & Garver, C.E. (2002). Changes in women's sexual interests and their partners' mate retention tactics across the menstrual cycle: Evidence for shifting conflicts of interest. *Proceedings of the Royal Society of London, B, 269*, 975–982.

Gangestad, S.W., Thornhill, R., & Garver-Apgar, C.E. (2005). Female sexual interests across the ovulatory cycle depend on primary partner developmental instability. *Proceedings of the Royal Society of London, B, 272*, 2023–2027.

Haselton, M.G., & Gangestad, S.W. (in press). Conditional expression of female desires and male mate retention efforts across the human ovulatory cycle. *Hormones and Behavior*.

Haselton, M.G., & Miller, G.F. (in press). Evidence for ovulatory shifts in attraction to artistic and entrepreneurial excellence. *Human Nature*.

Johnston, V.S., Hagel, R., Franklin, M., Fink, B., & Grammer, K. (2001). Male facial attractiveness: Evidence for hormone mediated adaptive design. *Evolution and Human Behavior, 23*, 251–267.

Macrae, C.N., Alnwick, K.A., Milne, A.B., & Schloerscheidt, A.M. (2002). Person perception across the menstrual cycle: Hormonal influences on social-cognitive functioning. *Psychological Science, 13*, 532–536.

Penton-Voak, I.S., Perrett, D.I., Castles, D., Burt, M., Kobayashi, T., & Murray, L.K. (1999). Female preference for male faces changes cyclically. *Nature, 399*, 741–742.

Pillsworth, E.G., Haselton, M.G., & Buss, D.M. (2004). Ovulatory shifts in female sexual desire. *Journal of Sex Research, 41*, 55–65.

Puts, D.A. (2005). Mating context and menstrual phase affect women's preference for male voice pitch. *Evolution and Human Behavior, 26*, 388–397.

Thornhill, R., & Gangestad, S.W. (1999). The scent of symmetry: A human pheromone that signals fitness? *Evolution and Human Behavior, 20*, 175–201.

Thornhill, R., Gangestad, S.W., Miller, R., Scheyd, G., McCollough, J., & Franklin, M. (2003). MHC, symmetry and body scent attractiveness in men and women (Homo sapiens). *Behavioral Ecology, 14*, 668–678

This article has been reprinted as it originally appeared in *Current Directions in Psychological Science*. Citation information for this article as originally published appears above.

New Evolutionary Perspectives on Altruism: Multilevel-Selection and Costly-Signaling Theories

Francis T. McAndrew[1]

Department of Psychology, Knox College, Galesburg, Illinois

Abstract

Social psychological theories tend to be primarily concerned with the immediate causes of altruism, whereas evolutionary explanations focus more on the origins and ultimate functions of altruistic behavior. Recent developments in the evolutionary psychology of altruism promise an even richer understanding of this important category of social behaviors. Specifically, new perspectives offered by multilevel-selection theory and costly-signaling theory may help to shed light on some of the more problematic issues in the study of altruism.

Keywords

altruism; evolutionary theory; multilevel selection; costly signaling

When defining altruism, social psychologists usually focus on the intentions of the altruist (i.e., the act as a voluntary attempt to benefit other individuals), and their research has traditionally attempted to isolate the situational factors that determine when people will behave altruistically. Four decades of research have identified the importance of such factors as empathy, rewards, emotional states, social norms, and number of bystanders in influencing helping behavior.

However, social psychological models of altruism do not address the question of why basic motives such as empathy and various situational factors came to be so important. In fact, social psychologists continue to study altruism and other social behaviors with little reference to the origins and ultimate functions of those behaviors, which have been the primary concerns of sociobiologists.

Altruism has always been a thorny issue for evolutionary theorists; the idea of an organism engaging in a behavior that comes at a great personal cost and seems to benefit only other individuals was difficult for natural selection to explain. It was not until the concept of inclusive fitness was introduced by Hamilton (1964) that evolutionists had a satisfactory theoretical framework for discussing altruism. Inclusive fitness is often referred to as "kin selection," because according to this concept, natural selection favors behaviors that benefit others who share our genes, especially closely related kin. Hence, the mother who sacrifices her life so that her children survive may actually be engaging in a behavior that is genetically very adaptive, as the copies of her genes that reside in her children will in the long run lead to greater genetic fitness than if she alone had survived.

The concept of kin selection is somewhat limited in that it cannot explain the whole range of altruistic behaviors observed in humans and other animals. For example, it cannot account for altruistic acts aimed at other individuals known not to be genetic kin. Obviously, there are many situations in which we help others who are not related to us: We loan money and personal belongings to friends, we give rides to strangers who are hitchhiking, and we go out of our way to do favors for acquaintances who ask us for help. Fortunately, an alternative form of altruism, *reciprocal altruism* (Trivers, 1971), explains why these important and socially necessary behaviors occur frequently in our lives. Reciprocal altruism is defined as cooperative behavior among unrelated individuals that benefits everyone involved. Individual success at reciprocal altruism depends greatly on the ability to quickly identify others who will be good exchange partners and those who are cheaters.

Because humans are a supremely social species, the selection pressures faced by early humans in this regard must have been profound. It would have been evolutionary suicide to consistently behave in a selfless, altruistic manner toward unrelated individuals who took as much as they could get while offering little in return. Consequently, it should not be surprising that people do seem to have skill in identifying cheaters. For example, they recognize photographs of other individuals better if the people in the photographs were identified as "untrustworthy" the first time they were seen than if they had been described by other adjectives (Mealey, Daood, & Krage, 1996). Similarly, people are hesitant to enter into interpersonal relationships with other individuals who are known to be highly manipulative (Wilson, Near, & Miller, 1998). Just as we are primed to detect cheaters, we also seem to be primed to quickly recognize true altruists who will be trustworthy partners in social exchange (Brown & Moore, 2000).

MULTILEVEL-SELECTION THEORY

The concepts of kin selection and reciprocal altruism are the foundations of most evolutionary explanations of altruism, and a belief that it is generally inappropriate to talk about natural selection occurring at any level larger than that of the individual organism dominates the field at this time. However, in recent years, a growing number of researchers have come to believe that the concept of natural selection can be meaningfully applied at the group level, and they maintain that group selection may be more common and more important than previously thought (Boehm, 1999; Wilson, 1997).

This new perspective is called *multilevel-selection theory* (MST), and its primary spokesperson has been evolutionary biologist David Sloan Wilson. For Wilson, it is crucial to distinguish between the competition between individuals within the same group and the competition between individuals in different groups. Within-group selection follows the generally accepted idea that individual organisms (or collections of genes) are in direct selfish competition with each other. Group-level adaptations, in contrast, require thinking in terms of selection in which groups can be thought of as adaptive units in their own right. According to MST, groups do not evolve into adaptive units for all traits, but only for those traits that increase the fitness of some groups relative to other groups (Wilson, 1997). In a highly social species such as humans, an altruistic predisposition toward other group members independent of past reciprocal interactions with these individuals may have been just such a trait. Although such "knee jerk" altruism may appear to decrease the fitness of individual altruists, it may sometimes become adaptive because groups of altruists will be more fit than groups of nonaltruists under the right conditions (Wilson, 1997).

Consider what might happen if two groups that are in direct competition with each other have different concentrations of altruists and nonaltruists. If one group has a high concentration of altruists, the cooperation among the altruists might increase the success of the group, bestowing significant adaptive advantages on all the individuals within the group. If the rival group is dominated by nonaltruists, it might be at a disadvantage relative to the group dominated by altruists, which would diminish the fitness of all the individuals in the less altruistic group. Because the cooperative group would prosper at the expense of the selfish group, the net result would be an overall increase in the number of altruists in the population as a whole. Hence, MST offers a compelling explanation for how altruistic tendencies would evolve in situations in which the main selection pressure derives from intense competition between two or more competing groups, when the fortunes of each individual are closely tied to the success of his or her group. However, if groups are permanently isolated from each other and the competition that exists is entirely within the group, natural selection would eliminate the altruists from the groups in short order as they would be mercilessly exploited by selfish individuals. In this scenario, the evolution of altruism is better explained by a more discriminating brand of reciprocal altruism.

Some critics of MST have argued that although selection at the group level may have been theoretically possible, the conditions that would be necessary for it to occur almost never exist in the real world (Cronk, 1994). The validity of this criticism awaits the results of research designed specifically with this issue in mind. However, the more common attacks leveled against MST stem from a basic misunderstanding of what the theory is saying. Although MST is not inherently incompatible with more traditional evolutionary viewpoints, it is often presented as if this were the case. For example, many writers equate MST with long-discredited naive theories of group selection based on organisms acting for "the good of the species," and think that MST discounts the importance of natural selection that occurs in units smaller than groups. MST does not deny that selection at lower levels of organization is vitally important; on the contrary, MST maintains that selection at the individual level occurs at a faster pace than selection at the group level (Boehm, 1997). In fact, MST maintains that traits such as altruism are selected at the group level precisely because they are ultimately adaptive to individuals. The confusion apparently arises over the fact that it is the individual's membership in a group faced with particular selection pressures that causes the group to become the vehicle for behaviors that benefit each individual.

COSTLY-SIGNALING THEORY

How might one explain large philanthropic gifts to nonkin or even handouts to beggars that will never be reciprocated? None of the aforementioned explanations of altruism offer a ready answer. Costly-signaling theory (CST) has been developed to help account for these interesting charitable acts (Grafen, 1990; Zahavi, 1977). In some respects, CST is about truth in advertising. It proposes that individuals often engage in behaviors that are very costly as a way of signaling honest information about themselves. Such behaviors can benefit the signaler by increasing the likelihood that he or she will be chosen as a mate or an ally or that he or she will later be deferred to as dominant by would-be rivals. Costly signals can also benefit observers simply because they provide useful social information. Smith and Bird (2000) have described the four qualities that a behavior must have to qualify as a costly signal. First, the behavior must be easily observable by others. Second, it must be costly to the actor in resources, energy, or some other significant domain. Third, the signal must be a reliable indicator of some trait or characteristic of the signaler, such as health, intelligence, or access to resources. Finally, the behavior in question must lead to some advantage for the signaler.

CST suggests that extreme forms of philanthropy and altruism are conspicuous displays of resources that serve to reinforce one's status. After all, if one can afford to expend a great deal of money, energy, or time in a manner that seems to be irrelevant to one's selfish interests, then the resources that one has in reserve must be very great indeed. This type of "competitive altruism" can be a way of positioning oneself for access to resources during unforeseen future times of need (Boone, 1998). There is, in fact, evidence to support the belief that individuals who have a history of being magnanimous are rewarded by others when times get tough. Among the Ache of Paraguay, for example, individuals who shared more than average with others in good times received more food from more people when they were sick or injured than did those who had been less generous (Gurven, Allen-Arave, Hill, & Hurtado, 2000). Apparently, having everyone owe you for past unselfishness can be a good hedge against future calamities, and costly signaling may be an effective strategy for inducing reciprocal altruism.

Anthropological studies provide numerous examples of exaggerated displays of public generosity, but these studies have yet to follow through on verifying the advantages that accrue to the displayers. For example, on Ifaluk Atoll in Micronesia, males sometimes engage in torch fishing (luring flying fish into nets at night with torches) when other fishing techniques would actually be more efficient. Torch fishing is a difficult, time-intensive activity, but also a highly visible activity that serves to advertise a man's work ethic (Sosis, 2000). Similarly, Smith and Bird (2000) described a form of costly signaling among the Meriam, a Melanesian society located on an island off the coast of Australia. Two to 5 years after a death, the family of the deceased puts on an elaborate feast to coincide with the erection of an expensive and showy permanent tombstone. Gifts are given to all guests, along with prodigious amounts of food. Ideally, one of the main courses is turtle meat obtained through a dangerous, time-consuming turtle hunt. Successful turtle hunting requires careful coordination of effort and great physical agility, strength, and diving abilities because the turtle hunters have to jump from a boat onto moving turtles in open water. The ability to supply many turtles for the funeral feast serves as an honest signal of the physical quality of the males in the family. Everyone in the village is invited to the feast, and no reciprocation of any kind is expected.

CONCLUSIONS

The antagonism between experimental social psychology studies of altruism and evolutionary thinking is counterproductive and misplaced. The paradigms are not inherently adversarial, and each provides a valuable piece of the puzzle. The difference between traditional psychological explanations of altruism and evolutionary explanations is a matter of focus. Social psychological theories tend to be primarily concerned with the immediate causes of altruism, whereas evolutionary explanations focus more on the origins of altruistic behavior. Social psychological theories have effectively identified many of the emotional and situational factors associated with altruistic behaviors, and evolutionary perspectives have been more effective at providing a theoretical framework for understanding the origins and ultimate functions of altruistic behavior. The concepts of inclusive fitness, reciprocal altruism, costly signaling, and multilevel selection can provide new, rich frameworks from which experimental social psychologists can launch more theoretically based investigations of altruism.

A union of these two rich traditions can provide both the hypotheses and the methods needed to study some currently unresolved issues. For example, MST suggests that competition between groups added a new evolutionary dimension that would have changed the course of evolution for traits such as altruism. Anthropologists might explore the degree to which this appears to have occurred in early human groups, and social psychologists might use this idea as a springboard for studying the behavior of individuals in a variety of social and work groups. Similarly, anecdotal accounts of costly signaling are interesting, but more rigorous research is needed to determine if the outcomes of such behavior fall in line with what evolutionists would predict. In short, open-mindedness regarding different perspectives within evolutionary thinking and a willingness to combine an evolutionary perspective with the traditions of social psychology promise much for our understanding of the nature of human altruism.

Recommended Reading

Batson, C.D. (1998). Prosocial behavior and altruism. In D.T. Gilbert, S.T. Fiske, & G. Lindzey (Eds.), *The handbook of social psychology* (4th ed., pp. 282–316). New York: McGraw-Hill.

Hamilton, W.D. (1996). *The narrow roads of gene land*. Oxford, England: W.H. Freeman/Spektrum.

Kenrick, D.T., & Simpson, J.A. (1997). Why social psychology and evolutionary psychology need one another. In J.A. Simpson & D.T. Kenrick (Eds.), *Evolutionary social psychology* (pp. 1–20). Mahwah, NJ: Erlbaum.

Sober, E., & Wilson, D.S. (1998). *Unto others: The evolution and psychology of unselfish behavior*. Cambridge, MA: Harvard University Press.

Wilson, D.S., & Kniffin, K.M. (1999). Multilevel selection and the social transmission of behavior. *Human Nature, 10*, 291–310.

Note

1. Address correspondence to Frank T. McAndrew, Department of Psychology, Knox College, Galesburg, IL 61401-4999; e-mail: fmcandre@ knox.edu.

References

Boehm, C. (1997). Impact of the human egalitarian syndrome on Darwinian selection mechanics. *The American Naturalist, 150*, S100–S121.

Boehm, C. (1999). The natural selection of altruistic traits. *Human Nature, 10,* 205–252.

Boone, J.L. (1998). The evolution of magnanimity: When is it better to give than to receive? *Human Nature, 9,* 1–21.

Brown, W.M., & Moore, C. (2000). Is prospective altruist-detection an evolved solution to the adaptive problem of subtle cheating in cooperative ventures? Supportive evidence using the Wason Selection Task. *Evolution and Human Behavior, 21,* 25–38.

Cronk, L. (1994). Group selection's new clothes. *Behavioral and Brain Sciences, 17,* 615–617.

Grafen, A. (1990). Biological signals as handicaps. *Journal of Theoretical Biology, 144,* 517–546.

Gurven, M., Allen-Arave, W., Hill, K., & Hurtado, M. (2000). It's a wonderful life: Signaling generosity among the Ache of Paraguay. *Evolution and Human Behavior, 21,* 263–282.

Hamilton, W.D. (1964). The genetical theory of social behavior: I and II. *Journal of Theoretical Biology, 7,* 1–32.

Mealey, L., Daood, C., & Krage, M. (1996). Enhanced memory for faces of cheaters. *Evolution and Human Behavior, 17,* 119–128.

Smith, E.A., & Bird, R.L.B. (2000). Turtle hunting and tombstone opening: Public generosity as costly signaling. *Evolution and Human Behavior, 21,* 245–261.

Sosis, R. (2000). Costly signaling and torch fishing on Ifaluk Atoll. *Evolution and Human Behavior, 21,* 223–244.

Trivers, R.L. (1971). The evolution of reciprocal altruism. *Quarterly Review of Biology, 46,* 35–57.

Wilson, D.S. (1997). Altruism and organism: Disentangling the themes of Multilevel Selection Theory. *The American Naturalist, 150,* S122–S134.

Wilson, D.S., Near, D.C., & Miller, R.R. (1998). Individual differences in Machiavellianism as a mix of cooperative and exploitative strategies. *Evolution and Human Behavior, 19,* 203–212.

Zahavi, A. (1977). Reliability in communication systems and the evolution of altruism. In B. Stonehouse & C.M. Perrins (Eds.), *Evolutionary ecology* (pp. 253–259). London: MacMillan Press

This article has been reprinted as it originally appeared in *Current Directions in Psychological Science.* Citation information for this article as originally published appears above.

Evolutionary Psychology: The Wheat and the Chaff

Frans B.M. de Waal[1]

Yerkes Primate Research Center, Emory University, Atlanta, Georgia

Abstract

Evolutionary approaches are on the rise in the social sciences and have the potential to bring an all-encompassing conceptual framework to the study of human behavior. Together with neuroscience, which is digging the grave of mind-body dualism, evolutionary psychology is bound to undermine the still reigning human–animal dualism. If a Darwinian reshaping of the social sciences seems inevitable, even desirable, this should not be looked at as a hostile take-over. The underlying theme of this essay is that it is time for psychologists to join the Darwinian revolution, yet the essay also critically reviews current evolutionary psychology. It questions the loose application of adaptationist thinking and the fragmentation of the genome, behavior, and the brain. From biology we learn that not every species-typical trait is necessarily advantageous, and from neuroscience we learn that not every psychological ability or tendency necessarily needs to have its own specialized brain circuitry. But even if the concept of adaptation is hard to apply, psychologists would do well to start looking at human behavior in the light of evolution.

Keywords

evolution; adaptation; modularity; biology

Few topics are as hotly debated within psychology today as evolutionary psychology. It is not that the issues are new—some go back to William James and the heyday of social Darwinism—but evolutionary ideas about human behavior are being forwarded with new force, backed by innovative concepts derived from the study of animal behavior, at a time when the once-popular environmental and cultural explanations are increasingly recognized as inadequate.

The stated goal of evolutionary psychology is to provide an evolutionary account of human behavior. By hypothesizing about the selection pressures that have shaped behavior in the past, evolutionary psychologists expect to arrive at testable hypotheses about present behavior. Because evolutionary psychology does not focus on genetic explanations at the exclusion of other explanations, it is not genetically deterministic, even though it obviously emphasizes genetic evolution more than psychologists have been used to. Whereas its objectives are broad and laudable enough, evolutionary psychology is unfortunately better known for a few narrow theories about why women fall for rich guys, why stepfathers are not to be trusted, and how rape is only natural. Moreover, in the promotion of these ideas, theoretical convictions have often been more conspicuous than data. Nonetheless, there is no way around an evolutionary approach to human behavior. Although I take a critical approach to evolutionary psychology in this essay, my arguments should not be taken to mean that it has no future. On the contrary,

I see evolutionary psychology as an inevitable, even desirable development plagued by serious growing pains that need to be addressed for its own good.

Looking at the social sciences as a relative outsider, I see thousands of ideas that are barely interconnected (Staats, 1991). One could argue that they do not need to interconnect, yet this amounts to an admission that every area within the discipline is free to come up with its own explanations. This approach results in a serious lack of mooring to the thinking in psychology, a lack of an overarching scheme within which everything must make sense.

A younger generation of psychologists, anthropologists, and even economists and political scientists is gaining enthusiasm for a Darwinian framework, which has the potential to tie together the forest of hypotheses about human behavior now out there. My hope is that this generation will turn evolutionary psychology into a serious and rigorous science by being critical of its premises without abandoning the core idea that important aspects of human behavior have been naturally selected. In the end, evolutionary theory may serve as the umbrella idea so desperately needed in the social sciences (Wilson, 1998).

Even though psychology is at the forefront in moving closer to the life sciences, it has not yet freed itself from certain aspects of Western philosophy, which ultimately came out of the Christian tradition. Psychology is still burdened with ancient dualisms, such as those between body and mind, human and animal, and nature and culture. It will have to rid itself of these dualisms before it can fully integrate with the life sciences and their non-Christian, Aristotelian foundation. Whereas we can safely leave it to cognitive neuroscience to do away with any lingering mind-body dualism, and to students of animal culture to bridge the nature-culture gap, psychology will also need to get over its pervasive human-animal dualism.

DARWINISM 101

But before evolutionary psychology can be successful, social scientists will need training in evolutionary theory. Many of the problems surrounding evolutionary psychology have nothing to do with whether human behavior has been subject to evolution by natural selection—which to me is a given—but rather concern how broad or narrow a view of evolution one embraces. Many followers of evolutionary psychology overlook some of the simplest truths coming out of evolutionary theory.

Dobzhansky (1973) wrote an article with the now-famous title "Nothing in Biology Makes Sense Except in the Light of Evolution." This obviously means that leaving evolution out of basic science education constitutes a fatal deficiency. Because of continuing resistance to evolutionary theory, however, this deficiency unfortunately characterizes large parts of the U.S. public school system. After such an education, the young social scientist goes to the university, where the curriculum, with few exceptions, also neglects evolutionary theory. As a result, the way evolutionary theory is applied to human behavior is often riddled with curious errors. The most basic one is taking the existence of a trait to mean that it must be good for something, thus ignoring the warning of Williams (1966), a contemporary evolutionary biologist, that "adaptation is a special and onerous concept that should be used only when it is really necessary" (pp. 4–5).

An example straight out of the evolutionary psychology literature—and I could offer hundreds more—is found right in the opening sentence of a recent article. It states: "Both male facial hair and male pattern baldness are genetically based, suggesting that they contributed to fitness" (Muscarella & Cunningham, 1996, p. 99). Later the same article, we learn that male pattern baldness may signal social maturity, described as a friendly kind of dominance based on wisdom. Is this supposed to explain why we have an entire industry that removes hair from men's heads? Obviously, every man wants to look mature and wise!

The first common mistake in evolutionary explanations, then, to think that if something is genetically influenced it must serve purpose. Alzheimer's disease and cystic fibrosis have a genetic basis, as do many other diseases, but no one would argue that they contribute to fitness. In addition, many characteristics are by-products of others, and all that matters from an evolutionary perspective is that the entire set of traits serves survival and reproduction. Many individual traits are imperfectly designed or positively costly. A human example is our back: Our species not fully suited for an upright posture, hence many of us suffer back problems, such as hernias, slipped disks, and neck pain. Walking upright must have had great benefits for these costs to be tolerable, even though there exists no universally accepted theory of why we walk upright.

It is no wonder that biologists of ten refer to the evolutionary process as "tinkering." Ballast often remains visible in the end-product. Ironically, then, the natural world rampant with flawed designs that reflect the trouble evolution has had turning one form into another, such as a quadruped into a biped.

RAPE AS ADAPTATION

The lesson from the foregoing is that one cannot atomize the organism. One cannot single out a trait for an adaptive story, as is often done in evolutionary psychology. Rather, one needs to (a) consider the entire set of traits and (b) trace the organism's phylogeny, that is, the ancestral forms that produced it.

In moving this observation to human behavior, it is impossible to ignore the evolutionary psychology book that has raised most eyebrows. In *A Natural History of Rape*, Thornhill and Palmer (2000) postulated that rape is an adaptation; that is, rape may have been favored by natural selection because it furthered male reproduction. The authors extrapolated straight from Thornhill's insect studies, which showed that there are indeed species with male anatomical features that seem designed to force females into sexual contact. But these are flies, and in humans rape is part of a far larger picture. Rape occurs at the interface of sex and power, two rich and complex areas of human behavior that are obviously interconnected. It is hard to see how any serious treatment of rape can rip it from this larger context, explaining it as an isolated behavior, as Thornhill and Palmer tried to do.

To be called an adaptation, rape would need to have its own genetic basis separate from the genetic bases of other sexual tendencies, as well as personality characteristics, such as impulsivity or aggressivity. Rape would also need to offer special reproductive advantages, and have been favored by selection for this very reason. These are heavy requirements that raise a number of pressing questions. Do we know if rapists are genetically unique? What are the advantages of rape, if any, in terms of reproduction? Are there costs associated with rape? In relation to the latter question, imagine a small ancestral community in which a man raped the wives and daughters of other men. I do not think this man would have had good survival chances. And why do men sometimes rape partners who are perfectly willing to engage in consensual sex? Declaring rape an adaptation raises a multitude of questions, questions that Thornhill and Palmer have failed to answer.

A major problem with the strategy of singling out rape for evolutionary explanation is that the behavior is shown by only a small minority. The same criticism applies to Daly and Wilson's (1988) well-known work on infanticide by stepparents. They explained this category of infanticide as arising from a lack of shared genes with adoptive offspring. I would argue that in seeking to understand rare behavior we should never ignore the norm. If child abuse by stepfathers is evolutionarily explained, why do so many *more* stepfathers lovingly care for their children than abuse them? And if rape is such an advantageous reproductive strategy, why are there so many *more* men who do not rape than who do? I have called this the dilemma of the rarely exercised option: A Darwinian account of an atypical behavioral choice is incomplete without at least an equally good account of the typical choice (de Waal, 2000).

THE MODULE EXPLOSION

Followers of evolutionary psychology often talk about a gene for this or a brain module for that, seeking to dissect the whole to explain each part separately. If this cannot be done with the components of a watch spread out on the table, it most certainly cannot be done with the genome, the organism, and its behavior. As for the brain, the current trend to divide brain function into modules reminds me of early ethology, when there was no limit to the number of instincts one could propose: from self-preservation to aggression, and from sex to motherhood. In the 1950s, each species-typical tendency had its own instinct, and Konrad Lorenz's *Instinktlehre* (German for "instinct doctrine") even included a "parliament" of instincts to indicate how all components together influence decisions. These ideas applied mainly to nonhuman species, but human instincts have been proposed many times as well, most energetically by self-declared evolutionary psychologist McDougall (1908). Similarly, proponents of evolutionary psychology have compared the brain to a Swiss army knife to which evolution has one by one added modules for everything from face recognition, to tool use, preference for kin over nonkin, child care, friendship, detection of cheaters, and theory of mind[2] (Tooby & Cosmides, 1992).

One problem with this approach—apart from the fact that brain modules at any specific task level have yet to be demonstrated—is that this would make for an incredibly unwieldy brain, much like a computer to which a new chip would need to be added each time we install another program: one chip for word processing, one for games, one for spreadsheets, and so on. Instead, a computer is a multipurpose device that allows each application to draw on its full potential.

This is not to imply that the brain is a *tabula rasa*. It seems prepared to acquire certain skills more easily than others, and to be waiting for certain kinds of information. The studies by Tooby and Cosmides (1992) do indeed suggest such preparation, as do many animal studies, going back to the early work on imprinting, according to which ducks and geese are preprogrammed to pick up information about their species in the first days of life. What makes this happen is unclear, however, and the various labels now in use to indicate genetic influences on behavior—from biogrammar, to biological algorithm, brain module, epigenetic rule, and learning predisposition—are really not much better at solving the mystery than the good-old instinct concept. The term module, in particular, carries the connotation of a brain part that is self-contained, encapsulated, and localized, rendering the idea unpalatable to neuro-scientists (Panksepp & Panksepp, 2000). Quite possibly, our pre-paredness for particular sets of stimuli or problems (e.g., the facility with which we recognize faces; Gauthier & Tarr, 1997) boils down to learned stimulus relevance rather than specialized brain circuitry.

Williams (1966) was right to warn that adaptation is an onerous concept that should be applied parsimoniously. What evolutionary psychology needs to develop is a taste for multilevel thinking in which attention freely shifts between immediate (proximate) explanations of behavior, which are the traditional domain of psychology, and evolutionary (ultimate) explanations. In other words, it needs to address both the "how" questions of how things work and the "why" questions of why evolution favored a particular behavior—to put a little less evolution and a little more psychology into its explanations.

CONCLUSION

Current problems with evolutionary psychology may be serious, but they are not insurmountable. Evolutionary psychology is bound to overcome them. I dare predict that 50 years from now every psychology department will have Darwin's bearded portrait on the wall. Evolutionary approaches have the potential to introduce a conceptual framework that will accommodate or replace the current proliferation of disconnected theories in the study of human behavior.

Even though evolutionary psychology, like the rest of psychology, oftentimes acts as if the human species is a world apart, it cannot help but undermine its own anthropocentrism given the source of the theories that it is so eagerly adopting. They derive from scientists, such as Darwin, who first of all were naturalists. If evolutionary psychology embraces Edward Wilson it cannot help but get covered in ants, and if it embraces William Hamilton it cannot overlook the beetles and parasites that fascinated this brilliant biologist. With regard to animals closer to us, the parallels are even more striking. Chimpanzees, for example, engage in political alliances when jockeying for power, show empathy toward others in distress, establish an economy of services and favors, and reconcile with opponents after a fight by means of a kiss and embrace (Fig. 1; de Waal, 1982/1998, 1996). Because evolutionary explanations require close attention to phylogeny, and given that primatologists are used to behavioral complexity not unlike that of our own species, evolutionary psychology and primatology make natural partners.

The questions asked by evolutionary psychology may strike some readers as simplistic, yet they are here to stay. Questions about why we choose particular mates, avoid incest, and favor kin, and what modes of cooperation we engage in, for example, are not the traditional questions of psychology, yet they emerge naturally from an evolutionary perspective.

Fig. 1. Example of chimpanzees' use of eye contact and hand gestures to invite a reconciliation. This photograph shows the situation 10 min after a protracted, noisy conflict between two adult males at the Arnhem Zoo in the Netherlands. The challenged male (left) fled into the tree, but 10 min later his opponent stretched out a hand. Within seconds, the two males had a physical reunion and climbed down together to groom each other on the ground. Photograph by the author.

These basic questions are central to any evolutionary approach. Psychologists who do not like the simplicity of the answers currently coming out of evolutionary psychology should make an effort to improve them, to broaden its intellectual horizon, because all of psychology would stand to gain from a more enlightened evolutionary psychology.

Recommended Reading

de Waal, F.B.M. (1999). The end of nature versus nurture. *Scientific American, 281,* 94–99

de Waal, F.B.M. (2001). *The ape and the sushi master: Cultural reflections by a primatologist.* New York: Basic Books.

Mayr, E. (2001). *What evolution is.* New York: Basic Books.

Zimmer, C. (2001). *Evolution: The triumph of an idea.* New York: HarperCollins.

Acknowledgments—I thank Allison Berger and Virginia Holt for providing the transcript of my 2001 Focus on Science Plenary Address, which was presented at the annual meeting of the American Psychological Association in San Francisco and was on the topic of this essay. I am also grateful to Mauricio Papini and Scott Lilienfeld for comments on previous versions of the manuscript.

Notes

1. Address correspondence to Frans B.M. de Waal, Living Links, Yerkes Primate Research Center, Emory University, 954 N. Gatewood Rd., Atlanta, GA 30322.

2. Theory of mind means that one understands the mental states of others (a capacity that may be limited to humans and apes).

References

Daly, M., & Wilson, M. (1988). *Homicide*. Hawthorne, NY: Aldine de Gruyter.

de Waal, F.B.M. (1996). *Good natured: The origins of right and wrong in humans and other animals*. Cambridge, MA: Harvard University Press.

de Waal, F.B.M. (1998). *Chimpanzee politics*. Baltimore: Johns Hopkins University Press. (Original work published 1982)

de Waal, F.B.M. (2000, April 2). Survival of the rapist [Review of the book *A natural history of rape: Biological bases of sexual coercion*]. *New York Times Book Review*, pp. 24–25.

Dobzhansky, T. (1973). Nothing in biology makes sense except in the light of evolution. *American Biology Teacher, 35*, 125–129.

Gauthier, I., & Tarr, M.J. (1997). Becoming a "Greeble" expert: Exploring mechanisms for face recognition. *Vision Research, 37*, 1673–1682.

McDougall, W. (1908). *An introduction to social psychology*. New York: Putnam.

Muscarella, F., & Cunningham, M.R. (1996). The evolutionary significance and social perception of male pattern baldness and facial hair. *Ethology & Sociobiology, 17*, 99–117.

Panksepp, J., & Panksepp, J.B. (2000). The seven sins of evolutionary psychology. *Evolution and Cognition, 6*, 108–131.

Staats, A.W. (1991). Unified positivism and unification psychology: Fad or new field? *American Psychologist, 46*, 899–912.

Thornhill, R., & Palmer, C.T. (2000). *A natural history of rape: Biological bases of sexual coercion*. Cambridge, MA: MIT Press.

Tooby, J., & Cosmides, L. (1992). The psychological foundations of culture. In J. Barkow, L. Cosmides, & J. Tooby (Eds.), *The adapted mind: Evolutionary psychology and the generation of culture* (pp. 19–136). New York: Oxford University Press.

Williams, G. (1966). *Adaptation and natural selection*. Princeton, NJ: Princeton University Press.

Wilson, E.O. (1998). *Consilience: The unity of knowledge*. New York: Knopf.

Section 1: Critical Thinking Questions

1. Based on the article by Dick and Rose, it will soon be possible to identify children with genes that predispose them to schizophrenia, conduct disorders, and aggression. What are the ethical considerations associated with this knowledge? By understanding the gene x environment interactions on the development of traits, how can psychologists help resolve some of these ethical issues?

2. Bouchard suggests that genes influence a number of human psychological traits. A broad question in behavior genetics is the extent to which genes contribute to a given trait. What is the goal of knowing the contribution of genes versus the contribution of environment in understanding human behavior?

3. Intelligence is a hypothetical construct in psychology as indicated by Posthuma and de Geus. It can be operationally defined, then measured based on performance of certain cognitive tasks. Intelligence must be more than simply what is measured by an intelligence test, but what is it? About half of the variance associated with performance on multiple cognitive tasks is assigned to a general intelligence factor that remains unidentified. Given the imprecise concept of intelligence, is it possible to discover the genes underlying it? Or should we be satisfied to discover genes associated with various components of cognitive function?

4. In the article by Gangestad and coauthors the ovulation shift hypothesis suggests that women shift their pattern of attraction to men that are especially masculine when they are fertile (around the time of ovulation), especially if their partner is asymmetrical, an indication of less desirable genes. Describe some of the male adaptations to counter these shifts in attraction. How can these adaptations be used to describe jealousy, envy, or other psychological traits observed in men?

5. The article by de Waal provides a cautionary tale about assigning human traits as an adaptation or requiring a separate brain module. To determine that a trait is adaptive, one must show that individuals who possess such a trait leave more progeny then individuals who do not have the trait. Has this been done with human adaptations? What other approaches might be used to determine if a trait is adaptive?

This article has been reprinted as it originally appeared in *Current Directions in Psychological Science*. Citation information for this article as originally published appears above.

Section 2: Plasticity

The previous section described the process underlying changes in behavior over long periods of time. Section 2 is comprised of studies of plasticity, or changes in behavior over the course of an individual's life. How the nervous system changes its organization and function over time is termed plasticity. Historically, the adult brain was considered immutable. Neuroscientists now appreciate that brain organization changes throughout life in response to experience. In the first paper, Bryan Kolb, Robbin Gibb, and Terry Robinson give a lucid overview of plasticity of brain and behavior. The first evidence that the brain could be influenced by the environment was provided by research conducted in the mid-1960s that demonstrated enriched or impoverished environmental conditions could alter the connectivity among neurons and neurochemistry, as well as brain function in rats. This work on the early influences of environment on brain development and learning and memory formed the basis of Project Head Start, a pre-school program that aimed to provide enriched learning environments for at-risk children. Kolb and colleagues reviews recent research that indicates that many factors affect brain plasticity including pre- and postnatal experiences, psychoactive drugs, steroid hormones, growth factors, dietary factors, diseases, stress, and brain trauma. They present two examples in detail to help understand how these factors influence brain organization and function with the goal of understanding both typical and atypical behavior. Kolb and coauthors then address the important issue of *how* all of these factors influence brain and behavioral plasticity.

Estrogen is one factor that can affect brain plasticity and thereby influence cognition and behavior. However, the effects of this steroid hormone on plasticity and disease are not straightforward. In the second article of this section, Lisa Marriott and Gary Wenk document the conflict between epidemiological data indicating that estrogen replacement therapy reduces the risk (or delays the onset) of Alzheimer disease (AD), and three controlled, double-blind, randomized clinical studies that indicate chronic estrogen treatment fails to positively influence cognitive impairments associated with AD. What accounts for these conflicting data? Marriott and Wenk suggest that the timing of the hormone therapy is critical. Estrogen receptors are located on neurons and glia, as well as on immune cells within the brain. Estrogen treatment can have multiple effects on the brain that may be detrimental or beneficial depending on the timing or duration of administration. Animal studies indicate that chronic estrogen treatment does not ameliorate pre-existing cognitive impairments. It may be possible that estrogen delays the onset of AD, but does not affect disease progression when estrogen treatment begins after symptoms surface. Thus, the epidemiological evidence that estrogen is beneficial may have included women who had begun estrogen treatment immediately after the onset of menopause and prior to any AD symptoms. Marriott and Wenk speculate that the conflicting results of the epidemiological and clinical studies may reflect complex interactions between normally fluctuating hormones with brain immune cells that influence neuroinflammation.

Changes in behavior such as displayed during learning and memory presumably reflect plasticity in the underlying neural organization and function. Learning requires individuals to predict events in the environment. Out of all the noise bombarding the central nervous system via sensory inputs, individuals must sort out those stimuli that are relevant for predicting the future versus those stimuli that are largely irrelevant. Our brains must discern causes of behavior in anticipation of appropriate responses to stimuli. Traditionally, studies of predictive learning have fallen into two categories: (1) predictors based on stimuli (classical conditioning) and (2) predictors that are based upon the individual's behavior (operant [AKA instrumental] conditioning). In the third article of the Plasticity Section, Björn Brembs details the molecular and cellular mechanisms of learning in *Aplysia*, a marine snail. For the past 40 years *Aplysia* has served as an important model for classical conditioning. It has been an ideal model system because it has a relatively simple nervous system, yet displays classical and operant learning. Importantly, the neurons are large (up to 1 mm in diameter) which facilitates identification, as well as electrophysiological recording and stimulation. Brembs reviews research demonstrating that operant learning of feeding behavior in *Aplysia* is dependent upon dopamine and its interaction with a single neuron. This simple model may provide insights into the more complex world and nervous systems of vertebrates including humans.

Social factors are among the many extrinsic factors that modulate neural and behavioral plasticity. In the next article, Michael Beecher and John Burt examine the role of social interactions in bird song learning. The process of learning bird song is a powerful animal model for the process of learning language in humans, and unlike humans, young birds can be isolated or exposed to specific stimuli to understand the contribution of environmental factors to the intrinsic process of learning the tools to communicate. Beecher and Burt review the history of the study of bird song learning. They note that the original studies of bird song learning deliberately eliminated social factors by placing isolated young birds into a controlled environment in which a loudspeaker delivered the song of an unknown adult. This experimental model is highly reliable and has yielded important concepts including the "innate" song template and the early sensitive period. Some species cannot learn their songs from tapes in the lab; field studies indicate that young male song sparrows, for example, learn their various song types from the neighboring adult males—males with which the young males are likely to interact as adults. In the lab, it is clear that the young male learns the song he hears, but in nature, a young male may hear songs from many males. How does he learn to piece together his song and whose song does he choose to imitate? His song must contain components that say to the world, that he is a member of a certain population of a certain species, as well as convey his individuality. How social factors influence song learning remains unspecified, but this research question represents a fertile area of research.

Storing information in the brain to predict future events depends on neural plasticity. Changes in synaptic communication between neurons are critical for learning and memory. Thus far, the articles have emphasized brain plasticity in relation to learning, but retention of learned relationships (i.e., memory) also likely represents long-term changes in neural plasticity. In the final article of this section, Wickliffe Abraham addresses some of the current issues in the study of the neural mechanisms of long-term memory. There are two phases of memory consolidation: (1) cellular and (2) systems consolidation. Cellular consolidation requires protein synthesis—blocking protein synthesis during or immediately after learning interferes with memory formation. This likely reflects the construction of new physical connections between neurons, but also reflects a strengthening (long-term potentiation) or weakening (long-term depression) of networked neuronal activation. In Hebbian terms, "neurons that fire together, wire together." Systems consolidation reflects changes in how and where memories are stored. Over time (days to years), memories are less dependent on the brain structures (e.g., hippocampus) required for cellular consolidation. The memories are somehow exported to neural circuits elsewhere in the brain via a Hebbian strengthening of neuronal connectivity. Although we may think of our long-term memories as permanent, in fact, these memories are quite malleable over time, changing as new learning occurs. Abraham notes that synaptic plasticity can be modified to accommodate new learning. Such reconfiguration of synaptic connection strengths represents a neurobiological phenomenon that matches much psychological data that learning and memory are dynamic processes.

Brain Plasticity and Behavior

Bryan Kolb,[1] Robbin Gibb, and Terry E. Robinson

Canadian Centre for Behavioural Neuroscience, University of Lethbridge, Lethbridge, Alberta, Canada (B.K., R.G.), and Department of Psychology, University of Michigan, Ann Arbor, Michigan (T.E.R.)

Abstract

Although the brain was once seen as a rather static organ, it is now clear that the organization of brain circuitry is constantly changing as a function of experience. These changes are referred to as brain plasticity, and they are associated with functional changes that include phenomena such as memory, addiction, and recovery of function. Recent research has shown that brain plasticity and behavior can be influenced by a myriad of factors, including both pre- and postnatal experience, drugs, hormones, maturation, aging, diet, disease, and stress. Understanding how these factors influence brain organization and function is important not only for understanding both normal and abnormal behavior, but also for designing treatments for behavioral and psychological disorders ranging from addiction to stroke.

Keywords   •

addiction; recovery; experience; brain plasticity

One of the most intriguing questions in behavioral neuroscience concerns the manner in which the nervous system can modify its organization and ultimately its function throughout an individual's lifetime, a property that is often referred to as *plasticity*. The capacity to change is a fundamental characteristic of nervous systems and can be seen in even the simplest of organisms, such as the tiny worm *C. elegans*, whose nervous system has only 302 cells. When the nervous system changes, there is often a correlated change in behavior or psychological function. This behavioral change is known by names such as learning, memory, addiction, maturation, and recovery. Thus, for example, when people learn new motor skills, such as in playing a musical instrument, there are plastic changes in the structure of cells in the nervous system that underlie the motor skills. If the plastic changes are somehow prevented from occurring, the motor learning does not occur. Although psychologists have assumed that the nervous system is especially sensitive to experience during development, it is only recently that they have begun to appreciate the potential for plastic changes in the adult brain. Understanding brain plasticity is obviously of considerable interest both because it provides a window to understanding the development of the brain and behavior and because it allows insight into the causes of normal and abnormal behavior.

THE NATURE OF BRAIN PLASTICITY

The underlying assumption of studies of brain and behavioral plasticity is that if behavior changes, there must be some change in organization or properties of the neural circuitry that produces the behavior. Conversely, if neural networks are changed by experience, there must be some corresponding change in the functions mediated by those networks. For the investigator interested in understanding the factors that can change brain circuits, and ultimately behavior, a major challenge is to find and to quantify the changes. In principle, plastic changes in neuronal circuits are likely to reflect either modifications of existing circuits or the generation of new circuits. But how can researchers measure changes in neural circuitry? Because neural networks are composed of individual neurons, each of which connects with a subset of other neurons to form interconnected networks, the logical place to look for plastic changes is at the junctions between neurons, that is, at synapses. However, it is a daunting task to determine if synapses have been added or lost in a particular region, given that the human brain has something like 100 billion neurons and each neuron makes on average several thousand synapses. It is clearly impractical to scan the brain looking for altered synapses, so a small subset must be identified and examined in detail. But which synapses should be studied? Given that neuroscientists have a pretty good idea of what regions of the brain are involved in particular behaviors, they can narrow their search to the likely areas, but are still left with an extraordinarily complex system to examine. There is, however, a procedure that makes the job easier.

In the late 1800s, Camillo Golgi invented a technique for staining a random subset of neurons (1–5%) so that the cell bodies and the dendritic trees of individual cells can be visualized (Fig. 1). The dendrites of a cell function as the scaffolding for synapses, much as tree branches provide a location for leaves to grow and be exposed to sunlight. The usefulness of Golgi's technique can be understood by pursuing this arboreal metaphor. There are a number of ways one could estimate how many leaves are on a tree without counting every leaf. Thus, one could measure the total length of the tree's branches as well as the density of the leaves on a representative branch. Then, by simply multiplying branch length by leaf density, one could estimate total leafage. A similar procedure is used to estimate synapse number. About 95% of a cell's synapses are on its dendrites (the neuron's branches). Furthermore, there is a roughly linear relationship between the space available for synapses (dendritic surface) and the number of synapses, so researchers can presume that increases or decreases in dendritic surface reflect changes in synaptic organization.

FACTORS AFFECTING BRAIN PLASTICITY

By using Golgi-staining procedures, various investigators have shown that housing animals in complex versus simple environments produces widespread differences in the number of synapses in specific brain regions. In general, such experiments show that particular experiences embellish circuitry, whereas the absence of those experiences fails to do so (e.g., Greenough & Chang, 1989). Until recently, the impact of these neuropsychological experiments was surprisingly limited, in part because the environmental treatments were perceived as extreme and thus not characteristic of events experienced by the normal brain. It has become clear, however, not only that synaptic organization is changed by experience, but also that the scope of factors that can do this is much more extensive than anyone had

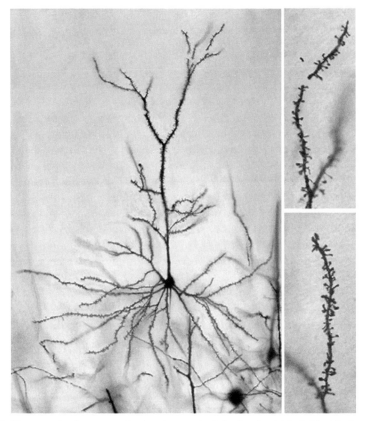

Fig. 1. Photograph of a neuron. In the view on the left, the dendritic field with the extensive dendritic network is visible. On the right are higher-power views of dendritic branches showing the spines, where most synapses are located. If there is an increase in dendritic length, spine density, or both, there are presumed to be more synapses in the neuron.

anticipated. Factors that are now known to affect neuronal structure and behavior include the following:

- experience (both leading pre- and postnatal)
- psychoactive drugs (e.g., amphetamine, morphine)
- gonadal hormones (e.g., estrogen, testosterone)
- anti-inflammatory agents (e.g., COX-2 inhibitors)
- growth factors (e.g., nerve growth factor)
- dietary factors (e.g., vitamin and mineral supplements)
- genetic factors (e.g., strain differences, genetically modified mice)
- disease (e.g., Parkinson's disease, schizophrenia, epilepsy, stroke)
- stress
- brain injury and leading disease

We discuss two examples to illustrate.

Early Experience

It is generally assumed that experiences early in life have different effects on behavior than similar experiences later in life. The reason for this difference is not understood, however. To investigate this question, we placed animals in complex environments either as juveniles, in adulthood, or in senescence (Kolb, Gibb, & Gorny, 2003). It was our expectation that there would be quantitative differences in the effects of experience on synaptic organization, but to our surprise, we also found *qualitative* differences. Thus, like many investigators before us, we found that the length of dendrites and the density of synapses were increased in neurons in the motor and sensory cortical regions in adult and aged animals housed in a complex environment (relative to a standard lab cage). In contrast, animals placed in the same environment as juveniles showed an increase in dendritic length but a decrease in spine density. In other words, the same environmental manipulation had qualitatively different effects on the organization of neuronal circuitry in juveniles than in adults.

To pursue this finding, we later gave infant animals 45 min of daily tactile stimulation with a little paintbrush (15 min three times per day) for the first 3 weeks of life. Our behavioral studies showed that this seemingly benign early experience enhanced motor and cognitive skills in adulthood. The anatomical studies showed, in addition, that in these animals there was a decrease in spine density but no change in dendritic length in cortical neurons—yet another pattern of experience-dependent neuronal change. (Parallel studies have shown other changes, too, including neurochemical changes, but these are beyond the current discussion.) Armed with these findings, we then asked whether prenatal experience might also change the structure of the brain months later in adulthood. Indeed, it does. For example, the offspring of a rat housed in a complex environment during the term of her pregnancy have increased synaptic space on neurons in the cerebral cortex in adulthood. Although we do not know how prenatal experiences alter the brain, it seems likely that some chemical response by the mother, be it hormonal or otherwise, can cross the placental barrier and alter the genetic signals in the developing brain.

Our studies showing that experience can uniquely affect the developing brain led us to wonder if the injured infant brain might be repaired by environmental treatments. We were not surprised to find that postinjury experience, such as tactile stroking, could modify both brain plasticity and behavior because we had come to believe that such experiences were powerful modulators of brain development (Kolb, Gibb, & Gorny, 2000). What was surprising, however, was that prenatal experience, such as housing the pregnant mother in a complex environment, could affect how the brain responded to an injury that it would not receive until after birth. In other words, pre-natal experience altered the brain's response to injury later in life. This type of study has profound implications for preemptive treatments of children at risk for a variety of neurological disorders.

Psychoactive Drugs

Many people who take stimulant drugs like nicotine, amphetamine, or cocaine do so for their potent psychoactive effects. The long-term behavioral consequences of abusing such psychoactive drugs are now well documented, but much less is known about how repeated exposure to these drugs alters the nervous system. One experimental demonstration of a very persistent form of drug experience-dependent plasticity is known as behavioral sensitization. For example, if a rat is given a small dose of amphetamine, it initially will show a small increase in motor activity (e.g., locomotion, rearing). When the rat is given the same dose on subsequent occasions, however, the increase in motor activity increases, or sensitizes, and the animal may remain sensitized for weeks, months, or even years, even if drug treatment is discontinued.

Changes in behavior that occur as a consequence of past experience, and can persist for months or years, like memories, are thought to be due to changes in patterns of synaptic organization. The parallels between drug-induced sensitization and memory led us to ask whether the neurons of animals sensitized to drugs of abuse exhibit long-lasting changes similar to those associated with memory (e.g., Robinson & Kolb, 1999). A comparison of the effects of amphetamine and saline treatments on the structure of neurons showed that neurons in amphetamine-treated brains had greater dendritic material, as well as more densely organized spines. These plastic changes were not found throughout the brain, however, but rather were localized to regions such as the prefrontal cortex and nucleus accumbens, both of which are thought to play a role in the rewarding properties of these drugs. Later studies have shown that these drug-induced changes are found not only when animals are given injections by an experimenter, but also when animals are trained to self-administer drugs, leading us to speculate that similar changes in synaptic organization will be found in human drug addicts.

Other Factors

All of the factors we listed earlier have effects that are conceptually similar to the two examples that we just discussed. For instance, brain injury disrupts the synaptic organization of the brain, and when there is functional improvement after the injury, there is a correlated reorganization of neural circuits (e.g., Kolb, 1995). But not all factors act the same way across the brain. For instance, estrogen stimulates synapse formation in some structures but reduces synapse number in other structures (e.g., Kolb, Forgie, Gibb, Gorny, & Rowntree, 1998), a pattern of change that can also be seen with some psychoactive drugs, such as morphine. In sum, it now appears that virtually any manipulation that produces an enduring change in behavior leaves an anatomical footprint in the brain.

CONCLUSIONS AND ISSUES

There are several conclusions to draw from our studies. First, experience alters the brain, and it does so in an age-related manner. Second, both pre- and postnatal experience have such effects, and these effects are long-lasting and can influence not only brain structure but also adult behavior. Third, seemingly similar experiences can alter neuronal circuits in different ways, although each of the alterations is manifest in behavioral change. Fourth, a variety of behavioral conditions, ranging from addiction to neurological and psychiatric disorders, are correlated with localized changes in neural circuits. Finally, therapies that are intended to alter behavior, such as treatment for addiction, stroke, or schizophrenia, are likely to be most effective if they are able to further reorganize relevant brain circuitry. Furthermore, studies of neuronal structure provide a simple method of screening for treatments that are likely to be effective in treating disorders such as dementia. Indeed, our studies show that the new generation of antiarthritic drugs (known as COX-2 inhibitors), which act to reduce inflammation, can reverse age-related synaptic loss and thus ought to be considered as useful treatments for age-related cognitive loss.

Although much is now known about brain plasticity and behavior, many theoretical issues remain. Knowing that a wide variety of experiences and agents can alter synaptic organization and behavior is important, but leads to a new question: How does this happen? This is not an easy question to answer, and it is certain that there is more than one answer. We provide a single example to illustrate.

Neurotrophic factors are a class of chemicals that are known to affect synaptic organization. An example is fibroblast growth factor-2 (FGF-2). The production of FGF-2 is increased by various experiences, such as complex housing and tactile stroking, as well as by drugs such as amphetamine. Thus, it is possible that experience stimulates the production of FGF-2 and this, in turn, increases synapse production. But again, the question is how. One hypothesis is that FGF-2 somehow alters the way different genes are expressed by specific neurons and this, in turn, affects the way synapses are generated or lost. In other words, factors that alter behavior, including experience, can do so by altering gene expression, a result that renders the traditional gene-versus-environment discussions meaningless.

Other issues revolve around the limits and permanence of plastic changes. After all, people encounter and learn new information daily. Is there some limit to how much cells can change? It seems unlikely that cells could continue to enlarge and add synapses indefinitely, but what controls this? We saw in our studies of experience-dependent changes in infants, juveniles, and adults that experience both adds and prunes synapses, but what are the rules governing when one or the other might occur? This question leads to another, which is whether plastic changes in response to different experiences might interact. For example, does exposure to a drug like nicotine affect how the brain changes in learning a motor skill like playing the piano? Consider, too, the issue of the permanence of plastic changes. If a person stops smoking, how long do the nicotine-induced plastic changes persist, and do they affect later changes?

One additional issue surrounds the role of plastic changes in disordered behavior. Thus, although most studies of plasticity imply that remodeling neural circuitry is a good thing, it is reasonable to wonder if plastic changes might also be the basis of pathological behavior. Less is known about this possibility, but it does seem likely. For example, drug addicts often show cognitive deficits, and it seems reasonable to propose that at least some of these deficits could arise from abnormal circuitry, especially in the frontal lobe.

In sum, the structure of the brain is constantly changing in response to an unexpectedly wide range of experiential factors. Understanding how the brain changes and the rules governing these changes is important not only for understanding both normal and abnormal behavior, but also for designing treatments for behavioral and psychological disorders ranging from addiction to stroke.

Recommended Reading

Kolb, B., & Whishaw, I.Q. (1998). Brain plasticity and behavior. *Annual Review of Psychology, 49*, 43–64.
Robinson, T.E., & Berridge, K.C. (in press). Addiction. *Annual Review of Psychology.*
Shaw, C.A., & McEachern, J.C. (2001). *Toward a theory of neuroplasticity.* New York: Taylor and Francis.

Acknowledgments—This research was supported by a Natural Sciences and Engineering Research Council grant to B.K. and a National Institute on Drug Abuse grant to T.E.R.

Note

1. Address correspondence to Bryan Kolb, CCBN, University of Lethbridge, Lethbridge, AB, Canada T1K 3M4.

References

Greenough, W.T., & Chang, F.F. (1989). Plasticity of synapse structure and pattern in the cerebral cortex. In A. Peters & E.G. Jones (Eds.), *Cerebral cortex: Vol. 7* (pp. 391–440). New York: Plenum Press.
Kolb, B. (1995). *Brain plasticity and behavior.* Mahwah, NJ: Erlbaum.
Kolb, B., Forgie, M., Gibb, R., Gorny, G., & Rowntree, S. (1998). Age, experience, and the changing brain. *Neuroscience and Biobehavioral Reviews, 22*, 143–159.
Kolb, B., Gibb, R., & Gorny, G. (2000). Cortical plasticity and the development of behavior after early frontal cortical injury. *Developmental Neuropsychology, 18*, 423–444.
Kolb, B., Gibb, R., & Gorny, G. (2003). Experience-dependent changes in dendritic arbor and spine density in neocortex vary with age and sex. *Neurobiology of Learning and Memory, 79*, 1–10.
Robinson, T.E., & Kolb, B. (1999). Alterations in the morphology of dendrites and dendritic spines in the nucleus accumbens and prefron-tal cortex following repeated treatment with amphetamine or cocaine. *European Journal of Neuroscience, 11*, 1598–1604.

Neurobiological Consequences of Long-Term Estrogen Therapy

L.K. Marriott and G.L. Wenk[1]

Division of Neural Systems, Memory & Aging, Arizona Research Laboratories, University of Arizona

Abstract

Postmenopausal women demonstrate an increased incidence of Alzheimer's disease (AD). Epidemiological evidence suggests that estrogen replacement therapy (ERT) may reduce the risk or delay the onset of AD, yet recent clinical trials found no cognitive benefits of ERT in women with mild to moderate AD. This review suggests that the timing of estrogen administration may explain these conflicting results. Chronic administration has neurobiological consequences that can affect neural and immune function, but a therapy designed to mimic the natural cycle of fluctuating hormones may more effectively slow the progression of AD in postmenopausal women.

Keywords

estrogen; Alzheimer's disease; luteinizing hormone (LH); immune; neuroprotection

Postmenopausal women demonstrate an increased incidence of Alzheimer's disease (AD), and many researchers have considered whether this heightened risk is linked to their low menopausal levels of the hormone estrogen. Indeed, epidemiological evidence suggests that postmenopausal estrogen replacement therapy (ERT) may reduce the risk and delay the onset of AD. Moreover, animal studies demonstrate that estrogen has beneficial effects on brain cell survival and cognition. Despite these positive indications, however, recent clinical trials found no benefits of ERT on cognitive function in women with mild to moderate AD (for a review, see Hogervorst, Williams, Budge, Riedel, & Jolles, 2000). In this review, we attempt to reconcile these conflicting findings, highlighting a potential misunderstanding of estrogen's action in the brain.

MENOPAUSE AND ERT

As women enter menopause, the amount of estrogen circulating in their blood declines, eventually reaching approximately 1% of the level found in younger women. This change results in numerous physiological consequences, including cognitive dysfunction, loss of attention, mood disorders, hot flushes, and increased risk of some diseases, including AD. ERTs were developed to compensate for diminished circulating hormones, thereby alleviating the undesirable symptoms associated with menopause. When epidemiological studies discovered that postmenopausal women taking estrogen had a reduced risk of developing AD, delayed onset of AD, and a milder progression of the disease, researchers undertook some initial studies to see whether women with AD might benefit from estrogen therapy. These early studies demonstrated improvements in attention, orientation, and mood (for a review, see Hogervorst et al., 2000), thereby instigating an extensive examination of estrogen outside its established role as a reproductive hormone. Animal studies supported the idea that short-term estrogen replacement might be beneficial by showing that cognition, neurotransmitter function, brain plasticity (the ability of brain cells to change), blood flow, and neuroprotection (the ability of nerve cells to survive a variety of toxic insults) were all enhanced by estrogen (for a review, see Norbury et al., 2003).

Three randomized, double-blind, placebo-controlled intervention studies in humans demonstrated less encouraging results regarding the effects of estrogen on the brain. In the largest of these studies, the effects of ERT were initially beneficial, much as in previous studies using smaller groups of patients and shorter treatment durations; however, over the longer term, performance on a scale measuring dementia declined significantly more among women receiving ERT than among those receiving a placebo (Mulnard et al., 2000). All three of these intervention studies concluded that ERT could not improve the cognitive abilities of women with mild to moderate AD (for a review, see Hogervorst et al., 2000). Thus, results of these clinical trials suggest that relatively short-term ERT has beneficial effects on cognitive function, but that these effects are attenuated, and possibly reversed, following much longer treatment regimens.

Investigators offered several hypotheses to reconcile the conflict in the findings of epidemiological, intervention, and animal studies. For example, intervention studies were criticized for their design and potential biases in subject selection. Researchers argued that women who typically take ERT are better educated, are healthier, and have a higher socioeconomic status than nonusers, and these factors have been associated with a reduced risk of AD. In contrast, the women enrolled in the ERT trials already had an ongoing disease process and may have been estrogen deprived for decades prior to receiving ERT, which may have altered the effectiveness of the therapy (for reviews, see Hogervorst et al., 2000, and Toran-Allerand, 2000).

CONSEQUENCES OF CHRONIC ESTROGEN

The positive and negative effects of estrogen appear to depend on the timing of estrogen exposure. Chronic administration of estrogen results in neurobiological consequences that can affect both neural and immune function. Premenopausal women experience cyclic fluctuations in estrogen levels that are not mimicked in postmenopausal women by the continuous replacement of estrogen through ERT.

Chronic Estrogen and Cognition

Animal experiments have shown that deficits in working memory (the temporary retention of information needed to solve a task) are not seen immediately following surgical removal of the ovaries (ovariectomy), which removes the major source of estrogen. Instead, working memory deficits develop after longer durations of estrogen withdrawal (for a review, see Markowska & Savonenko, 2002). Chronic administration of estrogen to ovariectomized animals does not improve their cognition if they already have detectable deficits when they begin the estrogen treatment

(Markowska & Savonenko, 2002). These results parallel the absence of cognitive benefits associated with ERT in postmenopausal women who already have cognitive deficits resulting from AD. However, estrogen levels fluctuate when constant administration is combined with injections of estrogen, and this combined treatment dramatically improved working memory in previously impaired ovariectomized animals (Markowska & Savonenko, 2002). These findings are consistent with the hypothesis that compared with constant estrogen levels, fluctuating levels may more effectively enhance cognition in postmenopausal women (Marriott, Hauss-Wegrzyniak, Benton, Vraniak, & Wenk, 2002).

Effects on Estrogen Receptors

Estrogen receptors are specialized proteins that respond to estrogen by initiating a variety of cellular responses. A prolonged period of menopause followed by the typical regimen of estrogen replacement can produce constant estrogen levels that may lead to a decrease in estrogen receptors' number or function (downregulation), which in turn may underlie the limited effectiveness of chronic ERT (Toran-Allerand, 2000). Estrogen receptors are distributed throughout the brain and located on both brain cells (neurons and glia) and immune cells. Therefore, it is not surprising that the downregulation of these receptors can have wide-ranging and dramatic effects on many neural, endocrine, and immune processes.

Chronic Estrogen Induces Reproductive Aging

The endocrine system is tightly regulated and requires a series of precisely timed hormonal signals. These signals are typically initiated in the hypothalamus and pituitary of the brain. For example, the induction of ovulation in healthy young animals and humans begins when the hypothalamus releases bursts of luteinizing hormone-releasing hormone (LHRH). LHRH stimulates production and pulsatile release of luteinizing hormone (LH) and follicle-stimulating hormone (FSH) from the pituitary gland. In turn, LH and FSH stimulate the production of steroid hormones and ovulation from the ovaries. The steroid hormones produced by the ovaries, such as estrogen and progesterone, control the reproductive cycle by acting on the hypothalamus and pituitary (for a review, see Hung et al., 2003). Thus, hormonal signals normally function in a pulsatile and tightly regulated manner. With aging, however, there is a dysregulation in these hormonal signals. Aging rodents experience a delayed onset and attenuation of LH pulses, as well as a chronic elevation of circulating estrogen, ultimately ending hormonal cycling and signaling the reproductive aging of the animal (for a review, see Tsai & Legan, 2001).

Continuous, long-term administration of estrogen to young ovariectomized rats suppresses the LH pulses, mimicking changes seen with normal aging (Tsai & Legan, 2001). The suppression of the LH pulses also induces alterations in hypothalamic and pituitary function. It has been suggested that reproductive aging in the rat is influenced more by the timing and duration of estrogen exposure than by true chronological age (Hung et al., 2003). In summary, the cessation of reproductive function in animals depends on a critical pattern of chronic estrogen exposure

(Desjardins, Beaudet, Meaney, & Brawer, 1995). In turn, reproductive aging can affect neural and immune function.

Irreversible Damage to the Hypothalamus

The hypothalamus is an important region for hormonal timing and control, and chronic estrogen can irreversibly damage it. For example, studies with rodents have shown that chronic estrogen can selectively destroy certain cells in the arcuate nucleus, a subregion of the hypothalamus. Specifically, more than 60% of β-endorphin neurons (brain cells that respond to β-endorphin, a type of opiate) are destroyed (for a review, see Desjardins et al., 1995). β-Endorphin and other opiates are important chemicals in the brain because they directly affect reproductive function and ovulation by strongly inhibiting the pattern of LHRH release, and subsequently LH release as well. The degeneration of β-endorphin neurons might be expected to increase LH concentrations. In fact, however, the loss of these neurons leads to compensatory changes that make the hypothalamus super-sensitive to residual β-endorphin and other naturally circulating opiates, thereby resulting in persistent inhibition of LH release and inducing reproductive aging of the animal.

The aging process shares many features with this hypothalamic pathology, including deficits in β-endorphin concentrations and β-endorphin cell loss (for a review, see Desjardins et al., 1995). Persistent suppression of LHRH and LH release, therefore, may underlie aspects of reproductive aging. The consequences of reproductive aging include alterations in endocrine and immune signals.

ENDOCRINE AND IMMUNE INTERACTIONS IN THE BRAIN

There is bidirectional communication between the endocrine and immune systems within the brain. Alterations in neuroendocrine signals can modulate immune function, just as alterations in immune function can have consequences for neuroendocrine function (Reichlin, 1998). Following hypothalamic damage induced by elevated estrogen levels, microglial cells (a type of immune cell in the brain) become activated (for a review, see Hung et al., 2003), releasing chemicals that can be either beneficial or destructive, depending on their timing and termination (Akiyama et al., 2000; Reichlin, 1998). For example, activated microglial cells release inflammatory cytokines, and chronic exposure to these chemicals can contribute to pathological conditions such as AD (Akiyama et al., 2000).

Interactions Affecting Neuroendocrine Function

LHRH and LH pulses are disrupted by activation of the body's inflammatory and stress pathways. Stimulation of inflammatory and stress pathways induces elevated levels of inflammatory cytokines, thereby suppressing LHRH and LH pulses and preventing ovulation (Karsch, Battaglia, Breen, Debus, & Harris, 2002). In addition, activation of the hypothalamic-pituitary-adrenal axis (the major stress pathway in the body, named for the structures it comprises) stimulates the adrenal gland to release stress hormones, including glucocorti-coids, that can have consequences on other processes, such as cognition and aspects of immune function. These relationships illustrate the extensive communication between the immune and endocrine systems within the brain (for a review, see Reichlin, 1998).

Interactions Affecting Neuroinflammation

AD is characterized by a process of chronic neuroinflammation (for a review, see Akiyama et al., 2000), and one of the hallmarks of the neuroinflammatory response is an elevation in numbers of activated microglia. Because the brains of AD patients show evidence of inflammation and the incidence of AD is elevated in postmenopausal women, we recently examined how the interaction of chronic neuroinflammation and either estrogen deprivation or chronic ERT affects cognitive function and the microglial response of rodents (Marriott et al., 2002).

Our results were similar to those of Markowska and Savonenko (2002), who showed that ovariectomy did not cause behavioral impairments unless deficits were already present, in that we found no cognitive impairment after ovariectomy. However, ovariectomized animals were impaired after they were administered either chronic estrogen or a treatment that caused chronic brain inflammation. Moreover, the cognitive deficit was exacerbated when chronic estrogen and inflammatory treatments were combined, a condition analogous to a postmenopausal woman with AD receiving ERT. Although a comparison between humans and rodents must be made with caution, it is interesting that continuous, long-term estrogen therapy immediately following ovariectomy in female rats led to an impairment that paralleled the cognitive deficit recently reported in postmenopausal women with AD who received continuous, long-term ERT initiated decades after the onset of menopause, after cognitive deficits were already present. However, we found no impairments in naturally cycling females receiving the same chronic inflammatory treatment that produced impairments in ovariectomized animals; these results are consistent with Markowska and Savonenko's finding that fluctuating estrogen improved working memory in previously impaired ovariectomized animals.

With regard to the microglial response, ovariectomized animals with chronic neuroinflammation showed a robust increase in activated microglia that was not affected by chronic administration of estrogen. The activated microglial cells were specifically localized to brain regions that regulate the autonomic nervous system, which modulates the internal state of the animal, including stress responses (e.g., the hypothalamic-pituitary-adrenal axis) and immune function. Interestingly, intact animals with neuroinflammation had approximately half the number of activated microglia, suggesting that fluctuating gonadal hormones can provide some protection from the consequences of chronic neuroinflammation.

Taken together, these results suggest that the consequences of chronic neuroinflammation, such as cognitive impairment and microglial response, depend on the internal state (including hormone status) of the animal. First, the data support other findings showing that fluctuating levels of gonadal hormones, such as estrogen, have a neuroprotective effect. Second, these results suggest that continuous, long-term ERT given to postmenopausal women with AD, or other diseases characterized by chronic neuroinflammation, may exacerbate existing cognitive impairments (Marriott et al., 2002).

TIMING IS EVERYTHING

Reproductive aging is a dysregulation of neuroendocrine signals that can affect neural and immune function. Continuous administration of hormones may mimic a component of this process by inducing inappropriate alterations in hypothalamic and pituitary function, such as suppression of pulsatile release of LHRH and LH. Bidirectional communication between the endocrine and immune systems may underlie aspects of the aging process, as dysfunctions in one system can have dramatic consequences in the other. These systems may work together to exacerbate dysfunctions associated with aging (for a review, see Straub, Miller, Scholmerich, & Zietz, 2000). Therefore, continuous, long-term administration of hormones, such as estrogen alone (Mulnard et al., 2000) or in combination with progestin (Shumaker et al., 2003), is likely to have negative consequences that may impair aspects of cognition and exacerbate existing diseases characterized by neuroinflammation, such as AD.

Epidemiological and intervention studies of chronic estrogen therapy have produced conflicting results. How can estrogen have deleterious effects when administered chronically to postmenopausal women yet seem to be beneficial in epidemiological studies using the same chronic ERT regimen? The answer may lie in a close examination of the timing of the initiation of estrogen therapy. Chronic estrogen cannot improve memory if cognitive deficits already exist (Markowska & Savonenko, 2002). It has been suggested that estrogen may decrease the risk of AD but may not alter the progression of AD if the disease process has already begun (Wise, Dubal, Wilson, Rau, & Liu, 2001). Thus, epidemiological studies may have included women who took ERT immediately following menopause, when cognitive deficits were not yet present and processes of chronic neuroinflammation stemming from the disease had not yet begun. ERT users tend to be better educated and healthier than women who do not take ERT, so epidemiological studies may skew their results by examining women who are taking ERT for noncognitive reasons (Hogervorst et al., 2000). Still, because chronic estrogen affects neural function negatively, through its effects on estrogen receptors, β-endorphin neurons, and LH pulses, the underlying explanations for the benefits seen in epidemiological studies remain unclear. The disparate results may be due to a modulatory interaction of gonadal hormones with neuroinflammation, which can regulate the output of the autonomic nervous system and the processes it controls, such as stress regulation and immune system function.

Estrogen has complex actions on the brain that may be beneficial or detrimental, depending on the timing of exposure. Current research suggests that continuous estrogen administration for long durations may have deleterious effects on endocrine and immune function, but that such effects may be mitigated by using a therapy designed to mimic the natural cycle of fluctuating hormones. Fluctuating administration of estrogen by itself, however, may be insufficient to protect against the consequences of neuroinflammation accompanying AD, as the physiology of young, intact animals is characterized by a more complex pattern of multiple fluctuating hormones. It may be necessary to mimic this physiology more closely in order to ameliorate the cognitive and neuroinflammatory components characteristic of AD.

Recommended Reading

Brinton, R.D. (2001). Cellular and molecular mechanisms of estrogen regulation of memory function and neuroprotection against Alzheimer's disease: Recent insights and remaining challenges. *Learning & Memory, 8,* 121–133.

Cholerton, B., Gleason, C.E., Baker, L.D., & Asthana, S. (2002). Estrogen and Alzheimer's disease: The story so far. *Drugs & Aging, 19,* 405–427.

Hung, A.J., Stanbury, M.G., Shanabrough, M., Horvath, T.L., Garcia-Segura, L.M., & Naftolin, F. (2003). (See References)

Acknowledgments—This work was supported by the U.S. Public Health Service (AG10546) and the Alzheimer's Association (IIRG-01-2654).

Note

1. Address correspondence to Gary L. Wenk, Neural Systems, Memory & Aging, 384 Life Sciences North, Tucson, AZ 85724-5115; e-mail: gary@nsma.arizona.edu.

References

Akiyama, H., Barger, S., Barnum, S., Bradt, B., Bauer, J., Cole, G.M., Cooper, N.R., Eikelenboom, P., Emmerling, M., Fiebich, B.L., Finch, C.E., Frautschy, S., Griffin, W.S., Hampel, H., Hull, M., Landreth, G., Lue, L., Mrak, R., Mackenzie, I.R., McGeer, P.L., O'Banion, M.K., Pachter, J., Pasinetti, G., Plata-Salaman, C., Rogers, J., Rydel, R., Shen, Y., Streit, W., Strohmeyer, R., Tooyoma, I., Van Muiswinkel, F.L., Veerhuis, R., Walker, D., Webster, S., Wegrzyniak, B., Wenk, G., & Wyss-Coray, T. (2000). Inflammation and Alzheimer's disease. *Neurobiology of Aging, 21,* 383–421.

Desjardins, G.C., Beaudet, A., Meaney, M.J., & Brawer, J.R. (1995). Estrogen-induced hypothalamic beta-endorphin neuron loss: A possible model of hypothalamic aging. *Experimental Gerontology, 30,* 253–267.

Hogervorst, E., Williams, J., Budge, M., Riedel, W., & Jolles, J. (2000). The nature of the effect of female gonadal hormone replacement therapy on cognitive function in post-menopausal women: A meta-analysis. *Neuroscience, 101,* 485–512.

Hung, A.J., Stanbury, M.G., Shanabrough, M., Horvath, T.L., Garcia-Segura, L.M., & Naftolin, F. (2003). Estrogen, synaptic plasticity and hypothalamic reproductive aging. *Experimental Gerontology, 38,* 53–59.

Karsch, F.J., Battaglia, D.F., Breen, K.M., Debus, N., & Harris, T.G. (2002). Mechanisms for ovarian cycle disruption by immune/inflammatory stress. *Stress, 5,* 101–112.

Markowska, A.L., & Savonenko, A.V. (2002). Effectiveness of estrogen replacement in restoration of cognitive function after long-term estrogen withdrawal in aging rats. *Journal of Neuroscience, 22,* 10985–10995.

Marriott, L.K., Hauss-Wegrzyniak, B., Benton, R.S., Vraniak, P., & Wenk, G.L. (2002). Long term estrogen therapy worsens the behavioral and neuropathological consequences of chronic brain inflammation. *Behavioral Neuroscience, 116,* 902–911.

Mulnard, R.A., Cotman, C.W., Kawas, C., van Dyck, C.H., Sano, M., Doody, R., Koss, E., Pfeiffer, E., Jin, S., Gamst, A., Grundman, M., Thomas, R., & Thal, L.J. (2000). Estrogen replacement therapy for treatment of mild to moderate Alzheimer disease: A randomized controlled trial. *Journal of the American Medical Association, 283,* 1007–1015.

Norbury, R., Cutter, W.J., Compton, J., Robertson, D.M., Craig, M., Whitehead, M., & Murphy, D.G. (2003). The neuroprotective effects of estrogen on the aging brain. *Experimental Gerontology, 38,* 109–117.

Reichlin, S. (1998). Neuroendocrinology. In J.D. Wilson, D.W. Foster, H.M. Kronenberg, & P.R. Larsen (Eds.), *Williams textbook of endocrinology* (9th ed., pp. 165–248). Philadelphia: W.B. Saunders.

Shumaker, S.A., Legault, C., Rapp, S.R., Thal, L.J., Wallace, R.B., Ockene, J.K., Hendrix, S.L., Jones, B.N., Assaf, A.R., Jackson, R.D., Kotchen, J.M., Wassertheil-Smoller, S., & Watctawski-Wende, J. (2003). Estrogen plus progestin and the incidence of dementia and mild cognitive impairment in postmenopausal women. *Journal of the American Medical Association, 289,* 2651–2661.

Straub, R.H., Miller, L.E., Scholmerich, J., & Zietz, B. (2000). Cytokines and hormones as possible links between endocrinosenescence and immunosenescence. *Journal of Neuroimmunology, 109,* 10–15.

Toran-Allerand, C.D. (2000). Estrogen as a treatment for Alzheimer disease. *Journal of the American Medical Association, 284,* 307–308.

Tsai, H.W., & Legan, S.J. (2001). Chronic elevation of estradiol in young ovariectomized rats causes aging-like loss of steroid-induced luteinizing hormone surges. *Biology of Reproduction, 64,* 684–688.

Wise, P.M., Dubal, D.B., Wilson, M.E., Rau, S.W., & Liu, Y. (2001). Estrogens: Trophic and protective factors in the adult brain. *Frontiers in Neuroendocrinology, 22,* 33–66.

This article has been reprinted as it originally appeared in *Current Directions in Psychological Science*. Citation information for this article as originally published appears above.

Electrical Signals of Memory and of the Awareness of Remembering

Ken A. Paller[1]

Northwestern University

Abstract

Learning factual information and accurately remembering specific experiences from the past are central to human intellectual and social life. These extraordinary abilities require computations on diverse sorts of information represented in the brain. Networks of neurons in the cerebral cortex are specialized for analyzing and representing such information, whereas the storage of facts and events within these networks depends fundamentally on linking multiple representational fragments together. This cross-cortical linking function is disrupted in patients with amnesia. Electrical measures of the brain in action, obtained while people perform feats of memory in laboratory settings, have been used to investigate the storage and retrieval of facts and episodes. Electrical signals associated with specific aspects of memory processing have been identified through research that constitutes part of a larger scientific endeavor aimed at understanding memory, the subjective experience of remembering that can accompany retrieval, and disorders of memory that can result from brain damage.

Keywords

declarative memory; priming; event-related potentials; ERPs; amnesia

What happens in your brain to allow you to remember a recent acquaintance, your favorite film, your last summer vacation, or your first kiss? Contemporary investigations of such phenomena are founded on systems for classifying types of memory. Many investigators focus on the category known as *declarative memory*, the ability to remember prior autobiographical episodes and complex facts (Squire, 1987). This ability can be demonstrated when an individual either retrieves learned information in a recall test or discriminates learned information from new information in a recognition test. Declarative memory provides each of us with a vast but imperfect storehouse of information, and a basis for our own life story.

What would constitute a comprehensive scientific understanding of declarative memory? Relevant research concerning declarative memory spans the gamut from neurobiological studies in animals to cognitive modeling in computers. A long-standing and venerable approach to exploring both the neural and the psychological underpinnings of memory is to investigate memory deficits in neurological patients.

NEUROCOGNITIVE FOUNDATIONS OF DECLARATIVE MEMORY

Patients with a selective memory dysfunction and otherwise preserved intellectual functions are uncommon, but analyses of such cases have been extraordinarily

Table 1. *Neuropsychological findings in patients with selective deficits in declarative memory*

Type of memory	Definition	Findings in amnesia
Declarative memory	Recall and recognition of episodes and facts (i.e., episodic memory and semantic memory)	Impairment in storage, producing deficits in new learning (anterograde amnesia) and in remembering information acquired prior to the illness or injury (retrograde amnesia)
Immediate memory	Information kept in mind by continuous rehearsal (e.g., verbal working memory)	Preserved
Nondeclarative memory		Generally preserved, but with some notable exceptions
Perceptual priming	Speeded or more accurate response to a specific stimulus, as a result of altered perceptual representations	Preserved if performance is not contaminated by declarative memory (i.e., not based on episodic retrieval during the implicit memory test)
Conceptual priming	Speeded or more accurate response to a specific stimulus, as a result of altered conceptual representations	Preserved in some cases, but further investigation is required, particularly across stimulus domains
Skills	Behaviors that improve gradually with practice, including cognitive skills (e.g., reading mirror-reversed text) and motor skills	Preserved when skill acquisition is accomplished without reliance on declarative memory (which is generally not the case for typical skills learned in everyday settings)
Classical conditioning	Learned associations between two stimuli, one of which elicits an automatic response	Generally preserved, especially when conditioned and unconditioned stimuli overlap temporally

Note. Not all subtypes of nondeclarative memory are listed.

informative. These amnesic patients generally have impairments in declarative memory, but not in certain other categories of memory, as listed in Table 1. Selective deficits in these patients imply that certain neural computations are essential for recalling and recognizing episodes and facts, but not for perceiving and manipulating the same sorts of information in other ways. An amnesic patient may carry on an intelligent and detailed conversation but, shortly afterward, be unable to remember that the conversation ever occurred.

Networks of neurons in the cerebral cortex (see Fig. 1) play a major role in perceiving and manipulating the information inherent in an episode, and alterations in connections between neurons in these same networks are thought to be responsible for declarative memory storage. A contemporary explanation for the disruption of declarative memory in amnesia postulates a core defect in a process of *cross-cortical storage*—the process whereby the fragments of an episode or the various features of a complex fact become connected together into a coherent

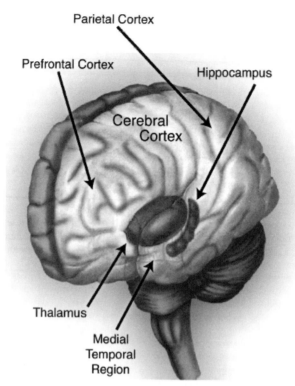

Fig. 1. Sketch of a human brain showing some of the brain regions involved in memory storage. The cerebral cortex is the large, outer portion of the brain with an infolded structure. It comprises two hemispheres, each of which includes parietal cortex at the top, prefrontal cortex behind the forehead, occipital cortex toward the back of the head, and temporal cortex at the side. The thalamus is a paired structure that would be hidden from view, but it can be seen on one side where the cortex is drawn as if it were transparent. Neurons in the thalamus are extensively interconnected with neurons in the cerebral cortex. The medial temporal region, which includes the hippocampus, would also be hidden from view but can be seen on one side through transparently illustrated temporal cortex. The hippocampus receives information indirectly from many cortical regions. Sensory information is analyzed in networks of neurons in occipital, parietal, and temporal cortex. Information relevant for remembering facts and episodes is represented in various cortical regions, and neurons in these regions are interconnected with each other and with neurons in the medial temporal region.

and sturdy representation in the brain (Paller, 2002). For example, fragments linked together in the cerebral cortex to form an enduring memory for an episode might include representations of sights, sounds, smells, a spatial layout of objects, people, actions, emotional coloring, a set of precipitating events, consequences of the episode, and so on. Representations of these different features are thought to depend on different cortical regions.

Storing declarative memories thus depends on linking cognitive representations instantiated not in a single brain region, but rather in many cortical networks specialized for different computations. The most fundamental characteristic of declarative memories is postulated to be their dependence on representations in multiple cortical zones that must be linked together. Although much remains to be learned about this process, memory binding is thought to be accomplished through mechanisms that alter the interconnectivity of cortical neurons through interactions with other brain regions (such as the hippocampus, adjacent cortex of the medial temporal region, and portions of the thalamus). Indeed, amnesia often results from damage to the hippocampus, medial temporal region, or thalamus.

Furthermore, cross-cortical storage is not finalized immediately following a learning episode, but rather, it can evolve over an extended time course as the information becomes integrated with knowledge already accrued, as well as with information acquired subsequently. This process of cross-cortical consolidation may continue for many years for a fact or event that is reevaluated, reinterpreted, and repeatedly integrated with other information. *Cross-cortical consolidation* of a declarative memory may proceed not only during waking, but during sleep as well. It may even continue beyond a point when the memory has become *cortically self-sufficient*, which is when critical storage sites in the cortex can support retrieval of the memory even if the hippocampus and adjacent structures are dysfunctional. Such brain damage leads to difficulties remembering declarative memories that are not cortically self-sufficient, including memories formed prior to the onset of amnesia (retrograde amnesia) and memories formed after the onset of amnesia (anterograde amnesia). Because memories are less likely to be cortically self-sufficient the more recently they were acquired, retrograde amnesia is typically worse for recently acquired information than for older information. Many amnesic patients can remember facts and episodes from their childhood and early adulthood as well as anyone else their age.

Normal declarative memory is a product of three stages of information processing. *Encoding* refers to the initial stage, when information arrives in the brain following sensory analysis or via imagination. The term encoding has been used to refer to the input and comprehension of this information (which is not problematic for amnesic patients), as well as to the transformation of the experience into a memory (which is impaired in amnesia).

Declarative memory formation may not be finalized at initial encoding, but rather can continue over a prolonged storage period, when memory is subject to change, consolidation, interference, distortion, and forgetting. *Storage* denotes this second stage of information processing.

The final stage, *retrieval*, takes place when a declarative memory is accessed and used. Amnesic patients are generally able to retrieve some declarative memories, particularly those already consolidated to the point of cortical self-sufficiency. However, memory retrieval can be quite demanding and require effortful search strategies, such as when one successfully searches for a relatively insignificant childhood memory. In such cases, contributions from a division of the cerebral cortex called prefrontal cortex (see Fig. 1) are especially important with respect to conducting a systematic search, evaluating products of retrieval, escaping from the present moment to bring a prior experience to mind, maintaining information in mind, inhibiting the intrusion of irrelevant information, constructing a remembered experience based on retrieved information, evaluating each bit of retrieved information to decide if it is plausible and appropriate with respect to current goals, and so on. Accordingly, prefrontal damage by itself can lead to memory retrieval difficulties, and when combined with medial temporal damage can lead to exacerbated memory deficits.

Although amnesic patients exhibit significant impairments in declarative memory, they can be entirely normal when it comes to other types of memory. Besides memory based on continuous rehearsal of information just encoded (i.e., immediate memory), preserved memory is also found for the category of *nondeclarative memory*—which is defined by exclusion as distinct from immediate memory and from declarative memory, and which is not accessible to conscious recollection (see Table 1 for examples). This evidence underscores the idea that declarative memory depends on special storage mechanisms. Nondeclarative memory differs from declarative memory in that it does not require the linking of distinct representations across multiple cortical zones. Often, tests of nondeclarative memory do not make explicit reference to prior learning episodes (such tests are called *implicit memory tests*, and memory demonstrated in these tests is sometimes called *implicit memory*). For instance, behavioral responses to a specific stimulus may be faster or more accurate as a result of prior experience, even when a person is unable to remember that prior experience. This behavioral effect constitutes *priming*, a key type of nondeclarative memory. Understanding the fundamental differences between declarative and nondeclarative memory can shed light on the neurocognitive mechanisms unique to declarative memory.

Furthermore, understanding special cases in which nondeclarative memory is not preserved in amnesia may provide pivotal insights into the core defect. Future tests of the conceptualization of declarative memory I have summarized here should determine whether priming is preserved in amnesia because of experience-induced neural changes within isolated cortical zones, and whether some subtypes of priming tend to be impaired in amnesia when priming requires changes in connections among neurons in different cortical zones.

ELECTROPHYSIOLOGY OF DECLARATIVE MEMORY

To gain further insight into the distinct cognitive functions that combine to support declarative memory, it will be crucial to be able to measure these functions independently. Indeed, electrical activity from the brain can be recorded noninvasively in healthy individuals, and relevant measures can be obtained on a millisecond-by-millisecond basis in order to test and advance theoretical proposals developed through neuropsychological studies of memory disorders.

The electroencephalogram (EEG) is a summation of electrical fields produced by activity in vast numbers of neurons and recorded using electrodes placed harmlessly on an individual's head. An event-related potential (ERP) is an average response to a class of events, such as one type of stimulus, and can be calculated by averaging EEG responses to multiple stimuli presented to the individual in a suitable experimental setting (see Friedman & Johnson, 2000). ERPs can be characterized in terms of their latency (when they occur relative to the onset of a stimulus), their polarity (positive or negative at the recording location relative to a distant reference location), their amplitude (size of a potential deflection), and their topography (distribution of potential amplitudes across the head). In the following sections, I describe research from my laboratory associating certain memory functions with particular ERP signals. Despite this emphasis on ERP research, the general approach advocated here also applies to research with other direct and indirect measures of brain activity, including measures of blood flow, metabolism, and magnetic fields.

TRANSFORMING EXPERIENCE INTO MEMORY

One way to investigate the formation of declarative memories is to examine neural activity at initial encoding and determine which neural activity predicts successful versus unsuccessful memory performance. Brain potentials that predict successful subsequent recall and recognition have been observed in many experiments. These potentials are generally positive over parietal or prefrontal brain regions and reach maximal amplitudes 400 to 800 ms or so after stimulus onset, with larger amplitudes for remembered than forgotten stimuli. Similar ERPs were observed in a few experiments in which electrodes were implanted in the medial temporal region in patients who were candidates for surgery to relieve medically intractable epilepsy. ERPs that predict whether a person will remember seeing a common object have also been identified, as have ERPs that predict whether a person will claim to have seen an object that was not actually seen but rather was imagined. To-be-remembered stimuli in all these ERP studies have included objects, faces, spoken names, environmental sounds, and, most often, words.

In one experiment, words were presented visually in an encoding phase followed by either an implicit or an explicit memory test (Paller, 1990). In the implicit memory test, participants were instructed to complete three-letter stems with the first word to come to mind. The number of completions that matched words from encoding, compared with a baseline rate of such completions, provided a measure of priming. In the explicit memory test, participants attempted to recall words from the encoding phase in order to complete the stems. ERPs from the encoding phase were more positive for words later recalled on the explicit memory test than for words not recalled. This systematic difference in brain potentials can be referred to as *Dm-recall* (an ERP Difference based on later memory performance on the *recall* test). In contrast, ERPs did not reliably predict later priming. These findings, along with others, are consistent with the idea that Dm-recall indexed encoding activity specific to declarative memory formation, most likely processing pertaining to the meaning of each word rather than its visual appearance.

In an experiment with faces, ERPs at initial encoding predicted not only whether later recognition would be successful, but also the experiential quality of the recognition experience (Yovel & Paller, 2004). Positive ERPs from parietal regions over both left and right hemispheres predicted successful recognition accompanied by retrieval of episodic detail, whereas only right-parietal ERPs predicted successful recognition without episodic detail, a phenomenon referred to as pure familiarity—when a face seems familiar but is not remembered.

Other studies of ERPs, electrical rhythms, functional magnetic resonance images of brain activity, and spiking from single neurons have suggested that many cortical regions can be involved in memory encoding and that activity in the hippocampus may be particularly relevant for the storage of declarative memories (e.g., Fell, Klaver, Elger, & Fernandez, 2002; Paller & McCarthy, 2002; Reber et al., 2002; Sederberg, Kahana, Howard, Donner, & Madsen, 2003).

Many different types of processing at encoding can promote successful memory storage. Accordingly, many avenues of investigation will be required for scientists to understand the formation and preservation of declarative memories. Measures of neural activity predictive of subsequent memory, such as Dm-recall, provide an inroad to this problem, and will ultimately be most useful if connections can be built between these measures and specific neurocognitive processes. This goal will require analyzing neural activity as a function of successful versus unsuccessful encoding in conjunction with manipulating various factors that systematically affect memory encoding and storage.

MEMORY RETRIEVAL

The efficacy of encoding and storage becomes evident only when stored information is subsequently accessed. In studies of retrieval, differences between ERP responses to new and old items in recognition tests (i.e., items not previously presented and those presented at encoding, respectively) have been researched in considerable detail. These *old-new ERP effects* generally take the form of positive shifts in ERPs to old items relative to ERPs to new items.

Early experimental results prompted a range of conclusions regarding the cognitive concomitants of these effects without leading to consensus. In retrospect, firm interpretations were difficult because discriminating old from new generally involves a variety of different cognitive processes and multiple brain potentials that overlap in time. As a result, functionally distinct brain signals within old-new ERP effects were difficult to isolate from one another.

For example, consider two memory phenomena that can co-occur when a person views a face: (a) retrieval of prior episodes involving the same face and (b) faster or more accurate processing of that face due to prior perceptual analysis of the same face (the behavioral phenomenon of *perceptual priming*). Special tactics are needed to isolate ERPs associated with these different sorts of memory. Indeed, it is notoriously difficult to prevent people from systematically recalling prior episodes when stimuli are repeated, and this incidental retrieval can con taminate neural analyses of priming.

One approach to this problem made use of a condition in which faces were encoded only to a minimal extent (Paller, Hutson, Miller, & Boehm, 2003). Each of these faces was presented at a central location for 100 ms while participants were required to make a difficult visual discrimination at another location. When the face disappeared, a masking stimulus appeared centrally to further limit face encoding. On a subsequent test, participants' ability to recognize these faces was nearly the same as would be expected if they were merely guessing which faces had been presented previously. However, priming was still observed for these faces in an implicit memory test. Thus, ERPs elicited by these faces were associated with priming uncontaminated by conscious remembering. In contrast, other faces were well remembered by the participants because they were initially presented for a longer duration and without the additional discrimination requirement that interfered with encoding. The two conditions thus provide a direct comparison between ERPs associated with conscious memory for faces and ERPs associated with priming. Recognizing a repeated face was associated with positive ERPs at the rear of the head 400 to 800 ms after face onset (Fig. 2a), whereas priming was associated with negative ERPs at the front of the head 200 to 400 ms after face onset (Fig. 2b).

In another experiment, we used a different strategy to isolate signals associated with face recollection (Paller, Bozic, Ranganath, Grabowecky, & Yamada, 1999). At encoding, participants attempted to memorize 20 faces accompanied by spoken vignettes (simulating actually meeting the individuals pictured) and were told to forget 20 other faces. Later recognition was superior for the former compared with the latter faces, but the magnitude of priming observed during implicit memory testing was the same for the two groups of faces. Comparing ERPs for the two kinds of faces therefore revealed an uncontaminated neural signal of face recollection (comparable to that shown in Fig. 2a). In a subsequent experiment, similar electrical signals were observed for remembering a face per se and for remembering a face along with corresponding biographical facts learned at encoding. Brain activity was observed over posterior regions in both situations, whereas additional activity that was slightly more anterior was observed only when biographical retrieval occurred. Subjects in these experiments were able to successfully recall person-specific information, which is an ability that depends on linking diverse sorts of information together—a prototypical example of declarative memory retrieval that would naturally give rise to conscious recollection.

AWARENESS OF REMEMBERING

Despite the strong connection between declarative memory and the experience of remembering, these phenomena need not always occur together. Declarative memory retrieval provides some of the necessary precursors for the awareness of remembering, but it is not sufficient to produce this experience. Rather, conscious memory depends on a further inference—the explicit thought that the current contents of consciousness are derived from memory retrieval.

Thus, dysfunctional cross-cortical storage in amnesia has an indirect impact on awareness of remembering. A strong, selective disruption of declarative memory also tends to disrupt awareness of remembering because memory for the spatiotemporal context of an episode is a critical factor that can help one to infer that a memory for a prior event has been retrieved (e.g., Johnson & Chalfonte, 1994). The ability to make such inferences is one of several retrieval functions dependent on prefrontal cortex (along with strategic search, evaluation, and keeping retrieved information in mind). Indeed, retrieval functions have been associated with ERPs over prefrontal cortex in many studies (e.g., Ranganath & Paller, 1999; Rugg & Wilding, 2000).

Neural signals of memory must thus be evaluated with respect to the possibility that declarative memory retrieval need not necessarily give rise to awareness of remembering. That is, sometimes a stimulus can seem familiar even in the absence of conscious remembering. Data relevant to understanding the difference between retrieval with and without conscious remembering were recently obtained by

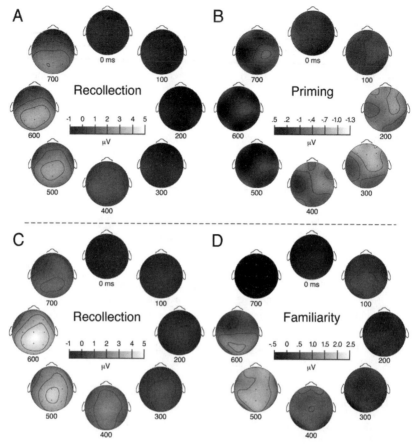

Fig. 2. Topographic maps of brain potentials associated with different memory experiences cued by faces: recollection (a, c), priming (b), and familiarity (d). In each panel, differences in potentials between two conditions are shown on schematic heads as if viewed from above (nose at the top), results are interpolated from 21 scalp locations (small circles), and measurements are displayed for eight intervals beginning at face onset (0 ms). Each of the eight maps represents a mean amplitude difference computed over a 100-ms interval beginning at the time shown. The largest differences are signified by the lightest shades of gray, although the microvolt scale is not the same in each panel. In (b), differences are negative potentials, whereas in the other panels, differences are positive. In (d), values beyond the negative range of the scale in the map for 700 to 800 ms are shown in black. Results shown in (a) and (b) are adapted from Paller, Hutson, Miller, and Boehm (2003). The recollection contrast is between remembered faces and new faces; the priming contrast is between primed but not remembered faces and new faces. Results shown in (c) and (d) are from Yovel and Paller (2004). The recollection contrast is between faces recognized with episodic recollection and new faces; the familiarity contrast is between faces recognized without episodic recollection and new faces. Color topographic maps are available in the original publications.

comparing the case in which a face provoked a full-blown recollective experience with the case in which a face provoked the unsubstantiated impression of memory known as pure familiarity (Yovel & Paller, 2004). Electrical signals associated with face-induced recollection (Fig. 2c) and face-induced pure familiarity (Fig. 2d) were similar, but amplitudes were reduced for pure familiarity. Notably, electrophysiological correlates of pure familiarity with faces and of priming with faces (Figs. 2d and Fig. 2b, respectively) were highly divergent, consistent with the notion that familiarity is not a straightforward outcome of priming, despite superficial similarities between familiarity and priming. Pure familiarity can instead be conceived of as a result of limited stimulus recognition without contextual retrieval adequate for triggering episodic recollection.

BORDER AREAS OF DECLARATIVE MEMORY

Current theories of memory address a variety of memory phenomena and their neural implementation, but many questions remain open. Some subtle but critical questions concern memory phenomena at the border between declarative and nondeclarative memory, such as several subtypes of priming. If amnesia fundamentally entails a disruption of memory functions dependent on cross-cortical storage, as proposed, then priming should remain preserved only if mediated within single cortical zones.

Conceptual priming is one subtype of priming that deserves further study; it is thought to arise from altered representations of the meaning of a stimulus rather than of the physical features of a stimulus. Conceptual priming can cross stimulus domains, such as when hearing a word primes its meaning so as to facilitate processing of the meaning when the word is subsequently read, or when reading the name of a famous person primes knowledge of his or her identity so as to facilitate processing of that person's identity when his or her face is subsequently viewed. Indeed, a putative electrical signal of conceptual priming with words was identified and shown to be preserved in patients with deficient declarative memory (Olichney et al., 2000; see also Yovel & Paller, 2004). This signal may reflect a component of exactly the type of memory that allows amnesic patients to engage fully in complex conversations, all the while maintaining their comprehension abilities and focus on the topic at hand.

CONCLUSIONS

Researchers now have the ability to record neural signals associated with several of the many processes that contribute to declarative and nondeclarative memory. These neural signals provide a window into the physiology of memory that will be essential for further explorations of the neurocognitive substrates of remembering.

Future efforts should be aimed at elucidating exactly how declarative memory differs from priming and other sorts of nondeclarative memory. What is unique about declarative encoding, storage, and retrieval? What memory processes support priming, and how do these processes differ from those that support declarative memory? Does remembering in the absence of contextual retrieval, as exemplified by pure familiarity experiences, rely on any memory processing in common with priming? What processing underlies priming phenomena that are impaired in amnesia?

A promising strategy to promote progress on these and related issues is to isolate and characterize neurophysiological events specifically responsible for memory. A variety of techniques for measuring brain activity can be used together to study human memory and memory disorders, and to provide data needed to advance and refine neurobiological hypotheses concerning memory, such as those I have outlined in this review. This approach may also lead to an eventual understanding of how neurocognitive processing gives rise to the conscious experience of remembering, and it may thus also provide clues to understanding subjective awareness in general.

Recommended Reading

Eichenbaum, H., & Cohen, N.J. (2001). *From conditioning to conscious recollection: Memory systems of the brain.* New York: Oxford University Press.

Münte, T.F., Urbach, T.P., Düzel, E., & Kutas, M. (2000). Event-related brain potentials in the study of human cognition and neuropsychology. In F. Boller, J. Grafman, & G. Rizzolatti (Eds.), *Handbook of neuropsychology, Vol. 1* (pp. 139–234). Amsterdam: Elsevier-Science.

Paller, K.A. (1997). Consolidating dispersed neocortical memories: The missing link in amnesia. In A.R. Mayes & J.J. Downes (Eds.), *Theories of organic amnesia* (pp. 73–88). East Sussex, England: Psychology Press. (Reprinted from *Memory, 5,* 73–88, 1997)

Paller, K.A., & Wagner, A.D. (2002). Observing the transformation of experience into memory. *Trends in Cognitive Sciences, 6,* 93–102.

Schacter, D.L. (1996). *Searching for memory: The brain, the mind, and the past.* New York: Basic Books.

Squire, L.R., & Kandel, E.R. (1999). *Memory: From mind to molecules.* New York: Scientific American Library.

Squire, L.R., & Schacter, D.L. (Eds.). (2002). *Neuropsychology of memory* (3rd ed.). New York: Guilford.

Acknowledgments—Research reported in this article was supported by Grant NS34639 from the National Institute of Neurological Disorders and Stroke. I thank Gary Paller for adapting multiple images to construct Figure 1.

Note

1. Address correspondence to Ken Paller, Department of Psychology, Northwestern University, 2029 Sheridan Rd., Evanston, IL 60208-2710; e-mail: kap@northwestern.edu.

References

Fell, J., Klaver, P., Elger, C.E., & Fernandez, G. (2002). The interaction of rhinal cortex and hippocampus in human declarative memory formation. *Reviews in the Neurosciences, 13,* 299–312.

Friedman, D., & Johnson, R., Jr. (2000). Event-related potential (ERP) studies of memory encoding and retrieval: A selective review. *Microscopy Research and Technique, 51,* 6–28.

Johnson, M.K., & Chalfonte, B.L. (1994). Binding complex memories: The role of reactivation and the hippocampus. In D.L. Schacter & E. Tulving (Eds.), *Memory systems 1994* (pp. 311–350). Cambridge, MA: MIT Press.

Olichney, J.M., Van Petten, C., Paller, K.A., Salmon, D.P., Iragui, V.J., & Kutas, M. (2000). Word repetition in amnesia: Electrophysiological measures of impaired and spared memory. *Brain, 123,* 1948–1963.

Paller, K.A. (1990). Recall and stem-completion priming have different electrophysiological correlates and are modified differentially by directed forgetting. *Journal of Experimental Psychology: Learning, Memory, and Cognition, 16,* 1021–1032.

Paller, K.A. (2002). Cross-cortical consolidation as the core defect in amnesia: Prospects for hypothesis-testing with neuropsychology and neuroimaging. In L.R. Squire & D.L. Schacter (Eds.), *Neuropsychology of memory* (3rd ed., pp. 73–87). New York: Guilford.

Paller, K.A., Bozic, V.S., Ranganath, C., Grabowecky, M., & Yamada, S. (1999). Brain waves following remembered faces index conscious recollection. *Cognitive Brain Research, 7,* 519–531.

Paller, K.A., Hutson, C.A., Miller, B.B., & Boehm, S.G. (2003). Neural manifestations of memory with and without awareness. *Neuron, 38,* 507–516.

Paller, K.A., & McCarthy, G. (2002). Field potentials in the human hippocampus during the encoding and recognition of visual stimuli. *Hippocampus, 12,* 415–420.

Ranganath, C., & Paller, K.A. (1999). Frontal brain potentials during recognition are modulated by requirements to retrieve perceptual detail. *Neuron, 22,* 605–613.

Reber, P.J., Siwiec, R.M., Gitelman, D.R., Parrish, T.B., Mesulam, M.-M., & Paller, K.A. (2002). Neural correlates of successful encoding identified using functional magnetic resonance imaging. *Journal of Neuroscience, 22,* 9541–9548.

Rugg, M.D., & Wilding, E.L. (2000). Retrieval processing and episodic memory. *Trends in Cognitive Sciences, 4,* 108–115.

Sederberg, P.B., Kahana, M.J., Howard, M.W., Donner, E., & Madsen, J.R. (2003). Theta and gamma oscillations during encoding predict subsequent recall. *Journal of Neuroscience, 23,* 10809–10814.

Squire, L.R. (1987). *Memory and brain.* New York: Oxford University Press.

Yovel, G., & Paller, K.A. (2004). The neural basis of the butcher-on-the-bus phenomenon: When a face seems familiar but is not remembered. *Neuro-Image, 21,* 789–800.

This article has been reprinted as it originally appeared in *Current Directions in Psychological Science*. Citation information for this article as originally published appears above.

The Role of Social Interaction in Bird Song Learning

Michael D. Beecher[1] and John M. Burt
University of Washington

Abstract

Bird song learning has become a powerful model system for studying learning because of its parallels with human speech learning, recent advances in understanding of its neurobiological basis, and the strong tradition of studying song learning in both the laboratory and the field. Most of the findings and concepts in the field derive from the tape-tutor experimental paradigm, in which the young bird is tutored by tape-recorded song delivered by a loudspeaker in an isolation chamber. This paradigm provides rigorous experimental control of auditory parameters, but strips song learning of any social context, and has slowed the realization that social factors might be critical to the process. In recent years, field research and lab studies using live birds as tutors have revealed that social factors play a preeminent role in song learning. In this article, we propose a new experimental paradigm—the virtual-tutor design, which permits precise manipulation of singing interactions between simulated tutors that the young bird "overhears," as well as direct singing interactions between the young bird and the simulated tutors. We suggest that this approach may permit researchers to analyze social factors in bird song learning, particularly those relating to auditory interactions, that have been difficult to analyze heretofore.

Keywords

social learning; bird song; animal communication

The parallels between bird song learning and human speech learning were first clearly noted by Marler (1970a), primarily on the basis of his own classic studies of song learning in white-crowned sparrows (Marler, 1970b). These parallels include (a) a sensitive period early in life, (b) innate predispositions for species-typical signals (in songbirds, this predisposition is dubbed the innate song template), (c) a memorization phase followed (or overlapped) by a motor phase in which the memorized signals are translated into production, and (d) the necessity of auditory feedback—hearing one's own voice—for memorized sensory information to be translated into vocal signals. The similarities between bird song learning and human speech learning, taken with the spectacular advances in the study of the neurobiology of song learning, have established bird song learning as perhaps the major model system of learning (for a review, see Brainard & Doupe, 2002).

In this article, we focus on one notable omission from Marler's list of parallels between bird song learning and human speech learning: the key role of social interaction in the learning process. The classic studies of Marler and other researchers on song learning in songbirds explicitly excluded social factors. In the *tape-tutor* paradigm used in these studies, the young bird is isolated in a sound-proof chamber at about the time he would normally leave the nest (10–20 days), and song is played to him through loudspeakers. This procedure indisputably provides more experimental control than would be possible with actual birds as the song tutors. From this Spartan paradigm came the important concepts of the sensitive period for learning and the innate song template. For example, Marler's tape-tutor experiments (1970b) showed that a white-crowned sparrow male develops normal species song only if the bird hears his own species' song during an early sensitive period, from age 10 to 50 days; the bird rejects other species' song heard during this period, as well as his own species' song heard after the sensitive period.

DISCOVERING SOCIAL FACTORS

Researchers first became aware of the importance of social factors in bird song learning when they discovered that individuals of some species will not learn from taped song, but instead require live birds as their song tutors. Particularly influential were the studies of Baptista and Petrinovich (e.g., 1984) showing that white-crowned sparrows learned more readily from live birds than tape tutors. Moreover, whereas the tape-tutor studies indicated that the sensitive period for white-crowned sparrows closes at approximately 50 days, and that songs of other species presented during the sensitive period are uniformly rejected (Marler, 1970b), Baptista and Petrinovich (1984) showed that a young white-crowned sparrow would learn song after this period, even if the tutor was not the same species, provided the tutor was live.

The other major impetus for the study of social factors came from field studies (e.g., Kroodsma, 1974). Although field studies could not provide the experimental control provided by laboratory studies, they naturally brought into focus the social variables that were controlled out of laboratory experiments. Moreover, field research challenged answers that tape-tutor studies had given to the simpler questions. For example, we have found that a young song sparrow in our population learns his eight or so different song types from birds in the neighborhood in which he will attempt to establish his own territory (Beecher, Campbell, & Stoddard, 1994). This pattern of learning songs from neighbors appears to be common in songbirds, and gives rise to patterns of song sharing within small neighborhood clusters. Furthermore, our field studies suggested that a song sparrow is capable of learning new songs at least into his first fall and perhaps the following spring, much later than suggested by tape-tutor experiments. Our lab experiments with live tutors simulating natural conditions confirmed that the sensitive period extends at least into the first fall (Nordby, Campbell, & Beecher, 2001). Finally, song sparrows seem to copy song types much more accurately in the field (see Fig. 1) than they do in lab tape-tutor experiments, in which they commonly develop new song types by rearranging imitated song elements.

WHAT ARE THE SOCIAL VARIABLES IN SONG LEARNING?

It is now widely accepted that social factors influence song learning. It is not at all clear, however, what precise aspects of social stimulation influence song development, and how they do it (Nelson, 1997). We suggest that the analysis of

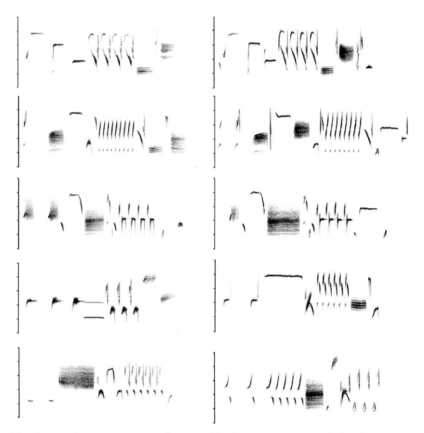

Fig. 1. Partial song repertoires of two neighboring song sparrows. Each column contains sonograms (vertical axis is frequency, 0–10 kHz; horizontal axis is time, songs are 2–3 s long) of five songs of one of the birds. We identified the bird whose songs are on the left as one of four probable song tutors of the younger bird whose songs are on the right. The songs in the top three rows are very similar. Thus, the two birds shared these song types. Each bird had six additional song types that the two did not share; four of those songs are shown in the bottom two rows.

social factors will be the major focus of the study of bird song learning in the next few decades, and we propose here a new approach and methodology for studying social factors in song learning.

If social factors are central to song learning, then a key question is how they determine which songs the young bird will select from all the songs he hears. The young bird hears many adult males of its species sing, and in the typical case, each of these adults sings multiple song types (in about three quarters of songbird species, males have song repertoires). Consequently, the young bird will hear many more songs than he can keep for his adult species-typical repertoire. There are two general ways social factors could influence song selection. First, young birds may observe interactions among the adult birds who are their potential song tutors and select tutors and songs on the basis of differences among these adults. One hypothesis is that young birds learn or retain songs of higher-status birds. Recent evidence has shown that both male and female songbirds "eavesdrop" on singing interactions of neighborhood males, and may make mating or other behavioral decisions based on information they extract concerning status relationships of the singing males (e.g., Otter et al., 1999). Thus, it is plausible that young males use this same kind of information to make tutor- and song-selection decisions in the song-learning process. To date, there is no direct evidence that they do so, but this may simply be because few investigators have yet examined this possibility.

The second major social determinant of song selection comprises factors relating directly to the social relationship of tutor and student, and probably depends on direct interactions between the two. For example, if the young bird is attempting to establish his territory next to a particular adult, learning that adult's songs may facilitate future interactions with him. We have shown that a young song sparrow learns the songs of adults who will be his neighbors in his first breeding season. We have also shown that sharing songs facilitates communication between neighbors, because neighbors preferentially use their shared songs to modulate territorial interactions (Burt, Campbell, & Beecher, 2001). Perhaps for this reason, birds who share more songs with their neighbors are more successful (i.e., enjoy longer territory tenures) than are those who share fewer songs (Beecher, Campbell, & Nordby, 2000).

THE VIRTUAL SONG TUTOR

Although field studies implicate some of the social variables that may be important in song learning, they fail to show how these variables might mediate the process of song learning. Precisely how do social interactions result in the young bird acquiring certain songs and not others? Here we sketch out an approach to investigating this question—the *virtual-tutor* design, which attempts to incorporate social factors that may be critical in the field into the controlled environment of a lab tape-tutor experiment. This approach returns to the basic design of the tape-tutor experiment, but uses modern computer techniques to simulate social, interactive tutors.

The virtual-tutor design we describe eliminates visual signals and manipulates only auditory variables. Although it has often been assumed that visual signals are a key part of the live tutor's effectiveness, there is little direct evidence that this is true, and some strong evidence to the contrary. For example, Slater, Eales, and Clayton (1988) found that zebra finch fledglings prevented from seeing by eye patches would still learn from a tutor if he was in the same cage. In one of our live-tutor experiments simulating natural conditions (Nordby et al., 2001), we found that our best tutor (of six) taught songs to many young birds who could hear him at a distance but not see him. Perhaps the effectiveness of purely auditory tutoring should not be surprising in view of the bird-human parallels: If a blind child can learn speech perfectly well, then perhaps a songbird can learn the songs of a tutor he hears and interacts with socially but cannot see.

As suggested in the previous section, two major classes of social variables can be manipulated in the virtual-tutor experiment: characteristics of tutor–tutor interactions observed (overheard) by the student and characteristics of tutor–student interactions. In our virtual-tutor design, different tutors are simulated by different loudspeakers in the chamber—for example, Tutor A always sings from the east loudspeaker, Tutor B from the north loudspeaker, and Tutor C from the west loudspeaker. This arrangement simulates a key feature of the natural environment of song sparrows (and the majority of songbird species): Birds are territorial, and thus different birds sing from different, predictable locations. Dominance interactions between the tutors can be simulated on the basis of communication rules derived from field studies. Although dominance patterns appear to vary from species to species, the following patterns are frequently observed and can be mimicked in the virtual-tutor experiment: A dominant bird will song-match another bird (switch to the same song type the other bird is singing), whereas a subordinate bird will switch off the type it was singing when matched; a dominant bird will sing over the song of a subordinate bird, whereas a subordinate bird will simply stop singing when so challenged by the song of a dominant bird. Will a young bird hearing these simulated interactions be more likely to learn the songs of the dominant tutor?

It seems likely that direct tutor–student interactions are the most important ones in song learning. It is straightforward to program the virtual tutor to respond to the song of the young bird. It is harder, but feasible, to program it to match song, that is, respond with the tutor song most like what the young bird has just sung. Intuitively, it seems likely that a responsive tutor of this sort would be an effective tutor. There are at least three possible dimensions to these interactions that might be critical.

First, perhaps it is critical for the tutor's song to be contingent on something the young bird has done. However, experiments have indicated that pure contingency that lacks social context—the bird triggers tutor song by hopping onto a particular perch or by pecking a key—does not seem to be an effective variable in song learning (experiments summarized in Houx & ten Cate, 1999). A second possibility is that it is critical for the tutor's song to consistently follow the student's song specifically, rather than some other aspect of his behavior. And a third possibility is that the similarity of the student's and tutor's songs is important because the tutor's song has a *shaping* function, serving as a model that the student moves his song toward over time. Clearly, vocal shaping is done by human tutors, as, for example, when a parent responds to an infant's efforts to say a word by repeating the word. Our second and third hypotheses could be distinguished in a virtual-tutor experiment comparing the relative effectiveness of a tutor that responds to the young bird's song with a random song from its repertoire and a tutor that responds with the closest-matching song in its repertoire; both reinforce the student's vocal efforts, but only the latter shapes them as well.

CONCLUSIONS

Live-tutor and field studies opened up the study of bird song learning by bringing social variables out of the closet, and they also challenged some of the generalizations about nonsocial variables, such as the timing of the sensitive period, that had been generated by the tape-tutor studies. Attempts to reconcile the differing views of song learning generated by these differing paradigms have generated considerable heat (e.g., Kroodsma, Baker, Baptista, & Petrinovich, 1985) and have resulted in a hybrid model of song learning that combines the purely auditory picture presented by tape-tutor studies with the social picture presented by live-tutor and field studies (Nelson & Marler, 1994).

But the most interesting question raised by the clashing paradigms has barely been addressed to date: How do social interactions result in the young bird acquiring certain songs and not others? Researchers have some idea of how nonsocial factors such as timing and dosage (how much song is heard) affect song learning, but virtually no idea of the critical social variables, nor how they may relate to auditory variables. The virtual-tutor paradigm provides a way to investigate social variables. In the best case, it will be possible to manipulate the variables of social tutoring, as researchers have previously been able to manipulate the nonsocial variables, in order to achieve comparable insights. Clearly, the ability to simulate natural social tutoring interactions without real birds will have its limitations, and these may ultimately constrain the virtual-tutor approach. Nevertheless, the prospect of reconciling the pictures of bird song learning derived from the tape-tutor and field traditions and of developing a powerful tool for analyzing social variables in song learning motivates us to press ahead with virtual-tutor experiments.

Recommended Reading

Baker, M.C. (2001). Bird song research: The past 100 years. *Bird Behavior, 14*, 3–50.
Beecher, M.D., Nordby, J.C., Campbell, S.E., Burt, J.M., Hill, C.E., & O'Loghlen, A.L. (1997). What is the function of song learning in songbirds? In D.H. Owings, M.D. Beecher, & N.S. Thompson (Eds.), *Perspectives in ethology: Vol. 12. Communication* (pp. 77–97). New York: Plenum Press.
Brainard, M.S., & Doupe, A.J. (2002). (See References)
Goldstein, M.H., King, A.P., & West, M.J. (2003). Social interaction shapes babbling: Testing parallels between birdsong and speech. *Proceedings of the National Academy of Sciences, USA, 100*, 8030–8035.
Snowdon, C.T., & Hausberger, M. (Eds.). (1997). *Social influences on vocal development.* Cambridge, England: Cambridge University Press.

Note

1. Address correspondence to Michael D. Beecher, Box 351525, Department of Psychology, University of Washington, Seattle, WA 98195; e-mail: beecher@u.washington.edu.

References

Baptista, L.F., & Petrinovich, L. (1984). Social interaction, sensitive phases and the song template hypothesis in the white-crowned sparrow. *Animal Behaviour, 32*, 172–181.
Beecher, M.D., Campbell, S.E., & Nordby, J.C. (2000). Territory tenure in song sparrows is related to song sharing with neighbours, but not to repertoire size. *Animal Behaviour, 59*, 29–37.
Beecher, M.D., Campbell, S.E., & Stoddard, P.K. (1994). Correlation of song learning and territory establishment strategies in the song sparrow. *Proceedings of the National Academy of Sciences, USA, 91*, 1450–1454.
Brainard, M.S., & Doupe, A.J. (2002). What songbirds teach us about learning. *Nature* (London), *417*, 351–358.

Burt, J.M., Campbell, S.E., & Beecher, M.D. (2001). Song type matching as threat: A test using interactive playback. *Animal Behaviour, 62*, 1163–1170.

Houx, B.B., & ten Cate, C. (1999). Song learning from playback in zebra finches: Is there an effect of operant contingency? *Animal Behaviour, 57*, 837–845.

Kroodsma, D.E. (1974). Song learning, dialects, and dispersal in the Bewick's wren. *Zeitschrift für Tierpsychologie, 35*, 352–380.

Kroodsma, D.E., Baker, M.C., Baptista, L.F., & Petrinovich, L. (1985). Vocal "dialects" in Nuttall's white-crowned sparrow. *Current Ornithology, 2*, 103–133.

Marler, P. (1970a). Birdsong and speech development: Could there be parallels? *American Scientist, 58*, 669–673.

Marler, P. (1970b). A comparative approach to vocal learning: Song development in white-crowned sparrows. *Journal of Comparative and Physiological Psychology Monographs, 71*, 1–25.

Nelson, D.A. (1997). Social interaction and sensitive phases for song learning: A critical review. In C.T. Snowdon & M. Hausberger (Eds.), *Social influences on vocal development* (pp. 7–22). Cambridge, England: Cambridge University Press.

Nelson, D.A., & Marler, P. (1994). Selection-based learning in bird song development. *Proceedings of the National Academy of Sciences, USA, 91*, 10498–10501.

Nordby, J.C., Campbell, S.E., & Beecher, M.D. (2001). Late song learning in song sparrows. *Animal Behaviour, 61*, 835–846.

Otter, K., McGregor, P.K., Terry, A.M.R., Burford, F.R.L., Peake, T.M., & Dabelsteen, T. (1999). Do female great tits (*Parus major*) assess males by eavesdropping? A field study using interactive song playback. *Proceedings of the Royal Society of London: Series B. Biological Sciences, 266*, 1305–1309.

Slater, P.J.B., Eales, L.A., & Clayton, N.S. (1988). Song learning in zebra finches: Progress and prospects. In J.S. Rosenblatt (Ed.), *Advances in the study of behavior, Vol. 18* (pp. 1–34). San Diego, CA: Academic Press.

Memory Maintenance: The Changing Nature of Neural Mechanisms

Wickliffe C. Abraham[1]

University of Otago, Dunedin, New Zealand

Abstract

Change in the synaptic communication between neurons—known as synaptic plasticity—plays a key role in learning and memory. It is not yet clear, however, whether the properties of synaptic plasticity are sufficient to account for long-term-memory maintenance. Recent studies have revealed that synaptic plasticity can indeed persist for weeks or months, as might be expected of a long-term-memory mechanism. However, memories encoded by neural systems are not static; they continue to evolve as new learning occurs. Furthermore, neural-network modeling has shown that synapses must be able to reconfigure their connection strengths during new learning if old information is to be preserved. Recent tests confirm that synapses, once modified, retain their capacity for further modification, indicating that they can indeed operate in the manner predicted to be necessary for memory maintenance in a dynamic learning network.

Keywords

synaptic plasticity; memory maintenance; neural networks; long-term potentiation

How is information learned, stored, and maintained in the brain? Historically, it has been supposed that these processes involve changes in the structure or function of neurons, particularly at the synaptic junctions through which they communicate. Thus, most theories postulate that synapses are likely sites of activity-induced change—known as plasticity—that could be responsible for reordering the communication between neurons during learning. By such restructuring, those same networks active during learning could then be readily re-engaged during memory retrieval. In Hebb's (1949) theory, synapses are strengthened as a function of neuronal co-activity, a principle now codified by the mnemonic "cells that fire together, wire together." In addition, more recent theories and empirical evidence suggest that a weakening of synaptic communication is also a memory mechanism. In this article, I will consider the properties and mechanisms of the synaptic plasticity that may underlie the maintenance of long-term memory, in light of recent advances in this area.

LONG-TERM POTENTIATION

In a landmark discovery, Bliss and Lømo (1973) reported that electrically induced neural activity can cause a persistent increase in the strength of transmission at the activated synapses (Fig. 1), a phenomenon termed long-term potentiation (LTP). There now exists a wealth of evidence supporting the working hypothesis that the molecular mechanisms underpinning LTP and its opposite synaptic

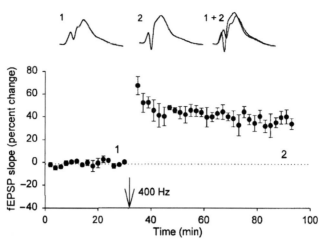

Fig. 1. Induction of long-term potentiation (LTP) in the rat hippocampus. Plotted are mean field excitatory postsynaptic potentials (fEPSP) generated by low-frequency electrical stimulation of an excitatory pathway in the hippocampus of 5 animals; fEPSPs are expressed as a percent change from the average baseline value (0–30 min). Brief high-frequency (400 Hz) stimulation (arrow) produced an increased synaptic potential, which remained potentiated for the duration of the experiment. Waveforms at top are average fEPSPs recorded from a single animal before and after high-frequency stimulation, at the times indicated by the numbers. (Calibration bars: 3 mV, 5 ms.)

change, long-term depression (LTD), are also engaged by the naturally occurring synaptic plasticity generated during learning (Martin, Grimwood & Morris, 2000). However, it is important to keep in mind that LTP and LTD are phenomena that are studied in the laboratory, using electrical stimulation to generate neural activity that is only a simulation of the neural activity that occurs during learning. Thus, while one approach to testing this hypothesis is to compare the relevant properties of LTP and memory, as I do below, it is necessary to be cautious in expecting too close a correspondence between the properties of plasticity at single synaptic junctions and the properties of memories that are distributed over networks of neurons and synapses.

A key question regarding any neural mechanism of memory has been whether it can last long enough to account for the longevity of long-term memory. Most studies of LTP persistence in animals typically have reported LTP to last from hours to weeks but ultimately decaying to baseline. However, LTP lasting stably for many months has now been reported (Abraham, Greenwood, Logan, Mason-Parker, & Dragunow, 2002). This is not to say that the potentiated synapses remain continuously active over this time, but that there is an enduring enhancement of their ability to communicate with the neurons to which they connect. Thus, it has been frequently hypothesized that if synaptic plasticity contributes to initial learning, its enduring persistence could underpin the memory retention for that learned event (Abraham, 2003). However, I will present recent findings that challenge this conventional wisdom and that point instead to a more dynamic view of the synaptic basis of memory maintenance.

MEMORY CONSOLIDATION

There is considerable evidence from both animal and human studies that, after learning, memory undergoes a time-dependent consolidation process such that it becomes resistant to treatments given post-training that can otherwise cause amnesia for the learned event. Many theorists now distinguish two forms of consolidation: cellular consolidation and systems consolidation.

The concept of cellular consolidation arose from animal studies showing that newly formed memories require the triggering of protein synthesis in order to survive longer than a few hours (Squire, 1986). Administration of a protein-synthesis inhibitor during or just after training impairs long-term retention of that memory without affecting initial learning or retention over the first few hours. This implies that, at a cellular level, neurons are triggered during training to make additional proteins that in some way help preserve the newly changed synaptic connection strengths. In a remarkable correspondence, LTP also shows a fundamental dependence on new protein synthesis in order to last longer than a few hours. The identity and function of the key proteins have yet to be fully characterized, but it is likely that the newly synthesized proteins contribute to changes in the fine structure of synapses, thereby locking in the functional changes that occur more immediately during learning. In another point of correspondence, the long-term persistence of LTP is best achieved by multiple episodes of synaptic activity spaced over time; likewise, memory retention is far superior after spaced training than after the same number of training trials occurring in rapid succession (DeZazzo & Tully, 1995).

Systems consolidation refers to a change in the way memories are stored, such that, with time, they lose reliance on the brain structures that were essential for successful retention early after learning. Systems consolidation studies have focused on structures in the brain's medial temporal lobe, such as the hippocampus. Many episodic- and spatial-memory tasks are dependent on the integrity of the hippocampus and related structures early after training, but eventually the information is consolidated in other brain regions, such that memory retention is unimpaired even if the hippocampus is completely removed (Wiltgen, Brown, Talton, & Silva et al., 2004). In contrast to cellular consolidation, however, systems consolidation can take days, weeks, or even years to be accomplished. It has been hypothesized that this lengthy consolidation period permits repeated cycling of activity between the hippocampus and neocortex, a major area for very-long-term memory storage, so that new information initially stored in the hippocampus can slowly be integrated into cortical networks without disrupting the information already stored there (McClelland, McNaughton, & O'Reilly, 1995).

MEMORY REACTIVATION, RECONSOLIDATION

The fact that consolidated memories are resistant to the disruptive effects of amnestic treatments has been construed as reflecting a permanent change in the function of the relevant synapses. It is a curious fact, therefore, that reactivation of consolidated memories—for example, by presentation of cues associated with the original learning—renders those memories susceptible once again to disruption by amnestic treatments such as protein-synthesis inhibitors or electroconvulsive shock (Misanin, Miller, & Lewis, 1968). This implies that a new wave of cellular-consolidation processes takes place following reactivation. Further, a new wave of systems consolidation may also take place, in some cases involving brain regions different from those critical for initial consolidation (Dudai & Eisenberg, 2004). Such reactivation effects may appear to be maladaptive, insofar as they put information at risk of being degraded after having initially been consolidated. However, this may be a necessary risk if new information from additional experiences or training trials is to be melded with the information already resident in the brain (see below). Taken together, the evidence for both consolidation and reconsolidation of memory suggests that the strength and identity of the synapses storing memories in the brain are likely to be continually undergoing change.

MAINTENANCE OF LTP VERSUS MAINTENANCE OF MEMORY

The capacity of LTP in the hippocampus and cortex of rodents to persist across months has been offered as strong support for its candidacy as a long-term-memory mechanism (Abraham et al., 2002). But is the capacity for long-term persistence a necessary prerequisite for a memory mechanism? The evidence for memory consolidation and reconsolidation suggests that memory maintenance is a dynamic process that may require more flexibility in synaptic efficacy than could be produced by a single bout of plasticity at the time of learning that is then stably preserved.

These considerations led us to address the question of why LTP can appear to persist so stably, particularly in the hippocampus, which is probably not a long-term information store. We hypothesized that this apparent stability may be a result of conducting our experiments in laboratory animals, typically housed in isolation from other animals and having limited learning opportunities. Indeed, we have recently shown that otherwise stably potentiated synapses are capable of further change, even long after the induction of LTP, if hippocampal neurons are activated in a significant way. In one set of experiments we used high-frequency stimulation (HFS) to establish saturated and persistent LTP in the synapses of the lateral perforant pathway, which connects the medial temporal cortex with the hippocampus. At either 21 or 100 days following LTP induction, HFS was delivered to a neighboring pathway. At either time point this procedure rapidly and completely reversed LTP in the lateral perforant path synapses (Abraham, 2003).

In a second set of experiments, stable LTP was induced in perforant path synapses, and then 2 weeks later animals were given periodic exposure to an enriched environment consisting of a large chamber with novel objects (changed daily), a novel food, and other animals. Exposure to the new environment for only 1 hour per day was sufficient to partially reverse the previously established LTP. Repeated overnight exposure led to a larger and more rapid reversal (Abraham et al., 2002). Interestingly, the LTP was harder to reverse if the environment treatment occurred 3 months rather than 2 weeks following LTP induction, implying that there had been a lengthy cellular consolidation process during that period. Taken together, our data indicate that LTP does not reflect a permanent change in synaptic strength, but rather that synapses operate as "sample and hold" devices such that plasticity, once induced, will be maintained until further relevant neural activity generates additional change. Importantly, the LTP-reversal effects bear formal similarity to the effects that interfering behavioral events have on the retention of long-term memory (Wixted, 2004).

The fact that both memory and synaptic plasticity remain changeable, even once apparently consolidated, casts serious doubt on the idea that memory retention requires preservation of a specific set of synaptic connection strengths. Instead, continued bouts of neural activity and synaptic plasticity long after learning may be necessary to maintain information in dynamic networks. Transgenic mice (i.e., mice genetically modified using molecular cloning technology) have been used to elegantly demonstrate that ongoing synaptic plasticity is very likely necessary for memory retention. For example, transgenic animals were created whereby it was possible to prevent LTP from occurring by stopping production of a critical protein (the NR1 subunit of the N-methyl-D-aspartate receptor). Inhibiting the synthesis of NR1 proteins for the first 1 to 2 weeks after training on a variety of hippocampus-dependent tasks impaired retention of those tasks (Shimizu, Tang, Rampon, & Tsien, 2000). Remarkably, when memories were allowed to consolidate for 6 months prior to inhibiting production of NR1, memory retention could still be impaired, but only when NR1 production was inhibited over a 4-week period (Cui et al., 2004). These findings imply that ongoing synaptic plasticity is necessary for even very-long-term retention of information, and again point to a prolonged consolidation process (Wixted, 2004). The results could imply that plasticity is necessary for restoring the synaptic strength changes that had occurred during learning but had passively or actively degraded over time. Alternatively, the ongoing plasticity may be needed to accommodate new information as it is acquired during daily life in the posttraining period. The latter possibility is supported by the network modeling I now describe.

NEURAL-NETWORK MODELING

Despite the rapidly growing advances in neuroscience, there is no technique that can directly assess whether learning-related changes in synaptic strengths are exactly preserved during memory retention. What is needed is an ability to repeatedly read out the strengths of the specific synapses involved in learning a task and to correlate those strengths with the ability to remember that information after various retention intervals or interfering events. Such a capacity is available, however, in computer-generated neural-network models.

The stability of connection strengths during repeated learning was tested in a standard artificial neural network using a learning algorithm known as back propagation (see Abraham & Robins, 2005, for details). The network was initially trained on 10 input–output pairings, equivalent to paired-associate learning, after which the strength of each connection in the network was noted. The network was then trained sequentially on 40 new input–output pairings, and after each new pairing the network was probed for its retention of the old information as well as for the degree of change in the connection strengths. As seen previously in the first generation of back-propagation models, learning new items caused "catastrophic interference" on the old items—that is, poor retention. Remarkably, however, this interference occurred with little change in the connection strengths. In contrast, under conditions whereby old information was preserved during new learning by being periodically rehearsed, connection strengths changed dramatically during new learning (Abraham & Robins, 2005). These findings strongly support the contention above that preservation of synaptic strength change is not a useful strategy for preserving information in networks that continue to learn. It appears instead that networks can generate many synaptic-strength solutions to solve a given input–output pairing and that during new learning a network must search to find a new solution that can accommodate both the new and the old information. Thus, in models at least, a memory is defined by the functional ability to generate the correct output pattern for a given input pattern, and not by a specific pattern of synaptic strengths within the network.

FINAL REMARKS

LTP and LTD are candidate mechanisms for memory, not least because of their capacity to stably persist over time. It is now apparent, however, that in networks that continue to learn, it is counterproductive for synaptic strengths to be permanently fixed after one learning episode. We propose a modified view, namely that synapses have a sample-and-hold capacity, such that strength changes that are induced during learning are stably maintained until such time as they must be modified to accommodate new information. This viewpoint suggests that a neural mechanism of memory should not be defined by its ability to persist for as long as the memory, not only because the synaptic loci and strengths may keep changing but also because the memory itself can keep changing, as psychologists have amply shown. Nonetheless, it remains important for psychologists and neuroscientists to continue refining their understanding of the synaptic basis of memory maintenance. For example, under what circumstances does learning-related synaptic plasticity overwrite old information, causing memory loss, and when does it participate in rewiring networks to preserve both types of information? Are there brain areas more suited to one of these processes than to the other, and if so, do the properties of synaptic plasticity differ between them? Such advances are necessary for informing the search for the molecular mechanisms underlying synaptic plasticity, a search that is critical for identifying the molecules to be targeted by therapeutic interventions to protect against the loss of memory abilities.

Recommended Reading

Abraham, W.C. (2003). (See References)
Cui, Z., Wang, H., Tan, Y., Zaia, K.A., Zhang, S., & Tsien, J.Z. (2004). (See References)
Martin, S.J., Grimwood, P.D., & Morris, R.G.M. (2000). (See References)

Acknowledgments—The author's work was supported by the New Zealand Health Research Council and the New Zealand Marsden Fund. I thank Dr. Anthony Robins for many helpful discussions.

Note

1. Address correspondence to Wickliffe Abraham, Department of Psychology, Box 56, University of Otago, Dunedin, New Zealand; e-mail: cabraham@psy.otago.ac.nz.

References

Abraham, W.C. (2003). How long will long-term potentiation last? *Philosophical Transactions of the Royal Society of London B, 358,* 735–744.

Abraham, W.C., Greenwood, J.M., Logan, B.L., Mason-Parker, S.E., & Dragunow, M. (2002). Induction and experience-dependent reversal of stable LTP lasting months in the hippocampus. *Journal of Neuroscience, 22,* 9626–9634.

Abraham, W.C., & Robins, A. (2005). Memory retention—the synaptic stability versus plasticity dilemma. *Trends in Neurosciences, 28,* 73–78.

Bliss, T.V.P., & Lømo, T. (1973). Long-lasting potentiation of synaptic transmission in the dentate area of the anaesthetized rabbit following stimulation of the perforant path. *Journal of Physiology, 232,* 331–356.

Cui, Z., Wang, H., Tan, Y., Zaia, K.A., Zhang, S., & Tsien, J.Z. (2004). Inducible and reversible NR1 knockout reveals crucial role of the NMDA receptor in preserving remote memories in the brain. *Neuron, 41,* 781–793.

DeZazzo, J., & Tully, T. (1995). Dissection of memory formation: From behavioral pharmacology to molecular genetics. *Trends in Neurosciences, 18,* 212–218.

Dudai, Y., & Eisenberg, M. (2004). Rites of passage of the engram: Reconsolidation and the lingering consolidation hypothesis. *Neuron, 44,* 93–100.

Hebb, D.O. (1949). *The organization of behavior.* New York: John Wiley & Sons, Inc.

McClelland, J.L., McNaughton, B.L., & O'Reilly, R.C. (1995). Why there are complementary learning systems in the hippocampus and neocortex: Insights from the successes and failures of connectionist models of learning and memory. *Psychological Reviews, 102,* 419–457.

Martin, S.J., Grimwood, P.D., & Morris, R.G.M. (2000). Synaptic plasticity and memory: An evaluation of the hypothesis. *Annual Review of Neuroscience, 23,* 649–711.

Misanin, J.R., Miller, R.R., & Lewis, D.J. (1968). Retrograde amnesia produced by electroconvulsive shock after reactivation of a consolidated memory trace. *Science, 160,* 554–555.

Shimizu, E., Tang, Y.-P., Rampon, C., & Tsien, J.Z. (2000). NMDA receptor-dependent synaptic reinforcement as a crucial process for memory consolidation. *Science, 290,* 1170–1174.

Squire, L.R. (1986). Mechanisms of memory. *Science, 232,* 1612–1619.

Wiltgen, B.J., Brown, R.A.M., Talton, L.E., & Silva, A.J. (2004). New circuits for old memories: The role of the neocortex in consolidation. *Neuron, 44,* 101–108.

Wixted, J.T. (2004). The psychology and neuroscience of forgetting. *Annual Review of Psychology, 55,* 235–269.

Section 2: Critical Thinking Questions

1. In the article by Kolb and colleagues, it is asserted "that if behavior changes, there must be some sort of organization or properties of the neural circuitry that produces the behavior." Given the complexities and enormities associated with human brain plasticity, what is the value of studying an organism as simple as *C. elegans* with only 302 neurons to understand human learning? What are the advantages and drawbacks of using animal models to understand human brain and behavior?

2. The article by Marriott and Wenk indicates that estrogen is important in maintaining optimal memory. After menopause, estrogen concentrations drop to nearly undetectable levels, and the risk of Alzheimer disease increases dramatically. If you were a physician, how would you advise a woman who wanted to take estrogens to prevent Alzheimer disease? What are the costs? What are the benefits? Would your advice differ if the patient already showed clinical signs of Alzheimer disease?

3. In the article by Brembs, the remarkable ability of a single B51 neuron to demonstrate operant conditioning is detailed. The case is made that because the

neurons cultured in a Petri dish show similar responses to yoked B51 neurons in the Aplysia that we can discover features of the nervous system by studying small components of isolated neurons. Given that many imaging studies in humans suggest that wide-ranging activation occurs during learning and other cognitive processes via neural networks, what is the value of studying single neurons in understanding behavior? Can the idea of distributed networks be resolved with the notion of functional brain centers?

4. Biopsychology is fractured by both field and lab biases. Field studies are generally more valid, but less reliable than lab studies, whereas lab studies are generally very reliable, but can be less valid than field studies. The article by Beecher and Burt provides a nice history of the use of speakers in sound-proof boxes to teach young birds songs leading to many insights about bird song learning. Despite the enormous usefulness of these controlled studies, field studies indicated the importance of social factors in song learning. What are the costs and benefits of lab studies compared with field studies of the biological bases of behavior? Are these two approaches complementary or antagonistic?

5. Why is it important to be able to adjust long-term memory stores? The article by Abraham indicates that neural-network models require synaptic connectivity strengths to adjust during new learning to maintain previous memories. What are some examples of psychological data that fit these neurobiological findings?

This article has been reprinted as it originally appeared in *Current Directions in Psychological Science*. Citation information for this article as originally published appears above.

Section 3: Resilience

The vernacular definition of resilience is the ability to recover form or shape. In biology, the ability to recover physiologically and behaviorally after a stressor is the cornerstone to survival. Individuals who are not resilient are likely to succumb prematurely to stress-related disorders. Although, some aspects of resilience are genetically determined, it is becoming increasingly clear that environment and previous experiences can act independently, or in conjunction with a genetic disposition, to shape resiliency.

In the first article, Jaap Koolhaas and colleagues assert that taking an evolutionary approach to studying stress in humans and other animals will lead to an improved understanding of the mechanisms underlying stress-related disorders. They suggest that in addition to face, construct, and predictive validity, researchers should consider ecological validity, when developing animal models for research. For stress research, the four variables that should be considered when assessing ecological validity are the nature, duration, frequency, and intensity of the stressor. Social stress is likely the most ecologically relevant and salient stressor for humans and other animals, although what constitutes social stress may vary greatly from species to species. Individuals within a species also vary considerably in their vulnerability to stress-related disorders, which may reflect individual differences in stress responsivity and/or coping strategies. Indeed, two of the other articles selected for this section highlight how pre-natal and early post-natal exposure to stress can have long-term influences on physiology, cognition, and behavior.

Janet DiPietro describes the very limited, but growing, literature suggesting that the psychological states of women during pregnancy can change the physiological and behavioral activity of their fetuses, and impact behavioral and cognitive development during early childhood. The biomedical perspective on stress is predominantly negative, however, this author proposes that the effects of pre-natal stress on the behavioral and cognitive development of children may be characterized by an inverted U-shaped curve; both low and high levels of arousal may be detrimental during development, whereas a moderate level of arousal may be advantageous during development.

The next article in this section, written by Charles Gillespie and Charles Nemeroff, reviews the role of childhood trauma and altered corticotrophin-releasing factor (CRF) regulation in the etiology of adult affective disorders. Among depressed patients, early childhood trauma is associated with elevated CRF if the stressor occurred before the age of 6, or decreased CRF if the stressor occurred during the perinatal period or pre-teen years. Again there seems to be an optimal level of CRF regulation, and that both suboptimal and supra-optimal CRF concentrations are associated with depression among individuals exposed to stress during development. Furthermore, the authors provide intriguing evidence that depressed patients who were exposed to early-life stress respond differently to standard therapies for affective disorders, and are more likely to relapse following treatment, than those who are depressed but without a history of early-life stress.

Although all of the articles in this section touch, to varying degrees, on the concept of neuroplasticity (physical or morphological changes in the brain in response to changes in the internal or external environment) the intersection between neuroplasticity and affect is the primary focus of the articles by Nathan Fox and his colleagues and Barry Jacobs. The Fox et al., article illustrates the potential for interaction between genes and the environment in shaping affect. Polymorphism in the promoter region of serotonin transporter (5HTTLPR) affects transcription of the serotonin transporter, in turn affecting serotonin reuptake at synapses throughout the brain; people with the short version of the allele are more vulnerable to stress-induced depression, impulsivity, and bulimia nervosa, than people with the long allele. Among 7-year-old children in supportive environments, temperaments are similar for those with the 5HTTLPR long and short alleles. Level of social support does not affect temperament among children with the long allele variant. However, in environments characterized as low in social support, expression of the short allele is associated with elevated and persistent fearfulness. These data provide clear evidence for an interaction between gene expression and social environment, what remains to be determined is how the brains of children with the short allele for 5HTTLPR change when they are raised in an environment with low rather than high caregiver support. Along the same vein, Jacobs proposes that neuroplasticity underlies both the onset and recovery from depression, and that there is a link between neurogenesis (birth of new neurons) and depression. Indeed, both chronic stress and elevated corticosteroids have been shown to suppress neurogenesis in rodents and primates, and induce depressive-like states in several species, including humans. In contrast, treatments that alleviate depression in humans (SSRIs and electroconvulsive shock), elevate neurogenesis in the brains of rodents. The temporal correspondence between the length of SSRI treatment required to induce neurogenesis and to alleviate depressive symptoms is intriguing also. However, establishing a causal link between neurogenesis and depressive behavior will be difficult to accomplish.

In the final article in this section, Robles and colleagues argue that proinflammatory cytokine expression is an important mechanism through which chronic stress and depression can exert effects on general health. Although traditionally glucocorticoids have been considered potent anti-inflammatory agents, a growing body of literature suggests that exposure to stress and elevation of endogenous glucocortioids may actually increase inflammation. The authors conceptualize the relationship between the brain and immune system as being bi-directional, emphasizing that the goal is to provide a balance between ongoing pro-inflammatory and anti-inflammatory processes. Exposure to chronic stress or depression interferes with the delicate balance, and by promoting inflammation can exacerbate affective disorders or precipitate other serious health conditions, such as cardiovascular disease. If so, then alleviating the depression or stress (or increasing resilience) should effectively reestablish the proper immunological balance and improve health outcomes.

Stress and Adaptation: Toward Ecologically Relevant Animal Models

Jaap M. Koolhaas,[1] Sietse F. de Boer, and Bauke Buwalda
Department of Behavioral Physiology, University of Groningen, Haren, The Netherlands

Abstract

Animal models have contributed considerably to the current understanding of mechanisms underlying the role of stress in health and disease. Despite the progress made already, much more can be made by more carefully exploiting animals' and humans' shared biology, using ecologically relevant models. This allows a fundamental analysis of factors modulating individual adaptive capacity and hence individual vulnerability to disease. This article highlights an emerging scientific approach that uses a framework of interpretation that is more biologically oriented than previous approaches, to evaluate both the adaptive and maladaptive nature of the stress response in relation to existing environmental demands.

Keywords

stress; adaptation; animal models; biology; behavior

A considerable part of our current knowledge of stress-related disorders in humans is based on animal models. The scientific rationale is that the underlying biological mechanisms are generally the same in animals and humans. This notion has stimulated a lot of research, starting with the early studies by Hans Selye (Selye, 1950). Right from its start, the field of stress research has been characterized by a fruitful interaction between human and animal studies. The introduction of a wide range of molecular and brain-imaging techniques has led to enormous progress during the last few decades. This is noticeable particularly in the study of physiological and molecular mechanisms underlying the stress response. We now know that the brain is an important target organ of stress hormones, leading to dynamic changes at the level of the molecular biology of the cell, which lead in turn to changes in gene expression and neuronal connectivity and consequently to changes in cognitive functioning, learning and memory processes, and activity of the neuroendocrine system itself (de Kloet, Joels, & Holsboer, 2005).

It is beyond the scope of this paper to summarize the state of the art in stress research. Rather, we will discuss some factors that, in our view, hamper a further integration of stress research in humans with studies using animal models. Despite the wealth of data and publications describing research at the molecular and physiological level, there is a paucity of theorizing at the conceptual level. We will discuss a conceptual framework of stress and adaptation based on underlying biological principles shared between humans and animals. Three issues will be addressed. First, the debate on the significance of animal models in stress research often centers on the validity of the models. By definition, an animal model will never fully mimic the human situation, either with respect to the stress-inducing stimuli or with respect to the symptoms evoked. However, much can be gained by more specifically addressing the biology of the species in question and its species-specific adaptations and constraints. Second, while human research has long recognized the importance of individual variation in stress vulnerability, studies using laboratory animals have considered variation only recently. In view of the biological function of individual variation in nature, we have to understand individual variation in terms of its biological function, genetic and developmental origin, and adaptive constraints. Finally, stress research generally belongs to the realm of the biomedical sciences. Consequently, in the interpretation of experimental results, maladaptive consequences of stress dominate, and possible beneficial and adaptive aspects are rarely discussed. Because the primary function of the stress response is to cope with environmental challenges, the interpretation of the consequences of the stress response should ideally be based on a proper cost–benefit analysis in relation to environmental demands.

VALIDITY OF ANIMAL MODELS

The validity of animal models for human disorders is generally evaluated using the criteria of face, construct, and predictive validity. Face validity means that a model should sufficiently mimic both the origins and the symptomatology of a human stress-related disorder. The criterion of construct validity requires that a model should be based on the same physiological and neurobiological mechanisms as the human disorder. Finally, predictive validity means that treatments that are effective in humans should also be effective in the animal model, without false negatives or false positives. Too often, drugs that are effective in preclinical animal research turn out to be ineffective clinically. These criteria are useful when one has a good understanding of the human disease to be modeled—i.e., the human disease is the gold standard. However, many of the human stress-related disorders are not understood very well. In that situation, a too-strict use of validity criteria may hinder scientific progress. For example, with respect to construct validity, animal-model research is often in advance of human research.

Many animal models fail with respect to face validity. Although animal models allow testing hypotheses using experimentally controlled stressors, often stressors that bear little or no relationship to the biology of the species—i.e., that do not resemble situations animals or humans may meet in everyday life—are used. Foot shocks, restraint, and loud noises are commonly used in many animal models. These certainly induce a behavioral and physiological stress response, but one may question the adaptive nature of those responses. There is a complete mismatch in such models between the stressor and the available repertoire of adaptive mechanisms. By definition, animals cannot adapt, and stress pathology will develop. However, the field of stress research has to move toward a more subtle understanding of the factors and processes underlying the development of stress pathology. Rather than pushing the animal toward a stress-physiological ceiling, it is more informative to explore the natural factors that determine and modulate the individual adaptive capacity and repertoire. To better understand the causal mechanisms of stress-related disorders, it is necessary to explore more carefully the limits of species-specific defense mechanisms developed in the course of evolution. We will refer to this as *ecological validity*. Regarding the ecological validity of a stressor, four variables are important: nature, frequency, duration, and intensity.

Nature of the Stressor

Central to modern stress research are the terms *controllability* and *predictability*. These terms date back to a series of experiments by Weiss in the late 1960s (Weiss, 1972). It is not so much the physical nature of an aversive stimulus that induces stress pathology but rather the degree to which the stimulus can be predicted and controlled. Although the concepts of controllability and predictability have strongly contributed to the present insights into the development of stress pathology, they are generally operationally defined as binary factors—e.g., full control or complete loss of control. However, in everyday-life situations, controllability is graded from absolute control to loss of control via various degrees of threat to control. Similar arguments hold for the factor of predictability. Few studies consider the importance of different degrees of controllability and predictability in the development of stress pathology. The biology of the species being studied and its natural adaptive capacity and defense repertoire can be used to design experiments with a more refined gradation of stressors.

Virtually all mammalian species, including humans, live in some form of social community. Disturbed social relations are by far the strongest stressors as measured by the magnitude of the physiological stress response. Studies in free-ranging social groups of animals indicate that the stability of the social environment is an important factor in health and disease. For example, in mice and monkeys it has been demonstrated that hypertension and cardiovascular abnormalities are more frequent in socially unstable groups and occur predominantly in dominant and subdominant males. Stomach ulcers are mainly found in social outcasts of colonies. Similarly, there is a clear relation between social position and immune-system-mediated disease.

The importance of social factors is also demonstrated by the stress-reducing or stress-buffering effects of social support, a phenomenon that has been known for a long time in humans but is poorly understood from a physiological point of view. Recent evidence shows that social support is clearly important in animals as well, allowing an in-depth study of the underlying mechanisms.

Although an increasing number of studies exploit the social nature of animals, it is surprising that the criterion of ecological validity is not used more widely. Few studies use, for example, changes in food availability or in workload to obtain food as stressors. After all, the controllability and predictability of food availability and the effort required to obtain food are crucial to survival in nature. Difficulties obtaining food may strongly challenge defense mechanisms. Moreover, in contrast to the widely employed aversive and noxious stimuli, the behavioral and physiological stress response that accompanies satisfying behavior and positive emotional contexts has hardly been studied in stress research.

Frequency, Duration, and Intensity of the Stressor

Apart from the nature of the stressor, its frequency, duration and intensity are also a matter of concern. The chronic character of stressors is generally considered as an important factor in various forms of stress pathology. However, many chronic-stress models in fact use a series of intermittent acute aversive stimuli that may change daily. Knowledge of the ecology of the model species can be used for the design of experiments aimed at creating a sustained challenge to adaptive mechanisms. For example, a situation of chronic stress can be created in a social environment by housing a subordinate male physically separated from but in close proximity to a dominant male. This has been successfully applied for a range of animal species including rats, mice, tree shrews, pigs, monkeys, and fish. All such studies point to common underlying biological principles in social stress and adaptation, independent of subtle species differences in social organization. These studies also show that stressors with a high ecological validity, such as social stress, are by far the strongest stressors as measured by the magnitude and duration of the physiological stress response. This suggests that the intensity of a stressor is not so much related to the physical nature of the stimulus (voltage, decibels), but rather to the degree to which it challenges adaptive defense mechanisms.

In humans, the development of posttraumatic stress disorders shows that acute stressors or major life events may have long-term consequences as well. This suggests that the time after exposure to a stressor may be important as a factor. Indeed, a single social defeat as a major life event in rats is sufficient to induce highly dynamic changes in behavior and stress physiology that may unfold over a period of time ranging from hours to days, weeks, or months (Koolhaas, Meerlo, de Boer, Strubbe, & Bohus, 1997). Consequently, the symptomatology changes over time after the single traumatic stress experience. It is tempting to label the various symptoms in terms of human pathology. However, it seems far more fruitful to avoid such a discussion and instead study the dynamics in behavior and physiology as a causal chain of processes, to see what one can hypothesize from this regarding the human traumatized patient.

INDIVIDUAL VARIATION AND COPING STRATEGIES

Individuals may differ considerably in their vulnerability to stress-related disorders. Factors that have been shown to affect the individual coping capacity in animals and human beings include genotype, development, adult experience, age, and social support. Several attempts have been made to classify individual variation in terms of personalities, temperaments, or coping styles that may predict the response to stressors. Basically, animal research finds suites of correlated behaviors that are consistent over time and across situations. For example, animals that actively control their territory using aggression will also actively control many aspects of their nonsocial environment. Various terms, such as boldness and shyness or proactive and reactive (or active and passive) coping, are used to characterize this dimension. Whatever terms are used, they all seem to share the same basic characteristics. Proactive coping or boldness is characterized by an active control of the environment—i.e., active avoidance, offensive aggression, nest building, etc. Reactive coping or shyness is characterized by a more ready acceptance of the environment as it is. Studies in rats and mice indicate that the most fundamental difference is the degree of behavioral flexibility. Reactively coping males are flexible, whereas proactive coping is characterized by rigidity and routine formation (Koolhaas et al., 1999). Recent field studies show that this individual variation in flexibility has clear evolutionary-fitness consequences in nature. It is tempting to consider this as the biological origin of human personalities and temperament as well (Sih, Bell, Johnson, & Ziemba, 2004).

From a biomedical point of view, the concept of coping strategies implies that individual animals are differentially vulnerable to stress-related disorders. In view of animals' differential physiological make-up, one may expect different types of stress pathology to develop under conditions in which a particular coping strategy fails. Indeed, individuals with different coping strategies differ in their susceptibility to cardiovascular pathology, ulcers, stereotyped behavior, impulsivity disorders, depression, and infectious disease (Veenema Meijer, de Kloet, & Koolhaas, 2003). This illustrates that individual variation in nature can be used to analyze constraints in individual adaptive capacity and individual vulnerability to breakdown in adaptation.

ADAPTIVE SIGNIFICANCE

Implicit in the interpretation of many stress experiments is that the observed changes somehow contribute to the development of pathology. However, one has to realize that the stress response has primarily an adaptive function. Therefore, a biological approach using more naturalistic stress models has to consider the adaptive nature of the stress response as well. The stress response is likely to be a trade-off between both short- and long-term benefits and the costs in terms of pathology and reduced evolutionary fitness. The bottom line is that the physiological stress response changes the organism. However, few studies address the question, under which environmental conditions is this change adaptive or maladaptive?

McEwen (1998) has developed the concept of *allostasis* to explain the dynamic interaction between an organism and its environment. Allostasis involves mechanisms that change the controlled physiological variable by predicting what level will be needed to meet anticipated demand. Natural selection has sculpted physiology and behavior to meet the most likely environmental demands plus a modest safety margin. Seen in terms of allostasis, an unusual physiological parameter value is not simply a failure to respond correctly to current demands but rather a response based on a prediction of the controllability of the stressor. This is clearly demonstrated by the rapid development of conditioned anticipatory stress responses with repeated exposure to a stressor. After all, it is much more cost efficient to prevent errors than it is to correct errors after they have occurred. A shift in the probability of demand will shift the integrated response. Indeed, mediators of allostasis (e.g., adrenal hormones and neurotransmitters) act on receptors in various tissues and organs to produce changes that are adaptive to behavior, metabolism, the immune system, and the cardiovascular system in the short term.

A fit organism is able to cope with a wide variety of conditions—i.e., it has a wide regulatory range of allostatic mechanisms. However, activation of these mechanisms outside this range can result in failure to habituate to repeated challenges, failure to shut off the physiological response when a challenge is over, and failure to mount an adequate response. This produces a state of chronic deviation of the regulatory system from its normal operating level. This new equilibrium (allostatic state) will be characterized by a narrower regulatory range and hence by an enhanced chance of overactivation. This overactivation is referred to as allostatic load, which can be described as the cumulative wear and tear to the brain and body (McEwen, 1998). If allostatic load is chronically high, pathologies may develop. The conceptual framework of allostasis has consequences for the interpretation of many stress experiments. Stress-induced changes in behavioral or neuroendocrine parameters are easily interpreted as signs of pathology. However, they can just as well reflect adequate and adaptive responses to existing environmental conditions. Unfortunately, few studies address this issue experimentally.

CONCLUDING REMARKS

Many human stress-related diseases like posttraumatic stress disorder, chronic fatigue, depression, or fibromyalgia, are far from understood. The contribution of animal studies in understanding these diseases in humans is large, but can be improved by more carefully exploring the biology animals and humans share. By using ecologically valid animal models, stress research will obtain a more subtle understanding of the biological principles and modulators involved when adaptive processes become pathological. These models inevitably address the fundamental question of the (mal)adaptive nature of stress-induced changes in behavior and physiology in relation to environmental demands. This line of reasoning has been successfully applied in evolutionary psychiatry (Nesse, 2001). The current article argues for an evolutionary approach to stress research in both animals and humans (Korte, Koolhaas, Wingfield, & McEwen, 2005).

Recommended Reading

de Kloet, E.R., & Derijk, R. (2004). Signaling pathways in brain involved in predisposition and pathogenesis of stress-related disease: Genetic and kinetic factors affecting the MR/GR balance. *Annals of the New York Academy of Sciences, 1032*, 14–34.
McEwen, B.S. (2004). Protection and damage from acute and chronic stress: Allostasis and allostatic overload and relevance to the pathophysiology of psychiatric disorders. *Annals of the New York Academy of Sciences, 1032*, 1–7.
Sapolsky, R.M. (2005). The influence of social hierarchy on primate health. *Science, 308*, 648–652.
Troisi, A. (2005). The concept of alternative strategies and its relevance to psychiatry and clinical psychology. *Neuroscience Biobehavior Review, 29*, 159–168.

Note

1. Address correspondence to Jaap M. Koolhaas, Department of Behavioral Physiology, University of Groningen, P.O. Box 14, 9750 AA Haren, The Netherlands; e-mail: j.m.koolhaas@rug.nl.

References

de Kloet, E.R., Joels, M., & Holsboer, F. (2005). Stress and the brain: From adaptation to disease. *Nature Reviews Neuroscience, 6*, 463–475.

Koolhaas, J.M., Korte, S.M., de Boer, S.F., van der Vegt, B.J., van Reenen, C.G., Hopster, H., de Jong, I.C., Ruis, M.A., & Blokhuis, H.J. (1999). Coping styles in animals: Current status in behavior and stress-physiology. *Neuroscience & Biobehavioral Reviews, 23*, 925–935.

Koolhaas, J.M., Meerlo, P., de Boer, S.F., Strubbe, J.H., & Bohus, B. (1997). The temporal dynamics of the stress response. *Neuroscience & Biobehavioral Reviews, 21*, 775–782.

Korte, S.M., Koolhaas, J.M., Wingfield, J.C., & McEwen, B.S. (2005). The Darwinian concept of stress: Benefits of allostasis and costs of allostatic load and the trade-offs in health and disease. *Neuroscience & Biobehavioral Reviews, 29*, 3–38.

McEwen, B.S. (1998). Stress, adaptation, and disease: Allostasis and allostatic load. *Annals of the New York Academy of Sciences, 840*, 33–44.

Nesse, R.M. (2001). On the difficulty of defining disease: A Darwinian perspective. *Medicine, Health Care and Philosophy, 4*, 37–46.

Selye, H. (1950). *Stress: The physiology and pathology of exposure to stress.* Montreal: Acta Medica.

Sih, A., Bell, A.M., Johnson, J.C., & Ziemba, R.E. (2004). Behavioral syndromes: An integrative overview. *Quarterly Review of Biology, 79*, 241–277.

Veenema, A.H., Meijer, O.C., de Kloet, E.R., & Koolhaas J.M. (2003). Genetic selection for coping style predicts stressor susceptibility. *Journal of Neuroendocrinology, 15*, 256–267.

Weiss, J.M. (1972). Influence of psychological variables on stress-induced pathology. In R. Porter & J. Knight (Eds.), *Physiology, emotion and psychosomatic illness: CIBA Foundation symposium* (Vol. 8, pp. 253–265). Amsterdam: Elsevier.

This article has been reprinted as it originally appeared in *Current Directions in Psychological Science*. Citation information for this article as originally published appears above.

The Role of Prenatal Maternal Stress in Child Development

Janet A. DiPietro[1]

Johns Hopkins University

Abstract

The notion that a woman's psychological state during pregnancy affects the fetus is a persistent cultural belief in many parts of the world. Recent results indicate that prenatal maternal distress in rodents and nonhuman primates negatively influences long-term learning, motor development, and behavior in their offspring. The applicability of these findings to human pregnancy and child development is considered in this article. Potential mechanisms through which maternal psychological functioning may alter development of the fetal nervous system are being identified by current research, but it is premature to conclude that maternal prenatal stress has negative consequences for child development. Mild stress may be a necessary condition for optimal development.

Keywords

pregnancy; fetus; fetal development; stress

"Ay ay, for this I draw in many a tear,
And stop the rising of blood-sucking sighs,
Lest with my sighs or tears I blast or drown
King Edward's fruit, true heir to the English Crown"

—Queen Elizabeth's response upon learning of her husband's imprisonment in
Shakespeare's *King Henry VI* (Part 3), Act IV, Scene IV

Since antiquity, people have thought that the emotions and experiences of a pregnant woman impinge on her developing fetus. Some of these notions, such as the idea that a severe fright marks a child with a prominent birthmark, no longer persist. However, the premise that maternal psychological distress has deleterious effects on the fetus is the focus of active scientific inquiry today. A resurgence of interest in the prenatal period as a staging period for later diseases, including psychiatric ones, has been fostered by the enormous attention devoted to the hypothesis of fetal programming advanced by D.J. Barker and his colleagues. Fetal programming implies that maternal and fetal factors that affect growth impart an indelible impression on adult organ function, including functioning of the brain and nervous system. That earlier circumstances, including those during the prenatal period, might affect later development is hardly newsworthy to developmentalists. In the 1930s, the Fels Research Institute initiated a longitudinal study of child development that commenced with intensive investigation of the fetal period.

Possible effects of maternal psychological distress during pregnancy range along a continuum from the immediate and disastrous (e.g., miscarriage) to the more subtle and long term (e.g., developmental disorders). Most existing research has focused on the effects of maternal distress on pregnancy itself. For example, there are numerous comprehensive reviews of research indicating that women who express greater distress during pregnancy give birth somewhat earlier to somewhat lighter babies than do women who are less distressed. The focus of this report is on the potential for maternal stress to generate more far-reaching effects on behavioral and cognitive development in childhood.

MECHANISMS AND EVIDENCE FROM ANIMAL STUDIES

There are no direct neural connections between the mother and the fetus. To have impact on the fetus, maternal psychological functioning must be translated into physiological effects. Three mechanisms by which this might occur are considered most frequently: alteration in maternal behaviors (e.g., substance abuse), reduction in blood flow such that the fetus is deprived of oxygen and nutrients, and transport of stress-related neurohormones to the fetus through the placenta. Stress-related neurohormones, such as cortisol, are necessary for normal fetal maturation and the birth process. However, relatively slight variations in these hormones, particularly early in pregnancy, have the potential to generate a cascade of effects that may result in changes to the fetus's own stress response system.

The most compelling evidence of a link between maternal psychological functioning and later development in offspring is found in animal studies. Stress responses in rodents can be reliably induced by a variety of experimental methods. Deliberate exposure of pregnant laboratory animals to stressful events (e.g., restraint) produces effects on offspring. These include deficits in motor development, learning behavior, and the ability to cope effectively in stressful situations. There is a tendency for the effects to be greater in female than in male offspring. Changes in brain structure and function of prenatally stressed animals have also been documented (Welberg & Seckl, 2001). Yet not all documented effects of prenatal stress are negative; mild stress has been observed to benefit, not damage, later learning in rats (Fujioka et al., 2001).

In a series of studies, pregnant rhesus monkeys that were exposed to repeated periods of loud noise were shown to bear offspring with delayed motor development and reduced attention in infancy. A constellation of negative behaviors, including enhanced responsiveness to stress and dysfunctional social behavior with peers, persisted through adolescence (Schneider & Moore, 2000). In general, studies of stress in nonhuman primates find males to be more affected than females. However, although a study comparing offspring of pregnant pigtailed macaques that were repeatedly stressed with offspring of nonstressed mothers did find that the behavior of prenatally stressed males was less mature than the behavior of non-prenatally stressed males, for females the results were reversed. The females born to the stressed mothers displayed more mature behavior than non-prenatally stressed females (Novak & Sackett, 1996). Thus, although most studies have reported detrimental consequences, reports of either no effects or beneficial ones make it clear that much is left to be learned about the specific characteristics of stressors that either accelerate or retard development.

DOES MATERNAL STRESS AFFECT DEVELOPMENT IN HUMANS?

Several important factors make it difficult to generalize results based on animal studies to humans. First, there are substantial physiological differences inherent to pregnancies in different species. Second, researchers are unable to control the events that transpire after birth in humans. Women who are psychologically stressed before pregnancy are also likely to be stressed after pregnancy, so it is critical that the role of social influences after birth be carefully distinguished from pregnancy effects that are transmitted biologically. Finally, the nature of the prenatal stress studied in animals and humans is very different, and this may pose the greatest barrier to the ability to generalize. In animal research, stressors are external events that are controlled in terms of duration, frequency, and intensity. The closest parallel in human studies is found in the few studies that have taken advantage of specific events, including an earthquake and the World Trade Center disaster, to study the effects on pregnancy in women residing in physical proximity. No such study has examined children's cognitive or behavioral outcomes. However, what is measured in virtually all human studies of "stress" during pregnancy is women's affect, mood, and emotional responses to daily circumstances in their lives. Maternal anxiety and, to a lesser extent, depression are prominent foci of research. Both may reflect emotional responses to stressful circumstances, but they also represent more persistent features of personality. Thus, not only are the physiological consequences and nature of prenatal stress different between animal and human studies, but when human studies detect an association between mothers' prenatal anxiety, for example, and their children's later behavior, it may be the result of shared genes or child-rearing practices related to maternal temperament.

Despite these concerns, there is a small but growing literature indicating that there is a relation between pregnant women's psychological distress and their children's behavioral outcomes. In one study, the ability of 8-month-old infants to pay attention during a developmental assessment was negatively correlated with the amount of anxiety their mothers reported about their pregnancy (Huizink, Robles de Medina, Mulder, Visser, & Buitelaar, 2002). This study is one of the few in which infants' behavior was rated by an independent observer and not a parent. Two separate studies with large numbers of participants found positive associations between maternal distress (primarily anxiety) in the first half of pregnancy and behavioral disorders or negative emotionality at preschool age (Martin, Noyes, Wisenbaker, & Huttunen, 2000; O'Connor, Heron, Golding, Beveridge, & Glover, 2002). Unfortunately, both relied on mothers' reports of their children's problems, so it is impossible to know whether the results simply indicate that anxious mothers perceive their children to be more difficult than nonanxious mothers do. However, new information about potential mechanisms whereby maternal stress might affect fetal development gives plausibility to these results. Maternal anxiety is associated with reduced blood flow to the fetus (Sjostrom, Valentin, Thelin, & Marsal, 1997), and fetal levels of stress hormones reflect those of their mothers (Gitau, Cameron, Fisk, & Glover, 1998).

Remarkably, this handful of published studies represents most of what we know about the effects of maternal distress on child development. There are several additional reports in the literature, but because of problems in methods or analysis, their results are not compelling. As the field matures, methodological, analytical, and interpretational standards will emerge over time.

THE NEXT LEVEL OF INVESTIGATION

The implicit assumption has been that prenatal stress and emotions have consequences for child development after birth because they have more immediate effects on the development of the nervous system before birth. Until recently, the fetal period of development was a black box. Although fetuses remain one of the few categories of research participants who can be neither directly viewed nor heard, opportunities to measure fetal development now exist. As pregnancy advances, the behavioral capabilities of the fetus become similar to those of a newborn infant, although the fetus is limited by the constraints of the uterus. Nonetheless, measurement of fetal motor activity, heart rate, and their relation to each other provides a fairly complete portrait of fetal development. New techniques present an opportunity to examine the manner in which the psychological state of the pregnant woman may affect development prior to birth, and perhaps permanently change the offspring's course of development.

In our first efforts to examine the link between fetal behavior and maternal stress, my colleagues and I relied on commonly used paper-and-pencil questionnaires to measure maternal psychological attributes. In a small study, we found that mothers' perception of experiencing daily hassles in everyday life was inversely related to the degree to which their fetuses' movement and heart rate were in synchrony. Such synchrony is an indicator of developing neural integration (DiPietro, Hodgson, Costigan, Hilton, & Johnson, 1996). In a second study, we found that mothers' emotional intensity, perception of their lives as stressful, and, in particular, feelings that they were more hassled than uplifted by their pregnancy were positively related to the activity level of their fetuses (DiPietro, Hilton, Hawkins, Costigan, & Pressman, 2002). We had previously reported that active fetuses tend to be active 1-year-olds, so fetal associations portend postnatal ones.

Measures of maternal stress and emotions that are based on mothers' self-reports are important only to the extent that they correspond to physiological signals that can be transmitted to the fetus; thus, they provide limited information. We turned to investigating the degree to which maternal physiological arousal, as measured by heart rate and electrical conductance of the skin, a measure of emotionality, is associated with fetal behavior. The results were unexpected in that fetal motor activity, even when it was imperceptible to women, stimulated transient increases in their heart rate and skin conductance.

It became apparent to us that the only way to truly examine the effect of stress on the fetus was to subject women to a standard, noninvasive stressor and measure the fetal response. The stressor we selected was a common cognitive challenge known as the Stroop Color-Word Test. In this test, subjects are asked to read color names that are printed in various colors and so must dissociate the color of the words from their meaning. The test is not aversive but reliably induces physiological arousal. In general, when pregnant women engaged in this task, fetal motor activity was suppressed, although individual responses varied.

The degree to which individual women and fetuses responded to the Stroop test was similar from the middle to the end of pregnancy. These results lead us to propose three hypotheses. First, women respond to stress in characteristic ways that fetuses are repeatedly exposed to over the course of pregnancy. This experience serves to sensitize the developing nervous system. Second, there are both short-term and longer-term adaptive responses to stress by the fetus, depending on the intensity and repetitiveness of the stimulation. Finally, the immediacy of the fetal response to the Stroop, as well as to maternal viewing of graphic scenes from a movie on labor and delivery, suggest an additional mechanism whereby maternal stress might affect the fetus. We propose that the fetus responds to changes in the sensory environment of the uterus that occur when maternal heart rate, blood pressure, and other internal functions are abruptly altered. This proposal cannot be readily tested, but hearing is among the first perceptual systems to develop prenatally, and it is well documented that the fetus can perceive sounds that emanate from both within and outside the uterus.

Our final foray into this area of inquiry has been to follow children who participated in our studies as fetuses. Recently, we completed developmental testing on approximately one hundred 2-year-old children. The results, as is often the case in fetal research, surprised us. Higher maternal anxiety midway through pregnancy was strongly associated with better motor and mental development scores on the Bayley Scales of Infant Development, a standard developmental assessment. These associations remained even after controlling statistically for other possible contributing factors, including level of maternal education and both anxiety and stress after giving birth. This finding is in the direction opposite to that which would be predicted on the basis of most, but not all, of the animal research. Yet it is consistent with what is known about the class of neurohormones known as glucocorticoids, which are produced during the stress response and also play a role in the maturation of body organs. Our results are also consistent with findings from a series of studies on physical stress. The newborns of pregnant women who exercised regularly were somewhat smaller than the newborns of women who did not exercise much, but showed better ability to remain alert and track stimuli; the children of the regular exercisers also had higher cognitive ability at age 5 (Clapp, 1996). Exercise and psychological distress do not necessarily have the same physiological consequences to the fetus, but the parallel is intriguing.

CONCLUSIONS

At this time, there is too little scientific evidence to establish that a woman's psychological state during pregnancy affects her child's developmental outcomes. It is premature to extend findings from animal studies to women and children, particularly given the disparity in the way the animal and human studies are designed. The question of whether maternal stress and affect serve to accelerate or inhibit maturation of the fetal nervous system, and postnatal development in turn, remains open. It has been proposed that a certain degree of stress during early childhood is required for optimal organization of the brain, because stress provokes periods of disruption to existing structures (Huether, 1998), and this may be true for the prenatal period as well.

The relation between maternal stress and children's development may ultimately be found to mirror the relation between arousal and performance, which is characterized by an inverted U-shaped curve. This function, often called the Yerkes-Dodson law, posits that both low and high levels of arousal are associated with performance decrements, whereas a moderate level is associated with enhanced performance. This model has been applied to a spectrum of psychological observations, and a parallel with prenatal maternal stress may exist as well. In other words, too much or too little stress may impede development, but a moderate level may be formative or optimal. The current intensive investigation in this research area should provide better understanding of the importance of the prenatal period for postnatal life as investigators direct their efforts toward determining how maternal psychological signals are received by the fetus.

Recommended Reading

Kofman, O. (2002). The role of prenatal stress in the etiology of developmental behavioral disorders. *Neuroscience and Biobehavioral Reviews, 26*, 457–470.
Mulder, E., Robles de Medina, P., Huizink, A., Van den Bergh, B., Buitelaar, J., & Visser, G. (2002). Prenatal maternal stress: Effects on pregnancy and the (unborn) child. *Early Human Development, 70*, 3–14.
Paarlberg, K.M., Vingerhoets, A., Passchier, J., Dekker, G., & van Geijn, H. (1995). Psychosocial factors and pregnancy outcome: A review with emphasis on methodological issues. *Journal of Psychosomatic Research, 39*, 563–595.
Wadhwa, P., Sandman, C., & Garite, T. (2001). The neurobiology of stress in human pregnancy: Implications for prematurity and development of the fetal central nervous system. *Progress in Brain Research, 133*, 131–142.

Acknowledgments—This work has been supported by Grant R01 HD5792 from the National Institute of Child Health and Development.

Note

1. Address correspondence to Janet DiPietro, Department of Population and Family Health Sciences, 624 N. Broadway, Johns Hopkins University, Baltimore, MD 21205; e-mail: jdipietr@jhsph.edu.

References

Clapp, J. (1996). Morphometric and neurodevelopmental outcome at age five years of the offspring of women who continued to exercise regularly throughout pregnancy. *Journal of Pediatrics, 129*, 856–863.
DiPietro, J., Hilton, S., Hawkins, M., Costigan, K., & Pressman, E. (2002). Maternal stress and affect influence fetal neurobehavioral development. *Developmental Psychology, 38*, 659–668.
DiPietro, J.A., Hodgson, D.M., Costigan, K.A., Hilton, S.C., & Johnson, T.R.B. (1996). Development of fetal movement-fetal heart rate coupling from 20 weeks through term. *Early Human Development, 44*, 139–151.
Fujioka, T., Fujioka, A., Tan, N., Chowdhury, G., Mouri, H., Sakata, Y., & Nakamura, S. (2001). Mild prenatal stress enhances learning performance in the non-adopted rat offspring. *Neuroscience, 103*, 301–307.
Gitau, R., Cameron, A., Fisk, N., & Glover, V. (1998). Fetal exposure to maternal cortisol. *Lancet, 352*, 707–708.

Huether, G. (1998). Stress and the adaptive self-organization of neuronal connectivity during early childhood. *International Journal of Neuroscience, 16*, 297–306.

Huizink, A., Robles de Medina, P., Mulder, E., Visser, G., & Buitelaar, J. (2002). Psychological measures of prenatal stress as predictors of infant temperament. *Journal of the American Academy of Child & Adolescent Psychiatry, 41*, 1078–1085.

Martin, R., Noyes, J., Wisenbaker, J., & Huttunen, M. (2000). Prediction of early childhood negative emotionality and inhibition from maternal distress during pregnancy. *Merrill-Palmer Quarterly, 45*, 370–391.

Novak, M., & Sackett, G. (1996). Reflexive and early neonatal development in offspring of pigtailed macaques exposed to prenatal psychosocial stress. *Developmental Psychobiology, 29*, 294.

O'Connor, T., Heron, J., Golding, J., Beveridge, M., & Glover, V. (2002). Maternal antenatal anxiety and children's behavioural/emotional problems at 4 years. *British Journal of Psychiatry, 180*, 502–508.

Schneider, M., & Moore, C. (2000). Effects of prenatal stress on development: A non-human primate model. In C. Nelson (Ed.), *Minnesota Symposium on Child Psychology: Vol. 31. The effects of early adversity on neurobehavioral development* (pp. 201–244). Mahwah, NJ: Erlbaum.

Sjostrom, K., Valentin, L., Thelin, T., & Marsal, K. (1997). Maternal anxiety in late pregnancy and fetal hemodynamics. *European Journal of Obstetrics and Gynecology, 74*, 149–155.

Welberg, L., & Seckl, J. (2001). Prenatal stress, glucocorticoids and the programming of the brain. *Journal of Neuroendocrinology, 13*, 113–128.

Corticotropin-Releasing Factor and the Psychobiology of Early-Life Stress

Charles F. Gillespie and Charles B. Nemeroff[1]

Department of Psychiatry & Behavioral Sciences, Emory University School of Medicine

Abstract

Trauma and neglect during childhood are increasingly appreciated as factors in the etiology of adult mood and anxiety disorders. Much has been learned about the role of stress biology in the persisting effects of early adverse experience on adult psychopathology. Here we present an overview of developmental trauma in the psychobiology of depression and anxiety. We emphasize the role of corticotropin-releasing factor in the pathophysiology of these disorders, focusing on the transduction of early life trauma into adult psychopathology.

Keywords

trauma; neglect; depression; stress; corticotropin-releasing factor

An epidemic of child abuse exists in the United States (reviewed in Gillespie & Nemeroff, 2005a). Conservative estimates suggest that every year more than 1,000,000 children experience sexual or physical abuse or severe neglect. Individuals abused in childhood are at elevated risk of depression during adulthood. Women abused in childhood attempt suicide at greater frequency and report greater numbers of depression, anxiety, somatic, and substance-abuse symptoms than do women who have not experienced such abuse. Further, child abuse and neglect also independently elevate risk for stress-related illnesses including cardiac disease, peptic ulcer, autoimmune disease, diabetes mellitus, and lung disease. While it is clear that many people abused or neglected as children will develop psychiatric and other forms of medical illness as adults, the variables that determine the form and magnitude of adult psychiatric and medical disease in these individuals remain uncertain.

The hypothesis that traumatic experiences during childhood result in adult mood and anxiety disorders was first disseminated in psychoanalytic theories of critical periods or phases disrupted by adverse experience during psychological development. Indeed, William Wordsworth's statement that "The child is father of the man" encapsulates this idea succinctly. More recently, the concept of the critical period as a temporal window through which environmental experience impacts brain development by effects on the timing and extent of gene expression has gained ascendance in clinical neuroscience.

The quest to understand the causes of depression has led to the development of numerous hypotheses regarding chemical or hormonal imbalances to explain the biological foundations of psychiatric illness. Over 40 years ago, a number of patients with depression were found to secrete excessive amounts of the steroid stress hormone cortisol (Gibbons & McHugh, 1962). The observation that patients with Cushing's disease or syndrome, endocrine diseases characterized by excessive secretion of cortisol, often also experience severe depression and anxiety, in conjunction with the finding of increased production and secretion of cortisol in healthy individuals exposed to stress, contributed to the modern *stress-diathesis* hypothesis of depression. In this model of illness, individual predisposition to excess reactivity of the neural and endocrine stress-response systems following exposure to environmental stressors is believed to play a significant role in both the initiation and relapse of certain forms of depression (reviewed in Gillespie & Nemeroff, 2005b).

Research with animals in the laboratory and clinical research with humans has yielded insight into the relationship between the neurobiology of stress and the physiology of depressive illness. Much of this work has focused on corticotropin-releasing factor (CRF) and other elements of the hypothalamic-pituitary-adrenal (HPA) axis, a collection of neural and endocrine structures that facilitate the response to stress, as mediating variables in this relationship between stress and depression (Fig. 1).

EARLY-LIFE STRESS AND DEPRESSION

A number of alterations of CRF and HPA-axis function have been observed in depressed patients (reviewed in Gillespie & Nemeroff, 2005a, 2005b). Elevated concentrations of CRF are found in the cerebrospinal fluid (CSF) of depressed patients and postmortem studies of individuals who have committed suicide have demonstrated decreased density of CRF receptors in the frontal cortex of the brain, decreased activity of the CRF receptor gene, and increased CRF concentrations in the frontal cortex as compared with control subjects. Effective treatment of depression normalizes the concentration of CSF CRF and other indices of HPA-axis activity measured by HPA-challenge tests (which assess normality of function within the HPA axis). This suggests that increased CSF CRF and enhanced activity of the HPA axis may be "state," rather than "trait," markers of depression. In this context, state refers to phenomena related to a particular phase of illness (e.g., depressed or in remission) as opposed to being present throughout all phases of illness as a trait of the illness or a marker for susceptibility to the development of illness. Clinically asymptomatic patients retaining elevated CSF CRF levels following treatment of depression are at increased risk for early relapse of depression, indicating perhaps that persistently elevated CSF CRF is a marker for vulnerability to early recurrence of depression.

Child abuse, neglect, or the loss of a parent during childhood are the most salient forms of early-life stress, although other forms of early-life stress, including accidents, surgeries, protracted illness, war- or terrorism-related events, natural disasters, and chaotic or unstable family environments, are also equally significant traumatic events. Trauma and/or neglect are common features in the history of many patients with depression, particularly those whose depression has been chronic. Certain types of depression may be the outcome of gene–environment interactions—that is, interaction between "nature," in the form of latent genetic vulnerability, and "nurture," in the form of stressful experiences early in life. Exposure to stress, particularly on a chronic basis, during early development is one way that

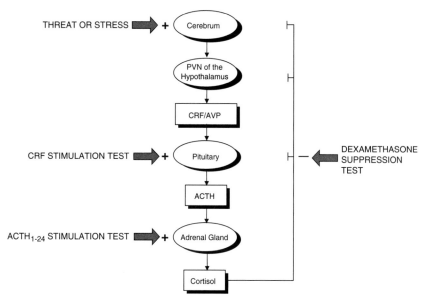

Fig. 1. Functional organization and assessment of the hypothalamic-pituitary-adrenal (HPA) axis. Information about threat or stress is relayed from the cerebrum to the paraventricular nucleus (PVN) of the hypothalamus. Neurons of the PVN secrete corticotropin-releasing factor (CRF) and arginine vasopressin (AVP) into blood vessels that transport these chemicals to the pituitary gland. Activation of CRF and AVP receptors on pituitary cells results in secretion of adrenocorticotrophic hormone (ACTH). ACTH released from the pituitary into the systemic circulatory system stimulates the production and release of cortisol from the adrenal gland. Cortisol provides feedback inhibition to the hypothalamus, pituitary gland, and other brain areas to inhibit further release of CRF and ACTH. Certain medical and psychiatric illnesses involve dysregulation of the HPA axis and result in insufficient or excessive secretion of CRF, ACTH, or cortisol; several endocrine challenge tests exist for functional assessment of the HPA axis to localize the site of pathology. The CRF stimulation test assesses pituitary function by measuring the secretion of ACTH into the bloodstream following standardized intravenous administration of CRF. The $ACTH_{1-24}$ stimulation test assesses adrenal secretion of cortisol following intravenous administration of $ACTH_{1-24}$. The dexamethasone suppression test assesses the adequacy of feedback inhibition to the pituitary, hypothalamus, and other brain areas such as the hippocampus that participate in the regulation of the HPA axis.

the environment influences susceptibility to depression in vulnerable individuals. As such, the biology of depression may also include the biology of early-life stress.

Animal models have provided insight into the consequences of early-life stress in adult humans. A consistent finding in animals exposed to early-life stress has been both short- and long-term adverse neurobiological and endocrine effects, as well as cognitive dysfunction and abnormal behavior associated with alterations of the physiology and genetic regulation of the CRF system (reviewed in Gutman & Nemeroff, 2003). For example, repeated brief separation of rat pups from their mothers is associated in adult animals with enhanced reactivity of the HPA axis to stress and increased activity of the CRF gene within areas of the brain that facilitate adaptation to stress or threat. Similar studies showed that infant bonnet macaques whose mothers faced variable and unpredictable foraging conditions for food later demonstrated chronically elevated concentrations of CRF in the CSF as adults. Thus, in two different species, the effects of early-life stress continue into adulthood in the form of persistent hyper-responsiveness of the HPA axis to environmental stress.

A limitation of the comparative approach to investigations of early-life stress is that much of the present animal literature models reduced, inconsistent, or absent interaction between parent and offspring during development but does not model abuse. Experimental deprivation paradigms are presumably stressful because they subtract care from the social environment during development. As such, they are more likely informative of the effects of "deficit states" such as neglect, instability of living environment, or parental loss on human physiology and behavior and complement the clinical literature on the consequences of child neglect. In contrast, much of what is known about the role of CRF in depression and the psychobiological consequences of child abuse has been derived from clinical research in humans.

To evaluate the relationship between childhood trauma, reactivity of the HPA axis, and adult psychopathology, Heim and colleagues (Heim et al., 2000) conducted a series of studies with adult women. The four groups of women in this study included women without psychiatric illness or history of early-life stress serving as a control group, depressed women without early-life stress, depressed women who did experience early-life stress, and nondepressed women who experienced early-life stress. Subjects participated in the Trier Social Stress Test (TSST), a laboratory psychosocial stress test that reliably activates the HPA axis. This test consists of a 10-minute speech and performance of mental arithmetic under the gaze of three members of the investigative team. Variables measured include heart rate, plasma adrenocorticotrophic hormone (ACTH), and cortisol concentrations at several intervals before, during, and after the test.

Abnormal ACTH responses during the TSST were observed exclusively in women who experienced early-life stress. The most striking results were found in the group of women with current major depression and a history of early-life stress. These women also more frequently held an additional diagnosis of post-traumatic stress disorder (PTSD) and demonstrated the largest ACTH and cortisol responses, as well as the largest increases in heart rate. In fact, the ACTH response of this group was nearly three times greater than that observed in the control group. In contrast, depressed women who had not been stressed in early life exhibited ACTH and cortisol responses comparable to healthy controls. Interestingly, elevated ACTH responses were also observed in women without current depression but with a history of early-life stress. Unlike depressed women with such a history, these women retained normal levels of cortisol release during the TSST despite an abnormal ACTH response. This suggests that, over time, the adrenal cortex has adapted to the excess release of ACTH during stress by reducing its secretion of cortisol in response to ACTH. More generally, these data indicate that childhood trauma exerts long-term effects on the responsiveness of the HPA axis to stress, effects that continue into adulthood. Functionally, these effects are likely to be a consequence of altered regulation between the brain and different components of the HPA axis.

The hypothesis that early-life stress alters the response of different components of the HPA axis to chemical signals was evaluated in a subsequent study (Heim, Newport, Bonsall, Miller, & Nemeroff, 2001). As in the Heim et al. (2000) study, the subjects in this study were women with and without early-life stress and depression. The HPA axis was assessed using two standardized endocrine challenge tests, the CRF stimulation test and the $ACTH_{1-24}$ stimulation test (Fig. 1). Unlike the TSST, which uses psychosocial stress to elicit a response of the HPA axis, endocrine challenge tests allow for very specific assessment of function within the different components of the HPA axis.

Women who had experienced early-life stress but who were not currently depressed exhibited an increased ACTH response following infusion of CRF. In contrast, depressed women with and without earlylife stress both exhibited a blunted ACTH response to intravenous infusion of CRF. With respect to the $ACTH_{1-24}$ stimulation test, women who had experienced early-life stress but were not currently depressed had lower plasma cortisol levels at baseline and after administration of $ACTH_{1-24}$ compared to depressed women with and without early-life stress. Similar to the findings of our previous study (Heim et al., 2000), women with major depressive disorder and a history of early-life stress were more likely to report current life stress and to fulfill diagnostic criteria for concurrent PTSD than were women who had experienced early-life stress but who were not currently depressed.

The data from the CRF stimulation test suggest that the pituitary gland is sensitized to CRF in abused women without depression. Conversely, the blunted ACTH response to CRF found in depressed women both with and without early-life stress may reflect adaptation by the pituitary, possibly through a reduction in the number of CRF receptors, to chronic hyper-secretion of CRF in response to current depression or life stress. While this particular finding may initially appear to conflict with data from our previous study (Heim et al., 2000) using the TSST (i.e., depressed women with early-life stress have an exaggerated ACTH response to the TSST but a blunted response to CRF infusion), it is important to appreciate that stress exposure and the CRF stimulation test are different ways of activating the HPA axis and are not directly comparable. The increased ACTH response to psychosocial stress observed in women with depression and early-life stress likely reflects involvement of multiple levels of neural systems and neurotransmitters mediating cognitive and emotional information that converge on the pituitary. The combined effects of such input may be able to override limitations on ACTH response imposed by reductions in the number of pituitary CRF receptors. Such reductions in the number of CRF receptors would limit the ACTH response to CRF infusion. Finally, and consistent with our previous study (Heim et al., 2000), we found reduced activity of the adrenal cortex, as evidenced by reduced secretion of cortisol, in response to ACTH infusion. This suggests that adaptation by the adrenal cortex to chronic hypersecretion of ACTH has taken place.

More recently, Carpenter and colleagues (Carpenter et al., 2004) evaluated the relationship between the perception of early-life stress and the CSF CRF concentration of drug-free patients with depression in comparison to matched healthy control subjects. The developmental timing of stress exposure was predictive of either relatively increased or decreased CSF CRF. Early-life stress before the age of 6 years was associated with elevated CSF CRF, whereas exposure to stressful events around the time of birth or in the preteen years was associated with decreased CSF CRF. Further, the individual's perception of trauma intensity was predictive of CSF CRF concentration (relative increase or decrease) independent of the presence or absence of depression. A limitation of this study was its retrospective design, which relies on participants' recall of past experiences not subject to independent confirmation. Additional studies using experimentally validated stress paradigms controlling for patient perception of trauma intensity may provide insight into the complex relationship between the subjective perception of trauma by an individual, the objective qualities of the trauma (duration, intensity, and frequency of neglect or abuse), and the individual's objective response to experimentally validated stressors.

These three clinical studies support the hypothesis that early-life stress results in an enduring sensitization of the HPA axis and the autonomic nervous system response to stress. That sensitization to stress in turn may elevate risk to develop depression or experience relapse of depression. Further, these data suggest that the developmental timing of early-life stress may have specific directional consequences with respect to the regulation of the HPA axis. However, a number of questions remain. For example, it is not clear whether individuals exposed to early-life stress that have PTSD but not depression differ from individuals with depression but not PTSD on the neuroendocrine profile generated by the TSST or HPA-axis challenge tests. In our sample of depressed women who experienced early-life stress, nearly 85% also had PTSD. From an experimental perspective, the presence of concurrent diagnoses of depression and PTSD makes recruitment of adequate sample sizes of discrete "depression only" and "PTSD only" subject groups in traumatized populations to perform these types of studies very difficult and the topic awaits further investigation. Clinically, patients with a history of early-life stress rarely have purely depressive or anxious symptoms, and both need to be addressed. Consequently, our appreciation of what constitutes the best standard of care is still evolving.

TREATMENT ISSUES

Evidence suggesting that depressed patients with early-life stress may be unique in their response to treatment continues to mount (reviewed in Craighead & Nemeroff, 2005). Early-life stress affects the response of patients with either dysthymia or depression to drug therapy. Compared to subjects without a history of early-life stress, depressed patients who experienced such stress exhibit increased rates of relapse following treatment of their depression. The course of depression in individuals with a history of early-life stress is often characterized by chronicity.

What is known about the treatment of depression in patients who experienced early-life stress? Keller and colleagues (Keller et al., 2000) conducted a large multicenter trial designed to compare the relative efficacy of pharmacotherapy (treatment with the antidepressant nefazodone) to psychotherapy or their combination in the treatment of chronic depression. Psychotherapy and pharmacotherapy were both comparible in efficacy but were less effective than the combination of the two in treating patients with chronic depression. However, a striking demographic feature of the study population was the widespread prevalence of early-life stress. Nearly one third of the subjects had experienced loss of a parent before age 15 years, 45% experienced childhood physical abuse, 16% experienced childhood sexual abuse, and 10% experienced neglect.

As a consequence of the results from the Keller et al. (2000) trial and the broad prevalence of early-life stress in that study population, Nemeroff and colleagues (Nemeroff et al., 2003) reanalyzed the data from this trial to determine whether a history of early-life stress in patients with chronic depression altered their response to pharmacotherapy or psychotherapy. Patients were stratified into groups based on the presence or absence of early-life stress and their response to treatment with psychotherapy or pharmacotherapy was reassessed. Patients with a history of early-life stress had a better response to psychotherapy alone compared to treatment with an antidepressant alone, using remission, the most stringent measure of treatment response, as the endpoint. Further, the combination of the antidepressant and psychotherapy was only slightly more effective than psychotherapy alone in the group of patients with early-life stress. These data suggest that a history of early-life stress is both common in the population of patients with chronic depression and that psychotherapy is a crucial component of treatment for depressed patients with such a history.

FUTURE DIRECTIONS

Thomas Edison once said "The doctor of the future will give no medicine, but will interest his patients in the care of the human body, in diet, and in the cause and prevention of disease." While we are not yet at the point predicted by Edison, we have gained considerable insight into the roots of depression at the intersection between the biology of CRF and early-life stress. This work has resulted in the discovery of candidate compounds for new pharmacological treatments for depression and anxiety in the form of CRF and glucocorticoid receptor antagonists. As social relationships are often the context of early life stress, it has also refined our appreciation of their importance in the cause, treatment, and prevention of psychiatric illness. Future research using the tools of psychiatric genetics may allow greater understanding of the gene–gene and gene–environment interactions during development that confer vulnerability or resilience to environmental stress and facilitate intervention with children or young adults at risk for developing trauma-related psychopathology.

Recommended Reading

Craighead, W.E., & Nemeroff, C.B. (2005). (See References)
Gillespie, C.F., & Nemeroff, C.B. (2005a). (See References)
Gutman, D.A., & Nemeroff, C.B. (2003). (See References)

Acknowledgments—Charles Gillespie was supported as a postdoctoral trainee on National Institutes of Health (NIH) Grant DA-015040. This research was supported by NIH Grants MH-42088 and MH-52899 to Charles Nemeroff and NIH Grant NCRRM01-RR00039 to Emory University. Dr. Gillespie has received funding from APIRE/Wyeth and NIDA. Dr. Nemeroff consults to, serves on the Speakers' Bureau and/or Board of Directors of, has been a grant recipient of, and/or owns equity in one or more of the following: Abbott Laboratories, Acadia Pharmaceuticals, AFSP, APIRE, AstraZeneca, BMC-JR LLC, Bristol-Myers-Squibb, CeNeRx, Corcept, Cypress Biosciences, Cyberonics, Eli Lilly, Entrepreneur's Fund, Forest Laboratories, George West Mental Health Foundation, GlaxoSmithKline, i3 DLN, Janssen Pharmaceutica, Lundbeck, NARSAD, Neuronetics, NIMH, NFMH, NovaDel Pharma, Otsuka, Pfizer Pharmaceuticals, Quintiles, Reevax, UCB Pharma, Wyeth-Ayerst.

Note

1. Address correspondence to Charles B. Nemeroff, Emory University School of Medicine, Department of Psychiatry & Behavioral Sciences, 101 Woodruff Circle, Suite 4000, Atlanta, GA 30322; e-mail: cnemero @emory.edu.

References

Carpenter, L.L., Tyrka, A.R., McDougle, C.J., Malison, R.T., Owens, M.J., Nemeroff, C.B., & Price, L.H. (2004). Cerebrospinal fluid corticotropin-releasing factor and perceived early-life stress in depressed patients and healthy control subjects. *Neuropsychopharmacology, 29*, 777–784.

Craighead, W.E., & Nemeroff, C.B. (2005). The impact of early trauma on response to psychotherapy. *Clinical Neuroscience Research, 4*, 405–411.

Gibbons, J.L., & McHugh, P.R. (1962). Plasma cortisol in depressive illness. *Journal of Psychiatric Research, 1*, 162–171.

Gillespie, C.F., & Nemeroff, C.B. (2005a). Early life stress and depression. *Current Psychiatry, 4*, 15–30.

Gillespie, C.F., & Nemeroff, C.B. (2005b). Hypercortisolemia and depression. *Psychosomatic Medicine, 67*(S1), 26–28.

Gutman, D.A., & Nemeroff, C.B. (2003). Persistent central nervous system effects of an adverse early environment: Clinical and preclinical studies. *Physiology and Behavior, 79*, 471–478.

Heim, C., Newport, D.J., Bonsall, R., Miller, A.H., & Nemeroff, C.B. (2001). Altered pituitary-adrenal axis responses to provocative challenge tests in adult survivors of childhood abuse. *American Journal of Psychiatry, 158*, 575–581.

Heim, C., Newport, D.J., Heit, S., Graham, Y.P., Wilcox, M., Bonsall, R., et al. (2000). Pituitary-adrenal and autonomic responses to stress in women after sexual and physical abuse in childhood. *JAMA: The Journal of the American Medical Association, 284*, 592–597.

Keller, M.B., McCullough, J.P., Klein, D.N., Arnow, B., Dunner, D.L., Gelenberg, A.J., et al. (2000). A comparison of nefazodone, the cognitive behavioral-analysis system of psychotherapy, and their combination for the treatment of chronic depression. *New England Journal of Medicine, 342*, 1462–1470.

Nemeroff, C.B., Heim, C.M., Thase, M.E., Klein, D.N., Rush, A.J., Schatzberg, A.F., et al. (2003). Differential responses to psychotherapy versus pharmacotherapy in patients with chronic forms of major depression and childhood trauma. *Proceedings of the National Academy of Sciences, USA, 100*, 14293–14296.

This article has been reprinted as it originally appeared in *Current Directions in Psychological Science*. Citation information for this article as originally published appears above.

Depression: The Brain Finally Gets Into the Act

Barry L. Jacobs[1]
Princeton University

Abstract

The theory of clinical depression presented here integrates etiological factors, changes in specific structural and cellular substrates, ensuing symptomatology, and treatment and prevention. According to this theory, important etiological factors, such as stress, can suppress the production of new neurons in the adult human brain, thereby precipitating or maintaining a depressive episode. Most current treatments for depression are known to elevate brain serotonin neurotransmission, and such increases in serotonin have been shown to significantly augment the ongoing rate of neurogenesis, providing the neural substrate for new cognitions to be formed, and thereby facilitating recovery from the depressive episode. This theory also points to treatments that augment neurogenesis as new therapeutic opportunities.

Keywords

serotonin; adult brain neurogenesis; stress; clinical depression

When the history of mental illness is written, the 20th century will be remembered primarily not for its biomedical advances, but as the period when depression (along with the other major psychopathologies) was finally considered to be a disease and not a failure of character or a weakness of will. In part, this change is attributable to putting to rest, at least in the scientific community, the dogma of Cartesian duality of mind and body. Given that the mind is the manifestation of the brain, depression could be considered to be a somatic disorder, along with pathologies of the heart, kidney, and other organs.

HISTORICAL CONTEXT

This new perspective laid open the problem of depression to assault by investigators utilizing the modern biomedical armamentarium. Because of recent scientific advances at both the basic research and the clinical levels, it is the 21st century that will be remembered as the time when the major mental illnesses were finally understood at a deep, basic biological level, and when their treatments, and even prevention, were finally at hand.[2]

In the early years of modern biological psychiatry and psychology (1950s–1970s), neurobiological theories of depression focused on changes in patients such as elevated plasma levels of cortisol and corticosterone (hormones released from the upper portion of the adrenal gland), alterations in neurotransmitter-breakdown products found in the urine or cerebrospinal fluid, or lowered levels of neurotransmitters measured in plasma. In most of these cases, there was a heavy reliance on measures outside the central nervous system because of the general inaccessibility of brain measures. Thus, the search for the neural basis or pathophysiology of depression, in terms of either neurochemical or neuroanatomical-structural changes, came up largely empty.

More recently proposed neurobiological theories of depression attempt to directly relate precipitating events to changes in the brain, to classic symptomatology, and to coherent treatment strategies and even prevention. Such theories are especially attractive because they attempt to deal with the totality of the disease in a consistent and integrated manner. These theories go beyond simply pointing to "dysfunction in the left hemisphere" or "hypoactivity in the frontal lobes" and attempt to elucidate the neural and molecular mechanism underlying depression (Duman, Heninger, & Nestler, 1997; Jacobs, van Praag, & Gage, 2000; Manji, Drevets, & Charney, 2001). My colleagues and I have proposed one such theory, which focuses on the importance of neural changes in the brain for both the onset of and the recovery from depression (Jacobs et al., 2000).

NEUROPLASTICITY

One of the great conceptual leaps of modern neuroscience has been the notion of neuroplasticity. This is the idea that the adult brain can physically or morphologically change, not only in response to powerful toxins or trauma, but also in response to even subtle treatments or conditions. No less an intellect than the great Spanish neuroanatomist and Nobelist Ramon y Cajal believed that the morphology of the adult brain was essentially fixed. Scientists now know that even modest changes in the internal or external world can lead to structural changes in the brain. In fact, it is fair to say that the watchword for neuroscience in the past 20 to 30 years has become "plasticity."

Research in neuroplasticity has now shown that not only can neuronal morphology be altered, but also the actual number of neurons in the brain is not fixed. In the field of neurogenesis (the birth of new neurons), the work of Altman stands out as seminal. Altman was truly a scientist before his time (Altman & Das, 1965). In the early 1960s, he reported that two regions of the mammalian brain (most of his work was in rats), the olfactory bulb and the granule cell layer of dentate gyrus (DG; part of the hippocampal formation, which is a critical structure in the laying down of new cognitions), continue to generate new neurons in adulthood. In the context of the prevailing dogma of the immutability of the adult brain, this claim was heretical. And thus, not surprisingly, Altman's work was largely ignored and forgotten. It required more than 20 years for this topic to be reopened and reinvigorated. In the 1980s, Nottebohm reported that the overall size of certain regions of the bird brain, and the number of neurons in those areas, changed seasonally. Moreover, the increase in the number of brain cells appeared to coincide with the learning of new songs (Nottebohm, 1985). More than 10 years later, research groups led by Gould and Gage extended the concept of DG neurogenesis from birds and small mammals to monkeys, and eventually to humans (Eriksson et al., 1998; Gould, Cameron, Daniels, Wooley, & McEwen, 1994).

ADULT BRAIN NEUROGENESIS

Most neurons in the mammalian brain and spinal cord are generated during the pre- and perinatal periods of development. However, at least in the olfactory bulb,

DG, and possibly some portions of the cerebral cortex areas, neurons continue to be born throughout life. These new neurons are derived primarily from progenitor cells that reside in the brain's subventricular zone, which lines the ventricles (fluid reservoirs of the brain), or in a layer of the hippocampal formation called the subgranular zone (lying immediately below the granule cell layer of the DG). Through a process that is as yet not well understood, a signal induces progenitor cells to enter the cell cycle and undergo mitosis (cell division). The entire process involves not only proliferation, but also migration and differentiation of brain cells. For the sake of economy, I use the terms proliferation and neurogenesis interchangeably because most new cells generated in the DG differentiate into neurons.

Our work in this field has focused on neurogenesis in the DG for several reasons: Neurogenesis occurs primarily in this structure, most studies of brain neurogenesis have been conducted on this region, this structure is known to play a critical role in brain information processing, and clinical evidence points to significant changes in the hippocampus in depression (as I discuss later). It is also well known that the hippocampus is linked to other brain structures, such as the amygdala, that play a more direct or central role in mood (affect).

STRESS

One of the cardinal features of depression is its recurrent nature. Some patients experience regular or periodic recurrence, whereas in other patients recurrence is aperiodic. It is tempting to speculate that such variation in mood might be attributable to the waning and waxing of some neural process in the brain.

In laboratory studies, the level of neurogenesis is quantified by treating animals with radioactive thymidine or bromodeoxyuridine (BrdU). These compounds are incorporated into the DNA of cells going through mitosis. Once these cells complete this process, their thymidine- or BrdU-labeled daughter cells in the brain can be identified and counted post mortem. A number of factors are known to positively and negatively influence neurogenesis in the DG. Stressors are the best known and most widely studied group of variables that strongly suppress DG neurogenesis. And almost always, this effect is attributable, in large part, to the release of hormones from the adrenal gland as part of the organism's general stress response. This fact was critical for our thinking, because stress and its related release of adrenal hormones are generally considered to be major etiological factors in clinical depression (Kendler, Karkowski, & Prescott, 1999).

SEROTONIN

The brain chemical most strongly associated with depression is serotonin (5-hydroxytryptamine). With the exception of psychotherapy, all effective treatments for depression are known to be directly or indirectly dependent on increasing brain serotonin. The best known of these are the eponymous SSRIs (serotonin-specific reuptake inhibitors), such as Paxil and Prozac. (These drugs act by preventing the serotonin that is released in the brain from being inactivated by being taken up by the brain cells that originally released it.) Thus, several years ago, we began to examine the effects of serotonin on cell proliferation in the DG of adult rats.

In our initial study, we found that the systemic administration of fenfluramine (which releases serotonin throughout the central nervous system) produced a powerful proliferative effect in the DG. We also found that this effect was completely prevented by prior administration of a drug that blocked serotonin's action at a specific site (5-HT$_{1A}$ receptor; Radley & Jacobs, 2002). Such drugs also significantly reduced spontaneous, or basal, levels of brain-cell production, suggesting that serotonin plays a role in DG cell proliferation under normal, or naturalistic, conditions. This line of work has been confirmed and extended by Daszuta and her colleagues (Brezun & Daszuta, 1999).

Next, we conducted an experiment that has the most direct relevance to the present theme. Systemic administration of the antidepressant drug fluoxetine (which is also known by the brand name Prozac) for 3 weeks produced a 70% increase in DG cell proliferation above that of control animals (Jacobs & Fornal, 1999). Two recent studies have confirmed and extended our results (Malberg, Eisch, Nestler, & Duman, 2000; Manev, Uz, Smalheiser, & Manev, 2001). They demonstrated that short-term administration of antidepressant drugs did not augment proliferation, an important finding because these drugs show clinical efficacy only after 4 to 6 weeks of daily administration. Electroconvulsive shocks (a powerful antidepressant treatment) given to rats also result in increased proliferation (Madsen et al., 2000).

The theory that follows from these experimental results is simple. Chronic, unremitting stress (a major etiological factor in depression) suppresses brain neurogenesis either by acting on adrenal hormones or by suppressing serotonin neurotransmission. This suppression of neurogenesis occurs most prominently in the hippocampus, but other brain areas may also be involved, either directly or indirectly. Recovery occurs, at least in part, when serotonin neurotransmission is increased, especially if the 5-HT$_{1A}$ receptor is activated, by any of a variety of methods (possibly including psychotherapy). Increased serotonin neurotransmission stimulates cell proliferation, and these recently born neurons provide the substrate for new cognitions to be formed.

This theory provides a ready explanation for the perplexing fact that antidepressant treatments typically require weeks to become effective. It is known that it takes several weeks for newly generated cells in the DG to fully mature and become integrated into the existing brain circuitry.

THE HIPPOCAMPUS

If this theory is valid, the hippocampus should show a special relationship to depression. A number of different pieces of evidence link clinical depression to changes in the hippocampus (Jacobs et al., 2000). However, this is not to suggest that change in the hippocampus is the only change in the brain associated with depression, nor do we suggest that alterations in the hippocampus underlie all of the observable aspects of depression.

Further clinical evidence supports an important role for the hippocampus in depression.

- The brains of depressed patients have smaller hippocampi than the brains of control subjects.
- Patients with Cushing's Syndrome (elevated levels of adrenal hormones in plasma) have a high incidence of depression. Additionally, patients administered such hormones for other medical reasons frequently become depressed.
- Temporal lobe epilepsy, which involves massive cell loss in and around the hippocampus, is often accompanied by depression.

DISCUSSION AND FUTURE DIRECTIONS

This work is firmly based on research in the burgeoning field of neurogenesis, which is a facet of stem-cell research, a topic that recently has become highly publicized and politicized. This area holds promise for treating human disease because it suggests that dead or damaged brain cells can be replaced with new, healthy neurons. Probably the most obvious candidate for this type of intervention is Parkinson's disease, in which the primary deficit is the loss of a particular type of brain cell (dopamine neurons) in a specific brain area (substantia nigra).

What would be a true test of the present theory? The first issue would be to determine whether DG neurogenesis wanes when patients go into depressive episodes and waxes as they emerge from these episodes (either spontaneously or following some type of therapy). Investigating this issue would require the development of new brain-imaging techniques, with greater resolution and specificity for particular cell types than is currently possible. Even if a relation between DG neurogenesis and waxing and waning of depression is confirmed in clinical studies, and I believe it will be, these data would be only correlative. In order to determine if there is a causal relationship between alterations of DG neurogenesis and depression, there would be a need to experimentally manipulate cell proliferation. Would the efficacy of antidepressant therapies be blunted by drugs that suppress neurogenesis? There would be obvious ethical concerns associated with such studies.

Perhaps researchers will find new drugs that more directly target augmentation of neurogenesis, and their potency as antidepressants could be evaluated. Also, nonpharmacological therapies that are known to affect neurogenesis, such as exercise, could be more fully evaluated for their antidepressant efficacy. Does the birth and death of brain cells lie at the heart of all types of clinical depression, regardless of etiology? If cell loss is critical, is it always mediated by increased release of adrenal hormones? If not, what other neurochemicals could mediate these deleterious effects and thus also become candidates for novel pharmacotherapies?

How important to depression are changes in neurogenesis in brain regions other than the hippocampus? The hippocampus is thought to be more involved in cognition than in affect or mood. However, a major difficulty that may be at the heart of depression is the patients' inability to form new cognitions about their condition and the future, and their resulting tendency to remain mired in a depressed state. Also, as mentioned earlier, the hippocampus has important connections to brain structures directly involved in mood (affect). Finally, there is no reason to restrict the present theory exclusively to the hippocampus, because neurogenesis may be a more general phenomenon in the brain.

In sum, this theory is representative of a new generation of approaches to understanding psychopathology from a specific neural perspective. Etiological factors lead to identifiable neural changes in particular brain structures, which in turn produce distinct symptomatology. This perspective suggests that therapies targeted at reversing these neural dysfunctions will be effective in treating mental illness.

Recommended Reading

Gross, C.G. (2000). Neurogenesis in the adult brain: Death of a dogma. *Nature Review Neuroscience, 1*, 67–73.

Jacobs, B.L., van Praag, H., & Gage, F.H. (2000). (See References)

Kendler, K.S., Gardner, C.O., & Prescott, C.A. (2002). Toward a comprehensive developmental model for major depression in women. *American Journal of Psychiatry, 15*, 1133–1145.

Acknowledgments—I thank Diane Ruble for helpful comments on an earlier draft of this manuscript. Preparation of this manuscript was supported by Grant MH 23433 from the National Institute of Mental Health.

Notes

1. Address correspondence to Barry L. Jacobs, Program in Neuroscience, Department of Psychology, Princeton University, Green Hall, Princeton, NJ 08544; e-mail: barryj@princeton.edu.

2. The importance of other aspects of psychiatric research in the past 50 years cannot be denied. This is the period in which psychopharmacology came into its own. In what many people consider a revolution, drugs were developed for the effective treatment of depression, bipolar illness, and schizophrenia.

References

Altman, J., & Das, G.D. (1965). Autoradiographic and histological evidence of postnatal hippocampal neurogenesis in rats. *Journal of Comparative Neurology, 124*, 319–335.

Brezun, J.M., & Daszuta, A. (1999). Depletion in serotonin decreases neuro-genesis in the dentate gyrus and the subventricular zone of adult rats. *Neuroscience, 89*, 999–1002.

Duman, R.S., Heninger, G.R., & Nestler, E.J. (1997). A molecular and cellular theory of depression. *Archives of General Psychiatry, 54*, 597–606.

Eriksson, P.S., Perfilieva, E., Björk-Eriksson, T., Alborn, A.M., Norberg, C., Peterson, D.A., & Gage, F.H. (1998). Neurogenesis in the adult human hippocampus. *Nature Medicine, 4*, 1313–1317.

Gould, E., Cameron, H.A., Daniels, D.C., Wooley, C.S., & McEwen, B.S. (1994). Adrenal hormones suppress cell division in the adult rat dentate gyrus. *Journal of Comparative Neurology, 340*, 551–565.

Jacobs, B.L., & Fornal, C.A. (1999). Chronic fluoxetine treatment increases hippocampal neurogenesis in rats: A novel theory of depression. *Society for Neuroscience Abstracts, 25*, 714.

Jacobs, B.L., van Praag, H., & Gage, F.H. (2000). Adult brain neurogenesis and psychiatry: A novel theory of depression. *Molecular Psychiatry, 5*, 262–269.

Kendler, K.S., Karkowski, L.M., & Prescott, C.A. (1999). Causal relationship between stressful life events and the onset of major depression. *American Journal of Psychiatry, 156*, 837–841.

Madsen, T.M., Treschow, A., Bengzon, J., Bolwig, T.G., Lindvall, O., & Tingström, A. (2000). Increased neurogenesis in a model of electroconvulsive therapy. *Biological Psychiatry, 47,* 1043–1049.

Malberg, J.E., Eisch, A.M., Nestler, E.J., & Duman, R.S. (2000). Chronic antidepressant treatment increases neurogenesis in adult rat hippocampus. *Journal of Neuroscience, 20,* 9104–9110.

Manev, H., Uz, T., Smalheiser, N.R., & Manev, R. (2001). Antidepressants alter cell proliferation in the adult brain in vivo and in neural cultures in vitro. *European Journal of Pharmacology, 411,* 67–70.

Manji, H.K., Drevets, W.C., & Charney, D.S. (2001). The cellular neurobiology of depression. *Nature Medicine, 7,* 541–547.

Nottebohm, F. (1985). Neuronal replacement in adulthood. *Annals of the New York Academy of Sciences, 457,* 143–161.

Radley, J.J., & Jacobs, B.L. (2002). 5-HT1A receptor antagonist administration decreases cell proliferation in the dentate gyrus. *Brain Research, 955,* 264–267.

This article has been reprinted as it originally appeared in *Current Directions in Psychological Science*. Citation information for this article as originally published appears above.

Plasticity for Affective Neurocircuitry: How the Environment Affects Gene Expression

Nathan A. Fox[1]
University of Maryland, College Park
Amie A. Hane
Williams College
Daniel S. Pine
The National Institutes of Health

Abstract

We (Fox et al., 2005) recently described a gene-by-environment interaction involving child temperament and maternal social support, finding heightened behavioral inhibition in children homozygous or heterozygous for the serotonin transporter (5HTTLPR) gene short allele whose mothers reported low social support. Here, we propose a model, Plasticity for Affective Neurocircuitry, that describes the manner in which genetic disposition and environmental circumstances may interact. Children with a persistently fearful temperament (and the 5HTTLPR short allele) are more likely to experience caregiving environments in which threat is highlighted. This in turn will exacerbate an attention bias that alters critical affective neurocircuitry to threat and enhances and maintains anxious behavior in the child.

Keywords

temperament; gene × environment interaction; attention bias to threat; parenting

Individual differences in the stress response represent stable aspects of behavior that emerge early in life and reflect aspects of brain function. While behavioral-genetic studies implicate genes and the environment in these differences, the manner in which specific genes and environmental events shape specific aspects of brain function remains poorly specified. Recent work provides important clues, however, concerning those specific pathways. In particular, emerging findings suggest that specific genes associated with the function of the neurotransmitter serotonin (5-HT) interact with social stressors during development to shape function in a neural circuit implicated in the stress response.

RESEARCH ON GENE × ENVIRONMENT INTERACTIONS

A series of recent research reports provides evidence for gene-by-environment (denoted gene × environment) interactions with a protein crucially involved in the effects of 5-HT on behavior. This protein regulates the fate of 5-HT released from neurons. Each of the genetically derived variants in this protein is known as an expression of a serotonin transporter protein polymorphism (5HTTLPR; Caspi et al., 2003; Kaufman et al., 2004). The 5HTTLPR gene has two major functional alleles: a long and a short, as well as another long-variant allele that behaves, functionally, like the short allele. Individuals who are homozygous have two copies of either the long or the short. Individuals who are heterozygous have one copy of each. In general, studies of gene × environment interaction with this particular gene suggest that individuals who are homozygous for the short allele of the 5HTTLPR and who are exposed to significant stress are more likely to exhibit significant maladaptive behavior than are individuals who are homozygous for the long allele and are exposed to similar levels of stress. Individuals who are heterozygous, having one copy of the long and one of the short allele, usually fall somewhere in the middle, exhibiting more maladaptive outcomes compared to individuals homozygous for the long, and somewhat fewer than individuals who are homozygous for the short allele.

For example, Caspi et al. (2003) found that individuals homozygous for the short allele of 5-HTTLPR and exposed to five or more stressful life events were more likely to experience a major depressive episode, compared to individuals homozygous for the long allele exposed to such stress. Kaufman et al. (2004) reported that children carrying the short allele who had a history of abuse were more likely to evidence depression if their caregivers reported that they themselves were under high stress. Both of these studies reported psychiatric outcomes as a result of this particular gene × environment interaction. Caspi et al. (2003) examined the probability of major depression. Kaufman et al. (2004) reported on depressive symptoms in the subjects.

In a recent paper, we (Fox et al., 2005) reported on a similar gene × environment interaction in young children who were selected for the temperamental characteristic of behavioral inhibition. Signs of behavioral inhibition are detectable within the first months of life. For example, infants displaying high motor reactivity and negative affect when presented with novel auditory and visual stimuli are more likely to display behavioral inhibition as toddlers and preschoolers (Fox, Henderson, Rubin, Calkins, & Schmidt, 2001). Behaviorally inhibited children cease their ongoing activity and withdraw to their caregiver's proximity when confronted with novel events. They are also likely to isolate themselves when confronted with unfamiliar peers or adults. This behavioral style appears early in life, is associated with physiological markers of stress, social reticence with unfamiliar peers, low self-concept in childhood, and may be a risk factor for later psychopathology (Perez-Edgar & Fox, 2005).

We examined the relationship between childhood behavior and two variants of the 5-HTTLPR. As noted above, this protein mediates 5-HT influences on behavior by regulating the fate of 5-HT released from neurons into the synaptic cleft, the space that separates two communicating neurons. We found that children with lower-activity variants of the 5-HTTLPR whose mothers reported experiencing low social support were more likely to display behavioral inhibition at age 7, relative to children with similar 5-HT genetics but whose mothers reported more social support. The gene × environment interaction suggested that children with high-activity forms of the gene were "protected" from manifesting inhibition, even if their mothers reported experiencing low social support. Moreover, while child 5HTTLPR strongly related to inhibition in children with low levels of social support, for children with high levels of social support, no such relationship with 5HTTLPR emerged.

These data extend the findings of previous work, reporting the interaction of environmental stress and genes in predicting behavioral outcomes. Unlike other studies, though, the Fox et al. (2005) study presents data on a sample of typically developing children with nonpsychiatric outcomes. But like the other papers it does not address the mechanisms or processes by which the environmental stressor(s) affect variations in genotype to create the particular phenotypic outcome.

NEUROBIOLOGY OF 5HTTLPR

The short and long forms of the 5HTTLPR produce proteins known as reuptake transporters. These proteins lie within the synapse, the space separating two communicating neurons, and they function to remove serotonin from the synapse after it has been released. 5-HT neurons removed from the brain and studied in the laboratory revealed that the different forms of 5-HT reuptake transporters associated with distinct genotypes act differently. This early work clearly demonstrated functional consequences of the 5HTTLPR. More recent work has begun to describe possible influences of the different polymorphisms or variations in the 5HTTLPR in the neural-system function of living primates and humans.

5-HT neurons, like neurons for other modulatory neurotransmitters, make connections with broadly distributed networks in the brain. 5-HT influences on behavior are thought to emerge through the neurotransmitter's effects on information processing. The neural architecture engaged in the service of processing dangerous stimuli has been mapped in particularly precise detail, and 5-HT is thought to modulate functioning in this circuit (Gross & Hen, 2004). The circuit encompasses the ventral prefrontal cortex (vPFC), an area involved in decision making, and the amygdala, a structure involved in the detection of salient events such as those that are novel or threatening. Both structures receive strong 5-HT innervations. Thus, the amygdala, vPFC, and connections between them constitute a neural circuit that has been labeled "vPFC–amygdala circuitry." Consistent with the laboratory evidence of its effects on serotonin reuptake, the 5HTTLPR also predicts functional aspects of this ventral prefrontal–amygdala circuitry (Pezawas et al., 2005).

One of the most important issues to resolve concerns the mapping of these 5 HT influences across development. Neuroimaging studies in humans demonstrate robust developmental influences on prefrontal–amygdala circuitry (Monk et al., 2003). Studies in animal models suggest that these influences result from developmental changes in 5-HT function (Gross & Hen, 2004). This suggests that the relationship between the 5HTTLPR and prefrontal–amygdala function is likely to change across development. Neuroimaging studies have yet to examine this issue.

Interestingly, animal models suggest that 5-HT effects on neural development emerge through interactions with the environment (Gross & Hen, 2004). Given these data, how then precisely does the action of the environment interact with the 5HTTLPR to shape brain function and behavior? In the specific case of behavioral inhibition, how does the mother's report of her social support influence the expression of her child's 5-HTT gene in a way that ultimately impacts the child's tendency to display inhibited behavior? We propose a model, called Plasticity for Affective Neurocircuitry, and suggest two possible complementary mechanisms, based upon work in the area of anxiety and our own developmental studies. The first deals with the manner in which caregivers interact with behaviorally inhibited children; the second, with the attention bias that may develop as a result of temperamental disposition, caregiver influence, or their interaction.

CAREGIVER BEHAVIOR AND SOCIAL SUPPORT

Research suggests that reported level of social support correlates with quality of caregiver behavior. Mothers who report high levels of social support tend to be more sensitive toward their infants (Crockenberg & McCluskey, 1986) and more satisfied with their role as a parent (Thompson & Walker, 2004). Additional evidence indicates that level of social support may be particularly important for mothers of temperamentally distress-prone infants. Crockenberg and her colleagues found that the positive association between social support and maternal sensitivity was only significant for irritable infants (Crockenberg & McCluskey, 1986). Pauli-Pott, Mertesacker, and Beckmann (2004) found that maternal insensitivity was predicted by the joint effect of infant negative emotionality and low social support. Hence, social support is a factor contributing to the quality of maternal caregiving behavior, particularly for inhibited children who have a history of negative reactivity in infancy and early childhood.

An emergent body of research indicates that the quality of the mother–child relationship mitigates the relation between early and later forms of behavioral inhibition, such that some parents of behaviorally inhibited children interact with their children in a manner that appears to exacerbate or maintain their child's temperament. In our own research, we have identified a unique group of children who consistently withdraw from novelty at age 4 months and who receive insensitive maternal caregiving due to this proneness to distress. For instance, Ghera, Hane, Malesa, and Fox (2006) found that infants who responded negatively to novel stimuli at age 4 months and who were viewed by their mothers as difficult to soothe received low levels of maternal sensitivity. Hane, Fox, Henderson, and Marshall (2006) found that 9-month-old infants who showed high levels of behavioral avoidance to ominous stimuli and a corresponding pattern of right frontal electroencephalogram (EEG) asymmetry (itself a determinant of continued inhibition across early childhood; see Fox et al., 2001), received low levels of maternal sensitivity. Hane and Fox (2006) reported that infants who received low-quality maternal caregiving behavior showed more fearfulness and less sociability in the laboratory, more negative affect while interacting in the home with their mothers, and a pattern of right frontal EEG asymmetry. Taken together, this research suggests that quality of maternal caregiving behavior shapes the development of behavioral inhibition, perhaps by altering the neural systems that underlie reactivity to stress and novelty (see a review by Parent et al., 2005, for parallels in research with rodents).

ATTENTION BIAS TO THREAT

A second mechanism through which experience may affect the neural systems underlying behavioral inhibition involves the development of attention bias to threat. A variety of data using a number of different experimental paradigms suggests that individuals who self-report a high degree of anxious symptoms or who are diagnosed with a number of different anxiety disorders display an attention bias to threat. When presented with visual stimuli reflecting threat, anxious individuals are more vigilant toward these stimuli and take longer to disengage from visual attention to them (Mogg, Millar, & Bradley, 2000). In humans, as in other species, the ability to detect threatening stimuli in the environment appears to provide an important adaptive advantage for safety and survival. The neural systems that are involved in threat detection have been well described in nonhuman primates, rats, and, through the use of functional neuroimaging, in humans (Monk et al., 2006). These systems encompass prefrontal–amygdala circuitry previously tied to threat responses and 5HTTLPR in humans.

An enhanced sensitivity to threat has been suggested as an underlying mechanism in anxiety disorders (MacLeod, Rutherford, Campbell, Ebsworthy, & Holker, 2002). A recent meta-analysis (Bar-Haim, Lamy, Pergamin, Bakermans-Kraneburg, & van IJzendoorn, 2007) suggests that the distribution of attention in anxious individuals may be part of a resource-allocation system that biases the individual to pay close attention to threat. Such biases may develop over time and be the result of a person's ongoing transaction with threatening or aversive stimuli. Moreover, studies using experimental approaches, at least in adults, suggest that these attention biases are causally implicated in the genesis of anxiety following exposure to stress (MacLeod et al., 2002). From this perspective, children born with a disposition to react intensively and with negative affect to stress or novelty may go on to show different patterns of behavior, depending on the degree to which they are exposed to overzealous, intrusive maternal behavior as opposed to a more sensitive, nurturing style.

The Plasticity for Affective Neurocircuitry model that we propose suggests that early temperament influences quality of the caregiving environment and quality of the environment in turn shapes attention bias to threat and mediates the relation between early temperament and later inhibition (see Fig.1). Rubin, Burgess, and Hastings (2002) showed that the relation between behavioral inhibition as a toddler and reticence at age 4 was significant and positive only for those children whose mothers were psychologically overcontrolling and derisive. Thus it appears that caregivers who highlight or identify negative events in their child's environment (often in an effort to control their child's behavior) may in fact be inadvertently promoting attention bias in the child. Evidence from studies of interactions between mothers and children with anxiety disorders supports this position. For example, Barrett, Rapee, and Dadds (1996) found that parental discussion of ambiguous situations was associated with increased perception of threat and the creation of avoidant plans of action in anxious children. Thus, from within the caregiving environment, children disposed to respond with negative affect to novelty or uncertainty may be further reinforced to bias their attention toward threat during the course of interactions with caregivers.

CONCLUSIONS

At the present time, there are preciously few data on the development of attention biases to evocative, threatening, or stressful stimuli. Research in this area

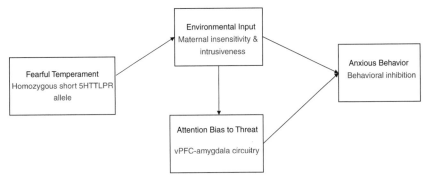

Fig. 1. Plasticity for Affective Neurocircuitry model. A child's genetically disposed fearful temperament (due to homozygosity for the short allele of the serotonin transporter, 5HTTLPR, gene) elicits and is elicited by caregiver behavior (maternal insensitivity and intrusiveness) to shape attention bias to threat and the underlying neural circuitry (in the ventral prefrontal cortex, vPFC, and amygdala) supporting this bias. Exaggerated attention bias contributes to the emergence and maintenance of anxious behaviors.

is clearly needed in order to understand the development of these attention processes and their effects on social behavior.

Research in the area of behavioral inhibition already highlights the importance of both biological dispositions and caregiving environments in shaping the social responses of the young child. Evidence of gene × environment interactions in this group of children marks another important step toward understanding the developmental mechanisms involved in the emergence of important variations in social behavior. The next steps involve process-focused research. Studies that carefully model the development of gene × environment interactions and the factors that mitigate the relevance of such interactions to key social outcomes are warranted; such studies would elucidate the mechanisms by which the environment influences the phenotypic expression of critical genes such as the 5HTTLPR and the degree to which phenotypes change across development. Hane and Fox (in press) suggest that early environmental experiences not only change the phenotypic expression of stress reactivity, but also prime the child to respond with a similar behavioral repertoire upon encountering like environmental stressors in the future. Hence, the child who is genetically vulnerable to anxiety and who has also developed a tendency to focus on threat vis à vis interactions with his or her caregivers may develop a strong attention threat bias that maintains anxious behavior well into adulthood.

Recommended Reading

Fox, N.A., Henderson, H.A., Marshall, P.J., Nichols, K.E., & Ghera, M.M. (2005). Behavioral inhibition: Linking biology and behavior within a developmental framework. *Annual Reviews of Psychology, 56,* 235–262.

Perez-Edgar, K., & Fox, N.A. (2005). Temperament and anxiety disorders. *Child Adolescent Clinics of North America, 14,* 681–705.

Pine, D.S., Cohen, P., Gurley, D., Brook, J., & Ma, Y. (1998). The risk of early-adulthood anxiety disorders in adolescents with anxiety and depressive disorders. *Archives of General Psychiatry, 55,* 56–64.

Pine, D.S., Klein, R.G., Mannuzza, S., Moulton, J.L., Lissek, S., Guardino, M., & Woldehawariat, G. (2005). Face-emotion processing in offspring at-risk for panic disorder. *Journal of the American Academy of Child and Adolescent Psychiatry, 44,* 664–672.

Note

1. Address correspondence to Nathan A. Fox, Department of Human Development, University of Maryland, College Park, MD 20742; e-mail: fox@umd.edu.

References

Bar-Haim, Y., Lamy, D., Pergamin, L., Bakermans-Kraneburg, M.J., & van IJzendoorn, M.H. (2007). Threat-related attentional bias in anxious and non-anxious individuals: A meta-analytic study. *Psychological Bulletin, 133,* 1–24.

Barrett, P.M., Rapee, R.M., & Dadds, M.M. (1996). Family enhancement of cognitive style in anxious and aggressive children. *Journal of Abnormal Child Psychology, 24,* 187–203.

Caspi, A., Snugden, K., Moffitt, T.E., Taylor, A., Craig, I.W., & Harrington, H., et al. (2003). Influence of life stress on depression: Moderation by a polymorphism in the 5-HTT gene. *Science, 301,* 386–389.

Crockenberg, S., & McCluskey, K. (1986). Change in maternal behavior during the baby's first year of life. *Child Development, 57,* 746–753.

Fox, N.A., Henderson, H.A., Rubin, K.H., Calkins, S.D., & Schmidt, L.A. (2001). Continuity and discontinuity of behavioral inhibition and exuberance: Psychophysiological and behavioral influences across the first four years of life. *Child Development, 72,* 1–21.

Fox, N.A., Nichols, K.E., Henderson, H.A., Rubin, K., Schmidt, L., Hamer, D., Ernst, M., & Pine, D.S. (2005). Evidence for a gene–environment interaction in predicting behavioral inhibition in middle childhood. *Psychological Science, 16,* 921–926.

Ghera, M.M., Hane, A.A., Malesa, E.M., & Fox, N.A. (2006). The role of infant soothability in the relation between infant negativity and maternal sensitivity. *Infant Behavior and Development, 29,* 289–293.

Gross, C., & Hen, R. (2004). The developmental origins of anxiety. *Nature Reviews Neuroscience, 5,* 545–552.

Hane, A.A., & Fox, N.A. (2006). Ordinary variations in maternal caregiving of human infants influence stress reactivity. *Psychological Science, 17,* 550–556.

Hane, A.A., & Fox, N.A. (in press). A closer look at the transactional nature of early social development: The relations among early caregiving environments, temperament, and early social development and the case for phenotypic plasticity. In F. Santoianni & C. Sabatano (Eds.), *Brain development in learning environments: Embodied and perceptual advancements.*

Hane, A.A., Fox, N.A., Henderson, H.A., & Marshall, P.J. (2006). *Setting the trajectories to social competence: The relations among temperamental reactivity, frontal EEG asymmetry and social behavior in infancy.* Unpublished manuscript.

Kaufman, J., Yang., B., Douglas-Palombeni, H., Houshyar, S., Lipschitz, D., Krystal, J.H., & Gerlernter, J. (2004). Social supports and serotonin transporter gene moderate depression in maltreated children. *Proceedings of the National Academy of Sciences, 101,* 17316–17321.

MacLeod, C., Rutherford, E., Campbell, L., Ebsworthy, G., & Holker, L. (2002). Selective attention and emotional vulnerability: Assessing the causal basis of their association through the experimental manipulation of attentional bias. *Journal of Abnormal Psychology, 111,* 107–123.

Mogg, K., Millar, N., & Bradley, B.P. (2000). Biases in eye movements to threatening facial expressions in generalized anxiety disorder and depressive disorder. *Journal of Abnormal Psychology, 109,* 695–704.

Monk, C., McClure, E.B., Nelson, E.B., Zarahn, E., Bilder, R.M., Leibenluft, E., Charney D.S., Ernst, M., & Pine, D.S. (2003). Adolescent immaturity in attention-related brain engagement to emotional facial expressions. *NeuroImage, 20,* 420–428.

Monk, C.S., Nelson, E.E., McClure, E.B., Mogg, K., Bradley, B.P., Leibenluft, E., Blair, R.J., Chen, G., Charney, D.S., Ernst, M., & Pine, D.S. (2006). Ventrolateral prefrontal cortex activation and attentional bias in response to angry faces in adolescents with generalized anxiety disorder. *American Journal of Psychiatry, 163,* 1091–1097.

Parent, C., Zhang, T., Caldji, C., Bagot, R., Champagne, F.A., Pruessner, J., Meaney, M.J. (2005). Maternal care and individual differences in defensive responses. *Current Directions in Psychological Science, 14,* 229–233.

Pauli-Pott, U., Mertesacker, B., & Beckmann, D. (2004). Predicting the development of infant emotionality from maternal characteristics. *Development and Psychopathology, 16,* 19–42.

Perez-Edgar, K., & Fox, N.A. (2005). A behavioral and electrophysiological study of children's selective attention under neutral and affective conditions. *Journal of Cognition and Development, 6,* 89–118.

Pezawas, L., Meyer-Lindenberg, A., Drabant, E.M., Verchinski, B.A., Munoz, K.E., Kolachana, B.S., Egan, M.F., Mattay, V.S., Hariri, A.R., & Weinberger, D.R. (2005). 5-HTTLPR polymorphism impacts human cingulated–amygdala interactions: A genetic susceptibility mechanism for depression. *Nature Neuroscience, 8,* 828–834.

Rubin, K.H., Burgess, K.B., & Hastings, P.D. (2002). Stability and social-behavioral consequences of toddlers' inhibited temperament and parenting behaviors. *Child Development, 73,* 483–495.

Thompson, S.D., & Walker, A.C. (2004). Satisfaction with parenting: A comparison between adolescent mothers and fathers. *Sex Roles, 50,* 677–687.

This article has been reprinted as it originally appeared in *Current Directions in Psychological Science.* Citation information for this article as originally published appears above.

Out of Balance: A New Look at Chronic Stress, Depression, and Immunity

Theodore F. Robles
Department of Psychology, The Ohio State University
Ronald Glaser
Department of Molecular Virology, Immunology, and Medical Genetics, The Ohio State University College of Medicine; The Ohio State Institute for Behavioral Medicine Research; The Ohio State University Comprehensive Cancer Center
Janice K. Kiecolt-Glaser[1]
The Ohio State Institute for Behavioral Medicine Research; The Ohio State University Comprehensive Cancer Center; Department of Psychiatry, The Ohio State University College of Medicine

Abstract

Chronic stress is typically associated with suppression of the immune system, including impaired responses to infectious disease and delayed wound healing. Recent work suggests that stress and depression can enhance production of proinflammatory cytokines, substances that regulate the body's immune response to infection and injury. We provide a broad framework relating stress and depression to a range of diseases whose onset and course may be influenced by proinflammatory cytokines, particularly the cytokine interleukin-6 (IL-6). IL-6 has been linked to a spectrum of chronic diseases associated with aging. Production of proinflammatory cytokines that influence these and other conditions can be directly stimulated by chronic stress and depression. We suggest that a key pathway through which chronic stress and depression influence health outcomes involves proinflammatory cytokines. We discuss the evidence for relationships between psychosocial factors and proinflammatory cytokines, and important health implications of these findings.

Keywords

chronic stress; depression; immunity; cytokines; inflammation

A long-standing idea in the field of psychoneuroimmunology (the study of interactions between the nervous system and the immune system) is that chronic stress suppresses the immune system. A recent review of the past 30 years of research on stress and immunity concluded that "the most chronic stressors were associated with the most global immunosuppression" (Segerstrom & Miller, 2004, p. 618). Our own research has previously demonstrated that immune suppression related to chronic stress has clinical implications, including impaired immune responses to infectious disease and delayed wound healing.

Currently, researchers are changing their thinking about the relations among chronic stress, depression, and immunity. Recent research suggests that chronic stress and depression may actually enhance certain immune responses. One immune response in question is *inflammation*, a broad term that refers to immune processes triggered by damage to cells and tissues. Such damage occurs in a variety of ways, including infection and injury. The immune system initiates inflammatory responses that are critical to resolving infections and repairing the damaged tissue.

Focusing on the inflammation-enhancing role of chronic stress and depression marks an important shift in how researchers conceptualize the complex interactions between the brain, behavior, and the immune system. Rather than supporting the model in which chronic stress and depression results in global immune suppression, the evidence reviewed here suggests a more complex and clinically relevant model in which chronic stress and depression result more generally in immune dysregulation. The body normally orchestrates a balanced response when faced with immunological challenges, but in the new model, chronic stress and depression disrupt this balance, suppressing some immune responses and enhancing others. This can have significant costs to an individual's physical health, including prolonged cell and tissue damage, increased vulnerability to acute and chronic diseases, and even premature aging.

CYTOKINES AND IMMUNE REGULATION

The key substances involved in regulating inflammatory responses to infection and injury are *cytokines*. Released by a variety of cells, cytokines are proteins that serve as intercellular signals regulating immune responses. Much like hormones of the endocrine system, cytokines transmit messages by interacting with receptors on cell surfaces and communicate over long distances in the body. Cytokines can be differentiated into two broad classes on the basis of their effects on the immune response: *proinflammatory* (promoting inflammation) and *anti-inflammatory* (restraining inflammation).

Proinflammatory cytokines, including interleukin-1 (IL-1), IL-6, and tumor necrosis factor-α (TNF-α), are produced by cells at the site of infection or injury (see Fig. 1). Subsequently, proinflammatory cytokines attract other immune cells to the affected site and prime them to activate and respond. Anti-inflammatory cytokines such as IL-4, IL-5, IL-10, and IL-13 dampen this immune response, inhibiting immune-cell activities, such as replication, activation, and synthesis of other cytokines.

Proinflammatory cytokines initiate a variety of responses that regulate inflammation, in addition to stimulating production of other cytokines. Specifically, certain proinflammatory cytokines act on the brain, as shown in Figure 1, affecting the endocrine system and behavior. For instance, proinflammatory cytokines stimulate the hypothalamic-pituitary-adrenal (HPA) axis, a cascade of hormones from the hypothalamus and pituitary gland that results in production of the glucocorticoid hormone cortisol. Glucocorticoid hormones are steroid hormones produced by the adrenal cortex that can have anti-inflammatory effects by reducing the synthesis of proinflammatory cytokines, and thus complete a negative feedback loop that helps control inflammation. Proinflammatory cytokines

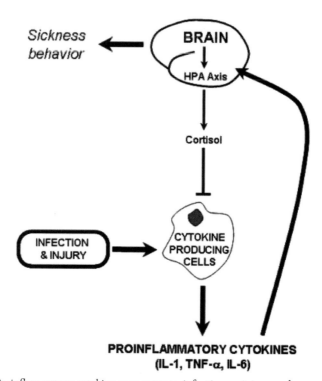

Fig. 1. Proinflammatory cytokine responses to infection or injury under normal conditions. Lines terminating in arrowheads denote stimulatory pathways, and lines terminating in flat lines denote inhibitory pathways. Infection and injury stimulate cells to secrete proinflammatory cytokines, including interleukin-1 (IL-1), tumor necrosis factor-α (TNF-α), and IL-6. These cytokines attract other cells to the site and stimulate them to respond. In addition, proinflammatory cytokines travel to the brain and stimulate the hypothalamic-pituitary-adrenal (HPA) axis. This results in cortisol production, which helps to control inflammation and prevent the immune system from over-responding. Proinflammatory cytokines in the brain also induce sickness behavior, which helps the body maximize physical resources required to combat infection.

also induce *sickness behavior*, a cluster of behaviors—including fever, decreased appetite, and reduced motor activity—that facilitate energy regulation (Maier & Watkins, 1998). By maximizing physical resources (energy, heat) required by the body to combat infection, sickness behavior is considered adaptive in helping the organism fight off infectious disease.

This review focuses on the proinflammatory cytokine IL-6, which has multiple effects on the immune, endocrine, and other tissue and organ systems, and thus serves as a good indicator of chronic inflammation. In addition, elevated IL-6 production is linked to key chronic diseases, such as cardiovascular disease and certain cancers, and to indices of physical health (Papanicolaou, Wilder, Manolagas, & Chrousos, 1998). Moreover, IL-6 production is related to psychosocial factors, including depression and chronic stress.

PSYCHOSOCIAL FACTORS AND PROINFLAMMATORY CYTOKINES

Several sociodemographic factors and health behaviors are related to elevated proinflammatory cytokines. Unlike other components of the immune system, which decline with age, IL-6 levels tend to increase with age (Papanicolaou et al., 1998). Men generally show higher levels of IL-6 than women, likely because of the effects of estrogen and androgens (Ershler & Keller, 2000). Higher IL-6 levels are associated with adverse health habits, including smoking, sedentary activity, and high body mass index; at the same time, elevated IL-6 levels are associated with higher rates of morbidity and mortality after controlling statistically for sociodemographic factors and health behaviors (Ferrucci et al., 1999).

As stated at the outset, the past 30 years of research on chronic stress and depression focused on immune suppression. Accordingly, one might expect that chronic stress and depression are related to suppressed production of proinflammatory cytokines. However, empirical evidence strongly suggests that major depression, depressive symptoms, and chronic stress enhance production of proinflammatory cytokines.

Major depression is related to enhanced proinflammatory cytokine levels, including IL-6, which can be reduced following successful treatment with antidepressant medications (Kenis & Maes, 2002). Elevated depressive symptoms also are related to elevated proinflammatory cytokine levels (e.g., Miller, Stetler, Carney, Freedland, & Banks, 2002). We recently found that higher levels of depressive symptoms were related to higher levels of IL-6 among older adults (Glaser, Robles, Sheridan, Malarkey, & Kiecolt-Glaser, 2003). More important, individuals reporting more depressive symptoms showed increased IL-6 levels 2 weeks after receiving a challenge to the immune system through an influenza virus vaccination, whereas there was little change in IL-6 among individuals reporting few or no depressive symptoms, as shown in Figure 2. In general, depressive symptoms were quite low in our sample of older adults, which suggests that even modest depressive symptoms may be sufficient in making the immune system hypersensitive to immunological challenges, resulting in amplified IL-6 production. Sensitization of inflammatory responses may have important health consequences, as amplified and prolonged inflammatory responses following infection and other immunological challenges could accelerate the progression of a range of age-related diseases. Overall, these data suggest that proinflammatory cytokines are a key mechanism whereby major depression and depressive symptoms may serve as a gateway to a broad array of health problems.

Chronic stressors are also related to elevated production of IL-6. A study found that women who were caring for a relative with Alzheimer's disease had higher levels of IL-6 than either women who were anticipating a housing relocation or women from the same community who experienced neither of these stressors (Lutgendorf et al., 1999). This finding was particularly noteworthy because the caregivers were 6 to 9 years younger, on average, than women in the other two groups. Given that IL-6 levels generally increase with age, what might be the impact of chronic stress on age-related increases in IL-6?

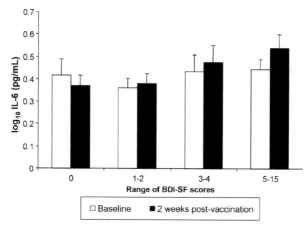

Fig. 2. Levels of interleukin-6 (IL-6) as a function of depressive symptoms in a sample of 119 older adults. IL-6 levels were measured before participants received an influenza virus vaccination (baseline, represented by the white bars) and 2 weeks after they were vaccinated (dark bars). Depression symptoms were measured using the short form of the Beck Depression Inventory (BDI-SF). Individuals reporting depressive symptoms showed an increase in IL-6 2 weeks following vaccination compared to individuals reporting few or no depressive symptoms. Error bars denote standard error of the mean. Redrawn after Glaser, R., Robles, T.F., Sheridan, J., Malarkey, W.B., & Kiecolt-Glaser, J.K. (2003).

We addressed this question by following older adults undergoing a chronic stressor for 6 years and assessing age-related change in their IL-6 levels during that period (Kiecolt-Glaser et al., 2003). Older adults experiencing the chronic stress of caring for a spouse with Alzheimer's disease showed an average rate of annual IL-6 increase that was about 4 times as large as that of noncaregivers. There were no systematic group differences in chronic health problems, medications, or health-relevant behaviors that might have accounted for the faster increase in IL-6 in caregivers. Moreover, the mean annual changes in IL-6 among former caregivers did not differ from that of current caregivers even several years after the death of the impaired spouse. Based on these findings, we suggest that chronic stressors may be capable of substantially augmenting normal age-related increases in proinflammatory cytokine production. Put simply, chronic stress may contribute to premature aging of the immune system.

PSYCHOSOCIAL FACTORS AND MECHANISTIC PATHWAYS

Apart from influencing health-related behaviors, how might psychosocial factors contribute to elevated production of proinflammatory cytokines? Figure 3 depicts four potential pathways. Several pathways (i.e., A, C, and D) involve dysregulation of signals coming from the endocrine system, specifically the HPA axis. Stress-related HPA activity results in elevated levels of glucocorticoid hormones, including cortisol. As previously mentioned, glucocorticoid hormones reduce the synthesis of proinflammatory cytokines and thereby help prevent the immune system from overshooting, or mounting an overreactive immune response that

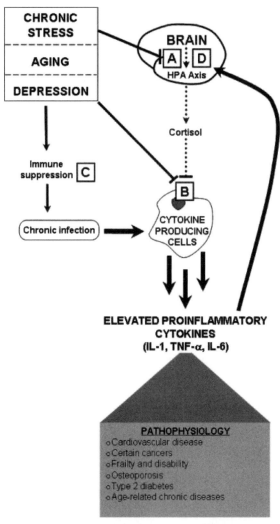

Fig. 3. A theoretical model depicting how psychosocial factors and aging contribute to immune dysregulation. Lines terminating in arrowheads denote stimulatory pathways, and lines terminating in flat lines denote inhibitory pathways. Dotted lines denote disrupted signaling pathways. In this model, chronic stress, depression, and aging contribute to elevated proinflammatory cytokines—interleukin-1 (IL-1), tumor necrosis factor-α (TNF-α), and IL-6—in four ways: (A) Psychosocial factors may disrupt the functioning of glucocorticoid hormones (such as cortisol) in the brain by reducing the number of glucocorticoid receptors in certain brain regions or disrupting receptor functioning, which may result in dysregulation of the hypothalamic-pituitary-adrenal (HPA) axis; (B) psychosocial factors may disrupt the functioning of glucocorticoid receptors on cytokine-producing cells, rendering those cells less sensitive to the anti-inflammatory effects of cortisol; (C) psychosocial factors may result in immune suppression, which inhibits the body's ability to fight off infection and injury, leading to chronic infections; and (D) proinflammatory cytokines may reduce the number of glucocorticoid receptors in the brain or disrupt the functioning of those receptors. All four mechanisms may eventually lead to elevated production of proinflammatory cytokines and, over time, contribute to chronic disease and pathophysiology.

could cause damage to cells and tissues, such as the damage observed in autoimmune diseases like multiple sclerosis or rheumatoid arthritis.

If glucocorticoid signals are disrupted, the result may be reduced restraint on the immune system and overproduction of proinflammatory cytokines. Figure 3, Path A depicts that chronic stressors and depression disrupt glucocorticoid signaling in the brain by altering the function of glucocorticoid receptors (Raison & Miller, 2003). Figure 3, Path B depicts that chronic stressors and depression may decrease the responsiveness of target tissues to cortisol. For instance, chronic stress is related to decreased sensitivity of immune cells to the anti-inflammatory effects of glucocorticoids (e.g., Miller, Cohen, & Ritchey, 2002).

Another pathway through which psychosocial factors may contribute to enhanced production of proinflammatory cytokines involves stress-related immune suppression (Fig. 3, Path C). Chronic stress impedes the immune response to infection, increasing risks for catching contagious diseases and having prolonged illness episodes, delaying wound healing, and increasing the risk for wound infection after injury. Thus, immune suppression may contribute to repeated, chronic, or slow-resolving infections or wounds, which subsequently enhance secretion of proinflammatory cytokines, a process that can serve to further inhibit certain aspects of immune responses. Finally, elevated proinflammatory cytokines may themselves impair cortisol signaling, and thus HPA axis regulation, by altering the functioning of glucocorticoid receptors in the brain (Fig. 3, Path D). As a result, elevated proinflammatory cytokines impair the ability of the HPA axis to regulate inflammatory processes, further enhancing proinflammatory cytokine production.

HEALTH IMPLICATIONS

Under normal conditions, elevated levels of proinflammatory cytokines are critical to resolving damage from infection and injury. However, chronic infections can result in persistent stimulation of immune and proinflammatory cytokine responses, leading to pathological effects (Hamerman, Berman, Albers, Brown, & Silver, 1999). For example, low levels of persistent inflammation may result when chronic infections such as periodontal disease, urinary tract infections, chronic pulmonary disease, and chronic renal disease continuously stimulate the immune system. In turn, chronic elevations in proinflammatory cytokines including IL-6 have substantially deleterious health implications, including links to a spectrum of conditions associated with aging. These conditions include cardiovascular disease, osteoporosis, arthritis, type 2 diabetes, certain cancers (including multiple myeloma, non-Hodgkin's lymphoma, and chronic lymphocytic leukemia), Alzheimer's disease, and periodontal disease (Ershler & Keller, 2000).

The association between cardiovascular disease and IL-6 has received increased attention in the past decade, in part because of the central role that IL-6 plays in promoting the production of C-reactive protein (CRP), recently recognized as an important risk factor for myocardial infarction (Papanicolaou et al., 1998). Elevations in both IL-6 and CRP levels are related to risk of future cardiovascular disease, myocardial infarction, and mortality, even in apparently healthy adults (Taubes, 2002).

More globally, chronic elevations in proinflammatory cytokines may be one key biological mechanism that fuels declines in physical function leading to frailty, disability, and, ultimately, death. Indeed, statistical analyses show that even after controlling for risk factors such as cholesterol levels, hypertension, and obesity, chronic IL-6 production continues to be an important indicator of physical decline among the very old (Ferrucci et al., 1999).

For these reasons, the role of chronic stress and depression in promoting IL-6 production should also have clinical relevance. Moreover, stress-related increases in proinflammatory cytokines may be particularly harmful for older adults. For instance, in our study of chronic-stress-related increases in IL-6, the average caregiver reached IL-6 levels that doubled his or her mortality risk by the age of 75; the average control participant in the study did not reach similar levels until the age of 90 (Kiecolt-Glaser et al., 2003).

CONCLUSION

Research has identified a key mechanism whereby chronic stress and depression may promote the development of chronic disease and speed aging of the immune system: elevated proinflammatory cytokine levels. This work demonstrates the shift in the field of psychoneuroimmunology away from focusing solely on chronic stress and immune suppression, toward integrating chronic stress and immune dysregulation in a model that emphasizes the balance between two important and adaptive mechanisms: inflammatory and anti-inflammatory responses.

Depression and chronic stress, by disrupting bidirectional communication between the brain and immune system, effectively damages the "brakes" that help restrain inflammatory responses, paving the way for increased production of proinflammatory cytokines through several distinct mechanisms. Depressive symptoms may increase production of proinflammatory cytokines following an infection or injury. Furthermore, chronic stress and depression accelerate age-related increases in production of proinflammatory cytokines, making these psychosocial stressors uniquely problematic for older adults.

Current work continues to establish relationships among chronic stress, depression, and proinflammatory cytokines. Future research must firmly establish proinflammatory cytokines as a key mediator between psychosocial factors and chronic disease. This requires longitudinal follow-up studies that not only track chronic stress, depression, and inflammation over time, but also include assessments of clinical indicators of chronic disease, such as coronary artery calcification in atherosclerosis. Ultimately, intervention studies will be needed to determine if treating chronic stress and depression can eventually restore immunological balance and affect health.

Recommended Reading

Irwin, M. (1999). Immune correlates of depression. In R. Dantzer, E.E. Wollmann, & R. Yirmiya (Eds.), *Cytokines, stress, and depression* (pp. 1–24). New York: Academic/ Plenum Publishers.

Kiecolt-Glaser, J.K., McGuire, L., Robles, T.F., & Glaser, R. (2002). Emotions, morbidity, and mortality: New perspectives from psychoneuroimmunology. *Annual Review of Psychology, 53*, 83–107.

Kiecolt-Glaser, J.K., McGuire, L., Robles, T.F., & Glaser, R. (2002). Psychoneuroim-munology: Psychological influences on immune function and health. *Journal of Consulting and Clinical Psychology, 70*, 537–547.

Miller, A.H. (1998). Neuroendocrine and immune system interactions in stress and depression. *Psychiatric Clinics of North America, 21*, 443–463.

Acknowledgments—Work on this article was supported by National Institutes of Health Grants P50 DE13749, P01 AG16321, AT002122, M01 RR034, and CA16058, and by a National Science Foundation Graduate Research Fellowship to the first author.

Note

1. Address correspondence to Janice K. Kiecolt-Glaser, Department of Psychiatry, Ohio State University College of Medicine, 1670 Upham Drive, Columbus, OH 43210-1228.

References

Ershler, W.B., & Keller, E.T. (2000). Age-associated increased interleukin-6 gene expression, late-life diseases, and frailty. *Annual Review of Medicine, 51*, 245–270.

Ferrucci, L., Harris, T., Guralnik, J., Tracy, R., Corti, M., Cohen, H., Penninx, B., Pahor, M., Wallace, R., & Havlik, R.J. (1999). Serum IL-6 level and the development of disability in older persons. *Journal of the American Geriatrics Society, 47*, 639–646.

Glaser, R., Robles, T.F., Sheridan, J., Malarkey, W.B., & Kiecolt-Glaser, J.K. (2003). Mild depressive symptoms are associated with amplified and prolonged inflammatory responses following influenza vaccination in older adults. *Archives of General Psychiatry, 60*, 1009–1014.

Hamerman, D., Berman, J.W., Albers, G.W., Brown, D.L., & Silver, D. (1999). Emerging evidence for inflammation in conditions frequently affecting older adults: Report of a symposium. *Journal of the American Geriatrics Society, 47*, 1016–1025.

Kenis, G., & Maes, M. (2002). Effects of antidepressants on the production of cytokines. *The International Journal of Neuropsychopharmacology, 5*, 401–412.

Kiecolt-Glaser, J.K., Preacher, K.J., MacCallum, R.C., Atkinson, C., Malarkey, W.B., & Glaser, R. (2003). Chronic stress and age-related increases in the proinflammatory cytokine interleukin-6. *Proceedings of the National Academy of Sciences, USA, 100*, 9090–9095.

Lutgendorf, S., Garand, L., Buckwalter, K.C., Reimer, T.T., Hong, S., & Lubaroff, D. (1999). Life stress, mood disturbance, and elevated interleukin-6 in healthy older women. *Journals of Gerontology Series A, Biological Sciences and Medical Sciences, 54A*, M434–M439.

Maier, S.F., & Watkins, L.R. (1998). Cytokines for psychologists: Implications of bidirectional immune-to-brain communication for understanding behavior, mood, and cognition. *Psychological Review, 105*, 83–107.

Miller, G.E., Cohen, S., & Ritchey, A.K. (2002). Chronic psychological stress and the regulation of proinflammatory cytokines: A glucocorticoid-resistance model. *Health Psychology, 21*, 531–541.

Miller, G.E., Stetler, C.A., Carney, R.M., Freedland, K.E., & Banks, W.A. (2002). Clinical depression and inflammatory risk markers for coronary heart disease. *American Journal of Cardiology, 90*, 1279–1283.

Papanicolaou, D.A., Wilder, R.L., Manolagas, S.C., & Chrousos, G.P. (1998). The pathophysiologic roles of interleukin-6 in human disease. *Annals of Internal Medicine, 128*, 127–137.

Raison, C.L., & Miller, A.H. (2003). When not enough is too much: The role of insufficient glucocorticoid signaling in the pathophysiology of stress-related disorders. *American Journal of Psychiatry, 160*, 1554–1565.

Segerstrom, S.C., & Miller, G.E. (2004). Psychological stress and the human immune system: A meta-analytic study of 30 years of inquiry. *Psychological Bulletin, 130*, 601–630.

Taubes, G. (2002). Does inflammation cut to the heart of the matter? *Science, 296*, 242–245.

Section 3: Critical Thinking Questions

1. Given that laboratory mice and rats have been selectively bred to thrive in an artificial environment (the lab) that is very different from the natural environment of their ancestors, is it possible to achieve ecological validity in experiments using these animals? What are the advantages and disadvantages of using inbred laboratory strains versus wild-caught animals or species that are not routinely used in laboratory studies (for example, lemmings).

2. What is the difference between establishing a correlation between two factors and establishing a causal relationship? In studies of stress effects on physiology and behavior in humans, do most studies establish correlations or causation?

3. Discuss strategies that can be used to tease apart pre-natal versus post-natal maternal influences on adult physiology and behavior in human and rodent studies.

4. Given that SSRIs alleviate depression by altering serotonin concentrations in synapses, is it reasonable to expect that the 5HTTLPR polymorphism also may modify the efficacy of SSRIs in treatment of depression? Why?

5. Medical conditions and treatments that are characterized by increased inflammation or cytokine production often precipitate depression. In these cases, it is a worrisome symptom or side effect. Is it possible that in nature, cytokine induced depressive-like behavior may actually be adaptive rather than maladaptive?

This article has been reprinted as it originally appeared in *Current Directions in Psychological Science*. Citation information for this article as originally published appears above.

Section 4: Drugs

The articles in the preceding two sections addressed plasticity and resilience in the brain, highlighting how experiences throughout life can alter brain structure and function. Exposure to commonly abused drugs, such as cocaine, amphetamine, opiates, nicotine, and alcohol, also can induce persistent changes in the brain, in turn affecting behavior. Furthermore, physical characteristics (sex, age, genotype, etc.), psychological state, past experiences, and environmental context can modify the behavioral and neurobiological effects of drugs. In the case of placebo effects, an inert substance produces measurable changes in brain activity and symptom relief in individuals who believe they have received an active drug. Likewise, drug-associated cues can acquire the ability to elicit changes in brain function, physiology, and behavior that resemble those induced by the drug itself (although typically at a lesser magnitude). Clearly, understanding how drugs affect the body, and successfully treating drug dependency, will require a holistic approach that takes into consideration not only the pharmacologic characteristics of the drug, but the circumstances under which it has been administered and the physiological, psychological and environmental factors that may have modified its effects.

The immediate and long-term effects of potentially addictive drugs on individuals are highly variable, and subject to pharmacological, psychological, and environmental influences. The first article in this section, by Hans Crombag and Terry Robinson, describes the interaction between drugs and the environment as an important factor influencing the behavioral and neurobiological changes that accompany repeated exposure to drugs of abuse. Historically, much of the effort in addiction research has focused on identifying the factors underlying the development of tolerance and physical dependence; in contrast, the current review focuses on factors that promote sensitization of motoric and neural responses to drugs. The authors argue that although associative learning (i.e., conditioning) and stress exposure play important roles in addiction, controlled studies indicate that the effects of a novel environment on the development of sensitization following repeated drug exposure can be dissociated from the effects of conditioning and exposure to stress-related hormones. Furthermore, the pattern of cocaine and amphetamine induced c-*fos* activation in regions of the brain that have been implicated in drug reinforcement differs in novel versus familiar environments. Thus, Crombag and Robinson propose that understanding how the environment contributes to individual differences in susceptibility to drug-induced sensitization may in turn illuminate the basis for individual differences in susceptibility to drug addiction and recidivism following sustained abstinence.

In the second article, Nick Goeders suggests that stress may increase vulnerability for drug abuse through a process analogous to sensitization.

Clinical studies report a high rate of co-occurrence between drug addiction and psychological trauma or elevated levels of life stress. Rodent studies confirm a causal relationship between stress and drug-taking behavior; exposure to stress, or corticosteroids (hormones released during stress), facilitates the acquisition of drug self-administration in naïve rats, and reinstates drug-seeking behavior in drug-exposed rats that have undergone extinction training. Furthermore, adrenalectomy, which eliminates endogenous corticosteroids, prevents the acquisition of drug self-administration at all doses. Taken together, these data suggest that stress and corticosteroids are important modulators of substance abuse. Because it is not possible to completely eliminate stress, focusing on reducing stress, building stress resilience, and normalizing circulating corticosteroid concentrations may reduce drug craving and relapse among individuals undergoing treatment for addiction.

Thomas Baker and colleagues focus on negative affect and drug craving during withdrawal as predictors of relapse in humans abstaining from nicotine. They postulate that withdrawal symptoms are elicited by two different types of deprivation: (1) pharmacological deprivation which occurs when drug levels drop within the body causing an escalation in negative symptoms, and (2) behavioral deprivation which occurs when drug users stop engaging in the self-administration rituals. Furthermore, they posit that early withdrawal symptoms are due primarily to pharmacologic withdrawal, whereas withdrawal symptoms that reemerge weeks or years following drug cessation are due primarily to behavioral withdrawal, and can be induced by drug craving or negative affect (regardless of cause). Based on the reviewed data, the authors propose that the efficacy of treatment for drug dependency could be improved if clients receive coping skills training prior to drug manipulation, and then once the drug-replacement phase begins, delivery is paired with the self-administration rituals.

Placebo treatment is effective in reducing symptoms in a large number health conditions. Through the review of placebo effects on brain activity and pain ratings, Wager demonstrates the potential for the mind to alter physiological states. For example, during anticipation of pain, placebo treatment increases brain activity in the anterior cingulated cortex, dorso lateral prefrontal cortex, and the orbitofrontal cortex, and more activity is associated with better amelioration of pain. The physiological and physiological mechanisms underlying placebo effects are largely unknown, although expectancy and self-efficacy appear to be important psychological components of the effect, and there is some evidence to suggest that activation of the endogenous opioid system may contribute to the physiological effects observed in placebo studies. Wager asserts that learning how much of a drug's effect is due to its pharmacological action versus expectancy, or an interaction between drug action and expectancy, is central to understanding how drugs affect the brain and behavior.

Drugs, Environment, Brain, and Behavior

Hans S. Crombag[1] and Terry E. Robinson[1]
University of Michigan, Ann Arbor

Abstract

The effects of psychoactive drugs are not just a function of their pharmacological actions, but are due to complex interactions among pharmacological, psychological, and environmental factors. We discuss here how drug-environment interactions determine the likelihood that addictive drugs produce a persistent form of neurobehavioral plasticity (sensitization) thought to be involved in the pathophysiology of addiction and relapse.

Keywords

sensitization; neuroplasticity; addiction; relapse; genes

In humans, the behavioral and subjective effects of drugs vary enormously, even within the same individual, because drug effects are due to complex interactions among pharmacological, psychological, and environmental factors—for instance, whether a drug is taken in a drug-associated environment (e.g., a "crack house"), whether drug paraphernalia (e.g., syringes, pipes) are present, and what expectation the individual has about the drug. That many Vietnam combat troops who became dependent on heroin while in Vietnam discontinued use upon their return to the United States illustrates the influence of environmental factors on drug use.

Early laboratory studies on drug-environment interactions typically used operant conditioning procedures to study the effects of different schedules of reinforcement (i.e., variations in when and how often behavior is reinforced). For example, in pigeons, the anesthetic pentobarbital either increases or decreases bar pressing to obtain food, depending on the schedule of reinforcement in place at the time the drug is administered. An especially compelling demonstration of how even a simple manipulation of environmental context can influence drug effects is the observation that the lethal dose of amphetamine in mice varies up to 10-fold depending on whether the drug is given in a large or small test cage, or to singly- or group-housed animals (see Kelleher & Morse, 1968, for reviews of the early literature).

Nonetheless, there has been very little work on how drug-environment interactions influence the behavioral and neurobiological effects of drugs of abuse, and there has been even less consideration of drug-environment interactions when drugs are administered repeatedly, as would be the case in developing addicts. In this article, we focus on how environmental conditions in which drugs are experienced modulate long-lasting changes in the brain (i.e., neuro-plasticity) that are caused by drug exposure—changes that are thought to be important in the transition to addiction and in relapse.

DRUGS CHANGE THE BRAIN

When a drug is taken repeatedly, some of its effects may decrease, or show tolerance, while other effects increase, or show sensitization. Historically, tolerance, and its role in the development of physical dependence, has been a central focus of research on addiction. However, increasing evidence suggests that long-lasting neurobiological changes related to sensitization play a critical role in addiction (Robinson & Berridge, 2003). This is in part because the behavioral and psychological drug effects that undergo sensitization include effects on motor activation (psychomotor sensitization), incentive motivation[2] (incentive sensitization), and the ability of drugs to sustain or reinforce drug-taking behavior (sensitization of drug reward). All of these behaviors and psychological processes are mediated in part by a neural circuit that involves the neurotransmitter dopamine and connects to many forebrain structures, in particular, the dorsal striatum, nucleus accumbens, pre-frontal cortex, and related neural circuitry. Indeed, it is generally recognized that these dopamine circuits are crucial for sensorimotor function and for the reward value of natural stimuli, such as food, drink, and sex, as well as drugs. It is not surprising, therefore, that sensitization-related neuroplastic changes have been found in many components of this circuitry, and it is hypothesized that these brain changes may render individuals hypersensitive to the incentive motivational effects of drugs and thereby contribute to the transition to addiction (Robinson & Berridge, 2003). Therefore, identifying factors that influence susceptibility to sensitization may help researchers understand some of the variability in susceptibility to drug addiction and relapse.

ENVIRONMENTAL MODULATION OF BEHAVIORAL SENSITIZATION

In a series of experiments, we and our colleagues have studied the influence of environmental context on the ability of drugs to produce psychomotor sensitization (Badiani, Browman, & Robinson, 1995). In these experiments, rats receive repeated injections of a drug in one of two conditions: either where they live (*home* condition) or in a distinct and relatively novel test cage (*novel* condition). (Note that the home and novel cages are physically identical, and the only difference between these conditions is in the relative novelty of the test environment where the rats receive drug treatments.) This simple environmental manipulation has a large effect on the ability of drugs to induce psychomotor sensitization, that is, the progressive increase in psychomotor activity produced by repeated drug treatment. Amphetamine, cocaine, and morphine produce much more robust sensitization when administered in the novel condition than when administered at home (Badiani, Browman, & Robinson, 1995; Badiani, Oates, & Robinson, 2000). Indeed, when all injection-related stimuli are eliminated by injecting the drug intravenously using remotely controlled pumps (i.e., injections are unsignaled), low to moderate doses of amphetamine given at home often fail to produce sensitization altogether (Browman, Badiani, & Robinson, 1998; Crombag et al., 2001; Crombag, Badiani, Maren, & Robinson, 2000; Crombag, Badiani, & Robinson, 1996). The results from one of these studies are shown in Figure 1a (note the progressive increase in psychomotor activation produced by amphetamine injections in the novel condition, but not in the home condition).

In follow-up studies, we found that environmental context does not determine sensitization in an all-or-none fashion but shifts the dose required to produce

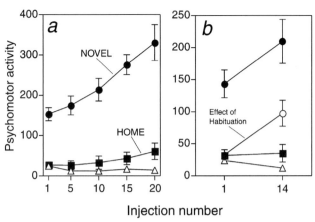

Fig. 1. Results of two independent studies in rats investigating the ability of environmental context to modulate the development of psychomotor sensitization. The level of psychomotor activity is graphed as a function of the number of unsignaled injections of amphetamine. The graph in (a) shows the psychomotor response by rats that received 20 injections (1 injection each day) of amphetamine in either the home (dark squares) or the novel (dark circles) condition. The triangle symbols show the response to control injections of saline. The graph in (b) shows the psychomotor response by rats that received 14 injections of amphetamine (results for first and last injection only are shown) in either the home (dark squares) or the novel (dark circles) condition, or after a 6- to 8-hr habituation to the novel environment prior to each injection (open circles). The triangle symbols show the response to control injections of saline. The graph in (a) is modified from Crombag, Badiani, Maren, and Robinson (2000) and has been adapted with permission of Elsevier. The graph in (b) is modified from Crombag et al. (2001) and has been adapted with permission of Nature Publishing Group.

sensitization. That is, when the dose is increased sufficiently, amphetamine and cocaine induce sensitization even at home (Browman et al., 1998).

Is It Conditioning?

How does this simple environmental manipulation exert such a profound effect on the susceptibility to psychomotor sensitization? One possibility is that when a drug is administered in a distinct test environment (the novel condition), that environment predicts the drug injection (i.e., becomes a conditioned stimulus) and reliably signals the experience of the drug's effects. In contrast, the home environment does not reliably signal drug administration because the rat lives there 24 hr a day. In other words, the differences in sensitization in the home and novel conditions might be due to facilitation of associative learning in the novel environment (Badiani, Browman, & Robinson, 1995; Crombag et al., 2000).[3] However, experiments do not support this interpretation. For example, drug treatment can be made predictable in the home condition by presenting discrete cues that predict administration of the drug (e.g., lights, tones), and this results in drug-environment conditioning, but has no influence on the development of sensitization (Crombag et al., 2000). Furthermore, degrading the predictive value of a novel environment by habituating the animals to it (i.e., keeping them there at times when the drug is not administered) eliminates drug-environment conditioning, but has no effect on the ability of the "novel" environment to promote sensitization (see Fig.1b—note that the response curve of the habituation condition is parallel to that of the novel condition, indicating an identical rate of sensitization).

Is It Stress?

Another possibility is that the novel environment facilitates sensitization because it acts as a stressor. Novel environments produce stresslike physiological and behavioral responses, and stressors enhance the behavioral and neurobiological responses to drugs. But when this hypothesis was tested, either by manipulating stress mechanisms surgically (by removing the adrenal glands, thereby preventing the release of "stress hormones" such as corticosterone; Badiani, Morano, Akil, & Robinson, 1995) or by habituating rats to the novel environment and making it less novel (see Fig. 1b; Crombag et al., 2001), sensitization was not affected. Habituation did, however, change the response to the first injection of the drug in the novel environment (Fig. 1b), as did adrenalectomy (Badiani, Morano, et al., 1995), suggesting that the effect of environment on the initial drug response is dissociable from its effects on sensitization.

ENVIRONMENT MODULATES DRUG EFFECTS IN THE BRAIN

Thus, relatively subtle variations in the environmental context in which drugs are repeatedly administered profoundly alter their long-term behavioral effects, and this is not readily accounted for by some immediate effect of the environment on stress or associative learning processes. Of course, stress and associative learning do have large effects on the actions of drugs, but it seems these processes do not account for the home-novel difference in sensitization.

Whatever the exact "psychological" difference between these two environments, environmental context has a profound effect on the neurobiological impact of drugs like amphetamine and cocaine, and this neurobiological effect may be directly responsible for the effect of environmental context on sensitization. How context influences the neurobiological actions of drugs has been studied by looking at activation of a class of genes in the brain, immediate early genes. The best known immediate early gene, c-fos, is readily activated by many forms of stimulation, including drugs, and because its activation is strongly correlated with neuronal activity, it provides a simple and sensitive indicator of where in the brain neurons are active.

Figure 2 shows the pattern of c-fos activation from one study in which rats were given a single injection of amphetamine or a control saline solution in a home or novel environment. It is obvious that the patterns of brain activation produced by amphetamine (i.e., areas where c-fos is activated following an injection of amphetamine) are very different depending on where the drug is administered. Three findings are particularly interesting: First, a novel environment by itself was sufficient to increase c-fos activation, but this activation occurred primarily

c-*fos* gene expression

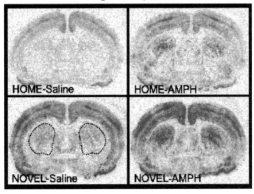

Fig. 2. Levels of c-*fos* activation in the brain after a single injection of amphetamine or saline solution in the home and the novel condition. The dashed outlines show the region of interest, the striatum, in both hemispheres. Darker shading indicates higher levels of c-*fos* activation. Photomicrograph provided by Susan M. Ferguson.

in the outer layers of the brain (i.e., in cerebral cortex; compare the saline response in the home vs. novel conditions). Second, the drug-environment interaction is most apparent in the areas of the brain that are critical for the psychomotor and rewarding effects of drugs, such as the dorsal striatum (compare the amphetamine response in the home vs. novel conditions). Third, in follow-up studies we have found that these differences are also present at the cellular level, in that the specific types of neurons that are activated by amphetamine or cocaine differ depending on environmental context (Badiani et al., 1998; Uslaner et al., 2001).

Although much work remains to be done, it is clear that the neuronal circuitry activated by drugs is powerfully modulated by changes in the environmental context in which the drugs are experienced. Presumably, these neurobiological effects contribute to the ability of drugs to sensitize brain regions that are involved in incentive motivational processes, and therefore play a role in the transition from casual drug use to the compulsive drug-seeking and drug-taking behavior seen in addiction (Robinson & Berridge, 2003).

ENVIRONMENTAL TRIGGERS OF RELAPSE

From a clinical perspective, understanding the factors involved in relapse in addicts is critically important. One reason for high rates of relapse may be that sensitization-related changes in brain reward systems are very persistent, if not permanent, rendering addicts highly susceptible to relapse even after long periods of abstinence (Robinson & Berridge, 2003). In addition, through associative learning processes, environmental stimuli (e.g., drug paraphernalia, drug-related environments) acquire the ability to activate these sensitized reward circuits, and become powerful incentives themselves.

In most animal studies, relapse is modeled using *reinstatement* procedures. In the first phase of these studies, an intravenous injection of a drug rewards rats for

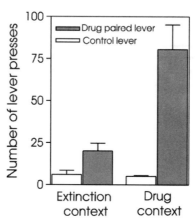

Fig. 3. Results of a reinstatement study with rats. The graph shows the number of lever presses made by the rats in a 2-hr session when they were either left in the extinction context or placed in the drug-associated context. Responding on a control lever that was not associated with delivery of the drug is shown for comparison. Modified from Crombag and Shaham (2002).

pressing a lever, and like many other species, rats learn to self-administer addictive drugs avidly.

Subsequently, the rats undergo extinction training sessions in which lever presses no longer result in the drug injection. Under these conditions, they typically show an initial burst in responding (called an extinction burst), followed by a steady decline in responding over test sessions. After extinction, lever-pressing behavior can be reinstated by drugs, by stressors, and also by environmental stimuli that have been associated with drug taking. In these types of experiments, the rate (and pattern) of responding observed under (nonreward) extinction conditions is typically used as a measure of drug seeking in rats.

For instance, in two experiments (Crombag, Grimm, & Shaham, 2002; Crombag & Shaham, 2002), when rats that had undergone extinction were reexposed to environmental stimuli associated with cocaine or speedball (a cocaine-heroin mixture), their rate of lever pressing returned to what it had been before extinction training (Fig. 3). Furthermore, this effect of environmental context was not seen when rats were pretreated with compounds that block the action of dopamine (Crombag et al., 2002). The fact that environmental stimuli associated with drug taking can activate brain reward circuits and trigger drug seeking may explain why relapse in humans is the rule, rather than the exception (and why contextual factors are so critical in relapse).

CONCLUSIONS AND ISSUES

In this brief review, we have emphasized that the context in which drugs of abuse are experienced has a large effect on their behavioral and neurobiological effects, and that drug-environment interactions powerfully modulate sensitization, which is thought to be involved in the transition to addiction. In addition, because environmental stimuli associated with drug taking can activate sensitized reward systems directly, they may contribute in a critical way to relapse.

Of course, many questions remain. For example, in all our studies on sensitization, we studied only the psychomotor-activating effects of drugs, and it is not known to what extent other drug effects are influenced in a similar manner. Paolone, Burdino, and Badiani (2003) reported recently that the home-novel manipulation modulates the development of sensitization to the psychomotor-activating effects of morphine, but does not modulate morphine's appetite-facilitating (prophasic) effects or analgesic effects. In addition, the lethal effects of high doses of cocaine are reduced when the drug is administered under novel conditions, relative to the home condition (Browman et al., 1998). Thus, not all drug effects and not all forms of drug-experience-dependent plasticity are modulated by environmental context in the same way. It will be especially important to directly determine if environmental context modulates sensitization to the incentive motivational effects of drugs of abuse.

A second issue concerns the mechanism (or mechanisms) by which the environment alters the susceptibility to sensitization, both at a behavioral-psychological level and at a neurobiological level. We have shown that drugs produce very different effects on the brain and engage different neural circuits depending on the context in which they are given (Badiani et al., 1998; Uslaner et al., 2001). But how alterations in cells and circuits lead to variation in the lasting effects of drugs on brain function and behavior is unknown. Certainly, the past few decades of research have provided an enormous increase in understanding of how addictive drugs alter neurochemical, cellular, and molecular processes in the brain. However, it now appears that to interpret such experimental findings, it will be important to consider some of the seemingly trivial aspects of the testing procedures that researchers use in their studies. Although behavioral scientists typically assess behavior in distinct and relatively novel test environments, many neuroscientists, for the sake of convenience, treat animals in their home cages. Therefore, it remains to be seen how well research findings on the neurobiology of addictive drugs integrate with those on the behavioral effects of these drugs.

The evidence reviewed here suggests that to fully understand the immediate and long-term consequences of addictive drugs on behavior and the brain will require a better appreciation of the environmental circumstances in which drugs are experienced. Indeed, when considering the problem of addiction, it is important to realize that although a large number of people experiment with potentially addictive drugs at some time, few develop an addiction. In other words, addiction is not an inevitable consequence of the mere self-administration of a potentially addictive drug. We suggest that complex interactions between drugs and environmental factors determine the likelihood that addictive drugs produce persistent alterations in neural circuits that contribute to the susceptibility to addiction and relapse.

Recommended Reading

Anagnostaras, S.G., & Robinson, T.E. (1996). Sensitization to the psychomotor stimulant effects of amphetamine: Modulation by associative learning. *Behavioral Neuroscience, 110*, 1397–1414.

Falk, J.L., & Feingold, D.A. (1987). Environmental and cultural factors in the behavioral action of drugs. In H.Y. Meltzer (Ed.), *Psychopharmacology: The third generation of progress* (pp. 1503–1510). New York: Raven Press.

Shalev, U., Grimm, J.W., & Shaham, Y. (2002). Neurobiology of relapse to heroin and cocaine seeking: A review. *Pharmacological Reviews, 54,* 1–42.

Stewart, J., & Badiani, A. (1993). Tolerance and sensitization to the behavioral effects of drugs. *Behavioural Pharmacology, 4,* 289–312.

Acknowledgments—We thank Susan M. Ferguson for providing the photomicrographs in Figure 2 and the many colleagues, in particular, Aldo Badiani and Yavin Shaham, who participated in the work summarized in this review.

Notes

1. Address correspondence to Hans S. Crombag or Terry E. Robinson, Department of Psychology, The University of Michigan, Ann Arbor, MI 48109-1109; e-mail: hcrombag @psy.jhu.edu or ter@umich.edu.

2. Incentive motivation refers to the psychological process by which objects, events, places, and their mental representations become attractive and wanted (incentive salience) and thereby acquire the ability to control goal-directed behavior.

3. For instance, some researchers have argued that through repeated pairing of the novel environment with the drug effects, environmental stimuli could acquire conditioned stimulus properties and thus the ability to elicit a conditioned "druglike" response. In this view, sensitization occurs because with repeated drug treatments the progressively increasing conditioned response adds to the unchanging unconditioned psychomotor drug effects.

References

Badiani, A., Browman, K.E., & Robinson, T.E. (1995). Influence of novel versus home environments on sensitization to the psychomotor stimulant effects of cocaine and amphetamine. *Brain Research, 674*(2), 291–298.

Badiani, A., Morano, M.I., Akil, H., & Robinson, T.E. (1995). Circulating adrenal hormones are not necessary for the development of sensitization to the psychomotor activating effects of amphetamine. *Brain Research, 673*(1), 13–24.

Badiani, A., Oates, M.M., Day, H.E., Watson, J., Akil, H., & Robinson, T.E. (1998). Amphetamine-induced behavior, dopamine release, and c-fos mRNA expression: Modulation by environmental novelty. *The Journal of Neuroscience, 10,* 10579–10593.

Badiani, A., Oates, M.M., & Robinson, T.E. (2000). Modulation of morphine sensitization in the rat by contextual stimuli. *Psychopharmacology, 151*(2–3), 273–282.

Browman, K.E., Badiani, A., & Robinson, T.E. (1998). The influence of environment on the induction of sensitization to the psychomotor activating effects of intravenous cocaine in rats is dose-dependent. *Psychopharmacology, 137*(1), 90–98.

Crombag, H.S., Badiani, A., Chan, J., Dell'Orco, J., Dineen, S.P., & Robinson, T.E. (2001). The ability of environmental context to facilitate psychomotor sensitization to amphetamine can be dissociated from its effect on acute drug responsiveness and on conditioned responding. *Neuropsychopharmacology, 24,* 680–690.

Crombag, H.S., Badiani, A., Maren, S., & Robinson, T.E. (2000). The role of contextual versus discrete drug-associated cues in promoting the induction of psychomotor sensitization to intravenous amphetamine. *Behavioural Brain Research, 116,* 1–22.

Crombag, H.S., Badiani, A., & Robinson, T.E. (1996). Signalled versus unsignalled intravenous amphetamine: Large differences in the acute psychomotor response and sensitization. *Brain Research, 722*(1–2), 227–231.

Crombag, H.S., Grimm, J.W., & Shaham, Y. (2002). Effect of dopamine receptor antagonists on renewal of cocaine seeking by reexposure to drug-associated contextual cues. *Neuropsychopharmacology, 27*, 1006–1015.

Crombag, H.S., & Shaham, Y. (2002). Renewal of drug seeking by contextual cues after prolonged extinction in rats. *Behavioral Neuroscience, 116*(1), 169–173.

Kelleher, R.T., & Morse, W.H. (1968). Determinants of the specificity of behavioral effects of drugs. *Ergebnisse der Physiologie, 60*, 1–56.

Paolone, G., Burdino, R., & Badiani, A. (2003). Dissociation in the modulatory effects of environmental novelty on the locomotor, analgesic, and eating response to acute and repeated morphine in the rat. *Psychopharmacology, 166*(2), 146–155.

Robinson, T.E., & Berridge, K.B. (2003). *Addiction. Annual Review of Psychology, 54*, 25–53.

Uslaner, J., Badiani, A., Day, H.E., Watson, S.J., Akil, H., & Robinson, T.E. (2001). Environmental context modulates the ability of cocaine and amphetamine to induce c-fos mRNA expression in the neocortex, caudate nucleus, and nucleus accumbens. *Brain Research, 920*(1–2), 106–116.

This article has been reprinted as it originally appeared in *Current Directions in Psychological Science*. Citation information for this article as originally published appears above.

Stress, Motivation, and Drug Addiction

Nick E. Goeders[1]

Departments of Pharmacology & Therapeutics and Psychiatry,
Louisiana State University Health Sciences Center

Abstract

A growing clinical literature indicates that there is a link between substance abuse and stress. One explanation for the high co-occurrence of stress-related disorders and drug addiction is the self-medication hypothesis, which suggests that a dually diagnosed person often uses the abused substance to cope with tension associated with life stressors or to relieve symptoms of anxiety and depression resulting from a traumatic event. However, another characteristic of self-administration is that drug delivery and its subsequent effects on the hypothalamic-pituitary-adrenal (HPA) axis are under the direct control of the individual. This controlled activation of the HPA axis may produce an internal state of arousal or stimulation that is actually sought by the individual. During abstinence, exposure to stressors or drug-associated cues can stimulate the HPA axis and thereby remind the individual about the effects of the abused substance, thus producing craving and promoting relapse. Stress reduction, either alone or in combination with pharmacotherapies targeting the HPA axis, may prove beneficial in reducing cravings and promoting abstinence in individuals seeking treatment for addiction.

Keywords

HPA axis; reward; vulnerability; stress; relapse

The mere mention of the word stress often conjures up images of heart disease, ulcers, and serious psychiatric disorders triggered through negative interactions with the environment. In reality, however, stress is not always associated with negative events. Selye (1975), who is generally accepted as the father of modern stress-related research, defined stress as the nonspecific response of the body to any demand placed upon it to adapt, whether that demand produces pleasure or pain. Accordingly, stress can result from a job promotion or the loss of a job, the birth of a child or the loss of a loved one, or any number of events, both positive and negative, that affect the daily life of an individual.

The two primary biological systems that are typically activated during and immediately after exposure to a stressor are the sympathetic nervous system and the hypothalamic-pituitary-adrenal (HPA) axis (Stratakis & Chrousos, 1995). The activation of these systems produces a stress response, or *stress cascade*, that is responsible for allowing the body to make the changes required to cope with the demands of a challenge. Sympathetic nervous system responses often include the release of the neurotransmitter norepinephrine, an increase in heart rate, a shift in blood flow to skeletal muscles, an increase in blood glucose, and a dilation of the pupils (for better vision), all in preparation for fight or flight (i.e., facing the stressor or attempting to escape from it). The HPA axis is initially activated by the secretion of corticotropin-releasing hormone (CRH) from the hypothalamus in response to a stressor (Goeders, 2002). CRH binds to receptors located in the anterior pituitary, causing the production of several substances, including adreno-corticotropin hormone (ACTH). When ACTH reaches the adrenal glands, it stimulates the biosynthesis and secretion of adrenocorticosteroids (i.e., cortisol in humans or corticosterone in rats). Cortisol travels through the bloodstream to produce a variety of effects throughout the body.

STRESS AND VULNERABILITY TO ADDICTION IN HUMANS

It is not ethical to conduct clinical studies on the effects of stress on the vulnerability for addiction in people without a history of drug abuse because no one should be intentionally put at risk for developing an addiction by being exposed to a substance with the potential for abuse. Therefore, scientists must rely on retrospective studies, and there is a growing body of clinical studies suggesting a link between stress and addiction. Combat veterans, especially those with posttraumatic stress disorder (PTSD), appear to have an elevated risk for substance abuse. Veterans with PTSD typically report more use of alcohol, cocaine, and heroin than veterans who do not meet the criteria for diagnosis of PTSD (Zaslav, 1994). However, people exposed to stressors other than combat, such as an unhappy marriage, dissatisfaction with employment, or harassment, also report higher-than-average rates of addiction. Sexual abuse, trauma, and sexual harassment are more likely to produce symptoms of PTSD and alcoholism or other addictions in women than in men (Newton-Taylor, DeWit, & Gliksman, 1998).

Despite these findings, however, it is difficult to determine if stressors, sexual trauma, or PTSD actually lead to subsequent substance use or if substance use contributes to the traumatic events or the development of PTSD in the first place. Obviously, not everyone who experiences trauma and PTSD is a substance abuser, and not every drug addict can trace his or her addiction to some specific stressor or traumatic event. Nevertheless, prevalence estimates suggest that the rate of substance abuse among individuals with PTSD may be as high as 60 to 80%, and the rate of PTSD among substance abusers is between 40 and 60% (Donovan, Padin-Rivera, & Kowaliw, 2001). These numbers show a clear relationship between PTSD and substance abuse. One explanation for the high co-occurrence of PTSD and drug addiction (i.e., dual diagnosis) is the self-medication hypothesis. According to this hypothesis, a dually diagnosed person often uses the abused substance to cope with tension associated with life stressors or to relieve or suppress symptoms of anxiety, irritability, and depression resulting from a traumatic event (Khantzian, 1985).

VULNERABILITY TO ADDICTION: ANIMAL STUDIES

It is much easier to conduct prospective studies on the effects of stress on the vulnerability for addiction in animals than in humans. These animal studies typically investigate the effects of stress on the propensity to learn drug-taking behavior (which is often referred to as the "acquisition" of drug taking). In a typical experiment, the animals come into contact with a drug and its potentially rewarding effects for the first time (Goeders, 2002), and the researcher investigates what dose or how much time is necessary for them to learn to make the response (e.g., a lever press) that leads to drug delivery, thereby producing reinforcement. Environmental events (e.g., stressors) that decrease the lowest dose that is recognized by an animal as a reinforcer (i.e., that leads to acquisition of the response) are considered to increase vulnerability to acquire drug-taking behavior. Another measure of acquisition is the time required for the animal to reach a specified behavioral criterion (e.g., a specified frequency of the response that leads to drug delivery).

The ability of stressors to alter the acquisition of drug taking in rats has received considerable attention (Goeders, 2002; Piazza & Le Moal, 1998). For example, studies have shown that sensitivity to amphetamine and cocaine is enhanced in rats exposed to stressors such as tail pinch and neonatal isolation. Electric shock to the feet is another stressor used in rat experiments. In a study on the effects of controllable versus uncontrollable stress, my colleagues and I modeled controllable stress by administering shocks whenever the rats made a particular response, and uncontrollable stress by administering shocks that were not contingent on the rats' behavior (Goeders, 2002). Rats that were exposed to uncontrollable stress were more sensitive to low doses of cocaine than rats that were exposed to controllable stress or that were not shocked at all; this finding demonstrates that control over a stressor can change the effects of that stressor on the vulnerability for drug taking (Goeders, 2002).

Given that uncontrollable stress made animals more sensitive to cocaine, my colleagues and I hypothesized that this process may have resulted from the stress-induced activation of the HPA axis. Because corticosterone (cortisol) is secreted as the final step of HPA-axis activation, we next studied the effects of daily injections of corticosterone on the acquisition of cocaine taking. These injections produced an increase in sensitivity to cocaine that was almost identical to what we saw with uncontrollable stress. In a related experiment, rats' adrenal glands were surgically removed (i.e., adrenalectomy) to effectively eliminate the final step in HPA-axis activation. These rats did not self-administer cocaine at any dose tested, even though they quickly learned to respond to obtain food pellets. Thus, the rats could still learn and perform the necessary lever-pressing response, but cocaine was apparently no longer rewarding. In another series of experiments, the synthesis of corticosterone was blocked with daily injections of ketoconazole, and this reduced both the rate of acquisition of cocaine self-administration and the number of rats that eventually reached the criterion for acquisition of this behavior. Taken together, these data suggest an important role for stress and the subsequent activation of the HPA axis in the vulnerability for drug taking.

How does exposure to a stressor increase the vulnerability for drug taking? This biological phenomenon likely occurs via a process analogous to sensitization, whereby repeated but intermittent injections of cocaine increase the behavioral and neurochemical responses to subsequent exposure to the drug (Piazza & Le Moal, 1998). Exposure to stressors or injections of corticosterone can also result in a sensitization to cocaine, and these effects are attenuated in rats that have had their adrenal glands removed or corticosterone synthesis inhibited. Although exposure to the stressor itself may be aversive in many cases, the net result is reflected as an increased sensitivity to the drug. This suggests that if individuals are particularly sensitive to stress or find themselves in an environment where they do not feel that they have adequate control over their stress, they may be especially likely to engage in substance abuse.

STRESS AND RELAPSE TO ADDICTION

Clinical studies of drug addicts have demonstrated that reexposure to the abused substance, exposure to stressors, or simply the presentation of stress-related imagery is a potent event for provoking relapse. However, simply exposing an addict to environmental stimuli or cues previously associated with drug taking can also produce intense drug craving (Robbins, Ehrman, Childress, & O'Brien, 1999). Such environmental stimuli include locations where the drug was purchased or used, the individuals the drug was purchased from or used with, and associated drug paraphernalia. In fact, the cycling, relapsing nature of addiction has been proposed to result, at least in part, from exposure to environmental cues that have been previously paired with drug use. Presumably, the repeated pairing of these cues with the chronic use of the drug can lead to a classical conditioning of the drug's effects, so that exposure to these stimuli following abstinence produces responses reminiscent of responses to the drug itself. These conditioned responses elicit increased desire or craving, thus leading to relapse.

Reinstatement is generally accepted as an animal model of the propensity to relapse to drug taking (Stewart, 2000). With this model, animals are taught to self-administer a drug until they reach a stable level of drug intake; they are then subjected to prolonged periods during which the response that previously resulted in drug delivery no longer does so (i.e., extinction). Once drug-taking behavior has extinguished, or following a specified period of abstinence, the rats are tested to see if specific stimuli will reinstate the response previously associated with drug taking (Goeders, 2002). Such reinstatement of drug-seeking behavior can be elicited by injections of the drug itself or by exposure to brief periods of intermittent electric shock to the feet (i.e., stress). In her review of reinstatement, Stewart (2000) described how norepinephrine and CRH are important for stress-induced reinstatement, which should be no surprise because norepinephrine and CRH are produced during the activation of the sympathetic nervous system and HPA axis, respectively.

Stimuli that were paired with the drug during self-administration can become environmental cues that can be presented following extinction to reinstate responding (See, 2002). Reinstatement that occurs under these conditions is referred to as cue-induced reinstatement. The fact that cue-induced reinstatement occurs suggests that exposure to a physical stressor or a "taste" of cocaine itself is not a necessary prerequisite for relapse. My colleagues and I have reported that the corticosterone synthesis inhibitor ketoconazole reverses the cue-induced reinstatement of cocaine seeking and also decreases the increases in corticosterone observed in the blood during reinstatement (Goeders, 2002). The CRH receptor blocker CP-154,526 also attenuates cue-induced reinstatement. Taken together, these data suggest an important role for the HPA axis in the ability of environmental cues to stimulate cocaine-seeking behavior in rats and relapse in humans. Treatment for relapse may therefore be improved by developing behavioral or pharmacological therapies that reduce HPA-axis responses induced by environmental cues previously associated with drug use.

IMPLICATIONS

Data obtained from both human and animal investigations indicate that exposure to stress increases the vulnerability for addiction. The animal literature suggests that stress increases reward associated with drugs such as cocaine and amphetamine through a process similar to sensitization. The growing literature on drug addiction indicates that there is a similar link between substance abuse and stress, as reflected in the high co-occurrence of PTSD and drug addiction. One explanation for this link is the self-medication hypothesis (Khantzian, 1985), according to which a dually diagnosed person often uses the abused substance to cope with tension associated with life stressors or to relieve or suppress symptoms of anxiety and depression resulting from a traumatic event. On the surface, however, this hypothesis may appear somewhat counterintuitive. Many abused substances (especially cocaine) can induce anxiety and panic in humans and anxiety-like responses in animals through direct effects on CRH release (Goeders, 1997, 2002). One might expect that this augmented HPA-axis activity would increase the aversive effects of the drug and reduce the motivation for it. During the acquisition of drug-taking behavior, however, exposure to aversive, stressful stimuli may actually sensitize individuals, making them more sensitive to the rewarding properties of the drug. Once drug taking has been acquired, the positive aspects of drug reward likely mitigate the drug's potential anxiety-like effects (Goeders, 2002).

However, another characteristic of self-administration is that drug delivery and its subsequent effects on the HPA axis are under the direct control of the individual. This is an important consideration because controllability and predictability of a stressor significantly decrease its aversive effects (Levine, 2000). If the individual controls when the drug is administered, he or she also controls when the activation of the HPA axis occurs. This controlled activation of the HPA axis may result in an internal state of arousal or stimulation that is rewarding to the individual (Goeders, 2002). This internal state may be analogous to the one produced during novelty or sensation seeking (e.g., in thrill seekers or sensation seekers), which may also be involved in drug reward (Wagner, 2001). Drug taking by some substance abusers may therefore be an attempt to seek out specific sensations, and the internal state produced may be very similar to that perceived by individuals who engage in risky, thrill-seeking behavior. Such sensation seekers have been reported to be at elevated risk for abusing a variety of substances, including cocaine, opioids, alcohol, cannabis, and nicotine.

Once an individual has stopped using a drug, exposure to stressors or drug-associated cues can stimulate the sympathetic nervous system and the HPA axis and thereby remind the individual about the effects of the abused substance, thus producing craving and promoting relapse (Goeders, 2002). Therefore, continued investigations into how stress and the subsequent activation of the HPA axis play a role in addiction will result in more effective and efficient treatments for substance abuse in humans. Stress-reduction and coping strategies, either alone or in combination with pharmacotherapies targeting the HPA axis, may prove beneficial in reducing cravings and promoting abstinence in individuals seeking treatment for addiction.

Recommended Reading

Goeders, N.E. (2002). (See References)

Piazza, P.V., & Le Moal, M. (1998). (See References)

Sarnyai, Z., Shaham, Y., & Heinrichs, S.C. (2001). The role of corticotropin-releasing factor in drug addiction. *Pharmacological Reviews, 53*, 209–243.

See, R.E. (2002). (See References)

Shalev, U., Grimm, J.W., & Shaham, Y. (2002). Neurobiology of relapse to heroin and cocaine seeking: A review. *Pharmacological Reviews, 54*, 1–42.

Acknowledgments—This work was supported by U.S. Public Health Service Grants DA06013 and DA13463 from the National Institute on Drug Abuse.

Note

1. Address correspondence to Nick E. Goeders, Department of Pharmacology & Therapeutics, LSU Health Sciences Center, P.O. Box 33932, 1501 Kings Highway, Shreveport, LA 71130-3932; e-mail: ngoede@lsuhsc.edu.

References

Donovan, B., Padin-Rivera, E., & Kowaliw, S. (2001). "Transcend": Initial outcomes from a posttraumatic stress disorder/substance abuse treatment program. *Journal of Trauma Stress, 14*, 757–772.

Goeders, N.E. (1997). A neuroendocrine role in cocaine reinforcement. *Psychoneuroendocrinology, 22*, 237–259.

Goeders, N.E. (2002). Stress and cocaine addiction. *Journal of Pharmacology and Experimental Therapeutics, 301*, 785–789.

Khantzian, E.J. (1985). The self-medication hypothesis of addictive disorders: Focus on heroin and cocaine dependence. *American Journal of Psychiatry, 142*, 1259–1264.

Levine, S. (2000). Influence of psychological variables on the activity of the hypothalamic-pituitary adrenal axis. *European Journal of Pharmacology, 405*, 149–160.

Newton-Taylor, B., DeWit, D., & Gliksman, L. (1998). Prevalence and factors associated with physical and sexual assault of female university students in Ontario. *Health Care for Women International, 19*, 155–164.

Piazza, P.V., & Le Moal, M. (1998). The role of stress in drug self-administration. *Trends in Pharmacological Science, 19*, 67–74.

Robbins, S.J., Ehrman, R.N., Childress, A.R., & O'Brien, C.P. (1999). Comparing levels of cocaine cue reactivity in male and female outpatients. *Drug and Alcohol Dependence, 53*, 223–230.

See, R.E. (2002). Neural substrates of conditioned-cued relapse to drug-seeking behavior. *Pharmacology Biochemistry and Behavior, 71*, 517–529.

Selye, H. (1975). Confusion and controversy in the stress field. *Journal of Human Stress, 1*, 37–44.

Stewart, J. (2000). Pathways to relapse: The neurobiology of drug- and stress-induced relapse to drug-taking. *Journal of Psychiatry and Neuroscience, 25*, 125–136.

Stratakis, C.A., & Chrousos, G.P. (1995). Neuroendocrinology and pathophysiology of the stress system. *Annals of the New York Academy of Sciences, 771*, 1–18.

Wagner, M.K. (2001). Behavioral characteristics related to substance abuse and risk-taking, sensation-seeking, anxiety sensitivity, and self-reinforcement. *Addictive Behaviors, 26*, 115–120.

Zaslav, M.R. (1994). Psychology of comorbid posttraumatic stress disorder and substance abuse: Lessons from combat veterans. *Journal of Psychoactive Drugs, 26*, 393–400.

Pharmacologic and Behavioral Withdrawal From Addictive Drugs

Timothy B. Baker[1], Sandra J. Japuntich, Joanne M. Hogle,
Danielle E. McCarthy, and John J. Curtin
University of Wisconsin-Madison

Abstract

Recent theories suggest that drug withdrawal does not motivate drug use and relapse. However, data now show that withdrawal produces complex changes over time in at least two symptoms (i.e., negative affect and urges) that are highly predictive of relapse. Evidence suggests that falling levels of the drug in the blood and interruption of the drug self-administration ritual both affect these symptoms. Both of these forms of withdrawal motivate renewed drug use in addicted individuals.

Keywords

smoking; tobacco dependence; tobacco withdrawal; drug withdrawal

Addicts have written powerfully about the "abstinence agony" that occurs when they stop using a drug. For instance, Sigmund Freud described quitting smoking as an "agony beyond human power to bear." One would assume from such accounts that drug withdrawal produces a powerful motive to resume or continue drug use. Indeed, movies and other popular accounts of addiction typically emphasize the role of withdrawal. However, current theoretical models of addiction downplay the role of drug withdrawal in the maintenance of addictive behaviors (Robinson & Berridge, 1993). Such models hold that withdrawal symptoms do not motivate relapse; for example, measures of withdrawal severity do not predict who is likely to relapse. Also, these models assert that withdrawal is brief and, therefore, cannot account for relapse that occurs long after drug use. Finally, these models assert that effective addiction treatments do not work via the suppression of withdrawal symptoms. These theoretical views of drug motivation emphasize incentive or reward processes rather than withdrawal.

In contrast to the claims of recent theories, addicted individuals typically report that withdrawal symptoms motivate them to relapse and that fear of withdrawal causes them to maintain drug use. There is now mounting evidence that the addicted individuals are correct—that withdrawal is a crucial motivator of their drug use. While drug use is no doubt determined by multiple factors, there is compelling evidence that, in the addicted individual, withdrawal potently influences the fluctuating course of drug motivation.

We believe that the motivational impact of withdrawal has been obscured by a failure to assess it sensitively and comprehensively. There are two reasons for this failure. One is that withdrawal is multidimensional, and only some elements, such as urges and negative affect, have motivational relevance. Unless studies focus on these symptoms, the motivational impact of withdrawal may be lost. The second reason is that most previous assessments of withdrawal have not adequately captured its dynamic symptom patterns, which may be both highly complex and persistent. These complex symptom patterns provide important clues regarding the nature and determinants of withdrawal. Withdrawal symptoms appear to reflect the effects of two distinct types of deprivation: deprivation of the drug molecule and deprivation of the drug-use instrumental response (such as injecting a drug or lighting and smoking a cigarette). A reduced level of the drug in the body, or *pharmacologic withdrawal*, results in the escalation of symptoms that has traditionally been labeled withdrawal. However, ceasing drug use also deprives the individual of a behavioral means of regulating or coping with escalating symptoms such as negative affect—in other words, it also causes *behavioral withdrawal*. At the heart of this model is the notion that the self-administration ritual per se quells withdrawal symptoms and that the absence of the ritual will actually exacerbate symptoms because of a disruption in symptom-regulatory processes. In theory, this disruption leads to very persistent and complex symptom profiles because symptoms may arise in response to cues that occur months after discontinuing drug use. This symptom dysregulation will persist until drug cues lose their associative strength (e.g., via extinction) and/or until the individual acquires a coping response that replaces use of the drug.

COMPONENTS OF WITHDRAWAL

Physical Signs

Previous views of withdrawal have been unduly influenced by characteristics of the physical symptoms of withdrawal. Each class of addictive drug produces a withdrawal syndrome that comprises different sorts of physical signs. For instance, ethanol withdrawal produces tremors, exaggerated reflexive behavior, and sometimes convulsions. Opiate withdrawal produces hypothermia, piloerection (gooseflesh), rhinnorhea (nasal discharge), and diarrhea. These signs all tend to follow the same rise-and-fall pattern after the discontinuation of drug use, with symptoms being largely absent within a couple of weeks after cessation.

Research has shown that these physical signs are not consistently related to drug motivation (e.g., Baker, Piper, McCarthy, Majeskie, & Fiore, 2004), supporting the idea that withdrawal is motivationally inert. However, the motivational irrelevance of these physical signs should not be surprising as they are so dissimilar across different types of drugs. If withdrawal has a motivational influence that is common to all addictive drugs, it seems sensible to look for this influence among the symptoms that are themselves common across drugs. Negative affect and drug urges are such symptoms.

Negative Affect

Many of the symptoms used to characterize withdrawal are, in fact, affective terms such as "irritable," "stressed," "anxious," and "depressed." Robust correlations are observed between measures of withdrawal and mood, and factor-analytic studies have demonstrated that affective items capture much of the reliable variance in withdrawal measures (Piasecki et al., 2000). Experimental manipulations of tobacco withdrawal in the laboratory prompt increases in self-reported and physiological indicators of negative affect (Hogle & Curtin, in press).

A listing of negative mood adjectives does not do justice to the affective consequences of withdrawal. Addicted individuals commonly report that giving up a drug seems like losing a dear friend or experiencing a death of a family member. We believe that this reflects a crucial part of the withdrawal syndrome: a feeling akin to social loss or separation distress. Indeed, at the neuropharmacologic and experiential levels, withdrawal produces effects similar to intense social loss (Panksepp, Herman, Connor, Bishop, & Scott, 1978). However, the relationship with the drug, once lost, can be reinstated at any time.

There is evidence that the emotional distress of withdrawal differs from other withdrawal elements in terms of both its motivational significance and its physiological substrata. For instance, researchers have shown that brain structures associated with the motivational components of the withdrawal syndrome (e.g., negative affect) show different sensitivity to the opioid antagonist, naloxone, than do brain structures associated with the somatic components (Frenois, Cador, Caille, Stinus, & Le Moine, 2002). In addition, research shows that it is the affective and not the somatic signs of withdrawal that are responsible for its motivational effects (Mucha, 1987; Piasecki et al., 2000). In sum, assessment strategies should target the affective elements of the withdrawal syndrome if the intent is to assess drug motivation or relapse vulnerability.

Urge/Craving

An urge may be viewed as the conscious recognition of the desire to use a drug. Since a variety of influences may stimulate such desire and make it available to consciousness, urges are not uniquely related to withdrawal (as negative affect is not uniquely related). However, urge measures appear to be sensitive indices of withdrawal and rise precipitously in response to abstinence (Baker et al., 2004).

There exist both biological and theoretical reasons to distinguish urges from the emotional components of withdrawal. First, urges and withdrawal-related affectivity appear to be associated with different physiologic substrata (e.g., Curtin, McCarthy, Piper, & Baker, 2006). Moreover, urges show different trajectories in response to drug removal and environmental events (McCarthy, Piasecki, Fiore, & Baker, in press). Finally, as we shall review momentarily, urges appear to exert their own distinct motivational influences.

EXTRACTING MEANING FROM COMPLEX WITHDRAWAL PROFILES

As noted earlier, most studies of withdrawal have assumed a standard pattern across time (waveform) for all symptoms and signs. This was used, either implicitly or explicitly, to justify simplistic measurement strategies. Researchers often used only a single measure of peak or average withdrawal, collapsing all symptoms together, to reflect the potentially meaningful information. Interviews with addicted individuals, however, indicate that they experience strong urges and negative affect many weeks after discontinuing drug use. This suggests that withdrawal

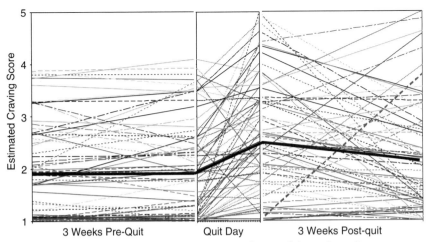

Fig. 1. Estimated cigarette-craving growth curves for 70 adult smokers. Craving ratings were collected multiple times per day for 3 weeks before and after the target quit date. The central panel labeled "Quit Day" reflects the change in craving ratings from just before to just after midnight on the quit day. The heavy black line represents the mean trend in craving ratings across individuals (from McCarthy, Piasecki, Fiore, & Baker, in press).

patterns should be assessed in a more comprehensive manner. Therefore, we measured profiles of withdrawal symptoms, especially urges and negative affect, so as to capture their average elevation, trajectories (e.g., whether symptoms are worsening or improving), rise times (how quickly symptoms increase following abstinence), durations, and reactivity to stressors and environmental events.

Waveforms of urges and affective symptoms show dramatic differences from one person to the next and possess motivational relevance (see Fig. 1; McCarthy, Piasecki et al., in press). When researchers measure withdrawal in a way that captures this variability, strong relations with smoking relapse are obtained. For instance, relapse to smoking is consistently and powerfully predicted by such measures as the rise time of craving, the average levels of craving and negative affect, and the duration of high levels of craving and negative affect (Baker et al., 2004). Moreover, such measurement strategies show that withdrawal symptoms are very persistent and predict the occurrence of relapses long after the initiation of the attempt to quit. Finally, these strategies have shown that suppression of withdrawal can indeed account for the therapeutic effects of drug treatments for addiction. For instance, recent studies show that smoking-cessation pharmacotherapies reduce relapse risk, at least in part, by suppressing negative affect and craving (McCarthy, Bolt, & Baker, in press). In sum, when researchers measure the temporal dynamics of urges and affective withdrawal symptoms, the resulting profiles provide insights into why addicted individuals persist in drug use and how treatments can help them quit.

WITHDRAWAL AS CONTROL-SYSTEM DYSREGULATION

The preceding discussion raises several questions. For instance, what could cause the highly variable and prolonged symptoms that are observed, and should these be considered withdrawal?

Dependent drug users cite affect regulation as a major reason for drug use, and research supports their claims. Addicted individuals have learned through repeated pairings of drug use with withdrawal relief that addictive drugs are extremely effective at quelling the affective distress and urges occasioned by withdrawal (Baker et al., 2004). It is not surprising, then, that when addicts stop using a drug they show evidence of symptom dys-regulation. Evidence of symptom dys-regulation is found in the prolonged and variable affective and urge symptoms noted earlier (e.g., Piasecki et al., 2000) and in smokers' amplified emotional and urge responses to environmental events (see Fig. 2; McCarthy, Piasecki et al., in press). In addition, laboratory research using both psychophysiological and neuroendocrine responses finds that smokers in withdrawal show disturbed patterns of emotion regulation in response to stressors (Hogle & Curtin, in press).

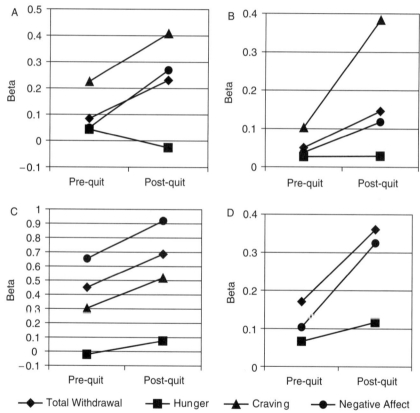

Fig. 2. The degree of association between four episodic events—smoking in the past 15 minutes (A), exposure to others' smoking since the last report (B), occurrence of stressful events since the last report (C), and occurrence of a strong urge or temptation to smoke since the last report (D)—and withdrawal symptoms. Episodic event coefficients (beta values) reflect changes in overall withdrawal summary scores (collapsed across specific symptoms) and hunger, smoking-urge (craving), and negative-affect (sadness, worry, and irritability) ratings associated with each of the events; these were estimated separately in the pre-quit and post-quit periods.

Thus, both self-report and physiological measures point to withdrawal-induced dysregulation of negative affect (Hogle & Curtin, in press; McCarthy, Piasecki et al., in press). If withdrawal varies in intensity, trajectory, and duration across individuals, is there a common mechanism that accounts for this variability? We believe that prolonged symptom dysregulation following withdrawal occurs because addicted individuals are withdrawn from both the self-administration ritual and from the drug molecule. That is, such individuals experience behavioral withdrawal as well as pharmacologic withdrawal. Pharmacologic withdrawal may be largely responsible for the characteristic rise and fall in withdrawal symptoms that occurs in the 1 to 2 weeks after initial drug abstinence, but we assert that behavioral withdrawal accounts for prolonged symptom persistence, the volatility and variability of symptoms, and exaggerated symptomatic reactivity to environmental events. In theory, the loss of a highly practiced and effective symptomatic control strategy should exert effects that occur again and again over a lengthy post-cessation period: Effects that persist until the organism has acquired new regulatory strategies or until once-evocative stimuli (e.g., drug cues) no longer elicit withdrawal responses. The organism may attempt to use nondrug coping strategies in response to symptomatic distress, but lack of practice may lead to inadequate affect regulation as compared to drug use.

The absence of a self-administration coping response leads to dysregulated symptomatic expression for several reasons. First, the lack of the drug per se leaves pharmacologic withdrawal untreated. Second, failure to use the self-administration ritual produces intense response conflict resulting in strong urges, frustration, and feelings of helplessness as the individual fights the urge to use the tried-and-true self-administration ritual (Curtin et al., 2006). Conflict between the well-learned drug-use response and a substitute response should elicit intrusive and effortful cognitive-control processes as well as frustration. Finally, the individual does not benefit from the positive conditioned associations (including anticipatory and placebo effects) that are activated by the ritual (Sayette et al., 2003).

If there is a behavioral withdrawal, there should be evidence that the self-administration ritual per se can suppress withdrawal symptoms in addicted individuals. Indeed, there is evidence that mere practice of the self-administration ritual, without any actual drug delivery, effectively suppresses withdrawal symptoms. For instance, heroin withdrawal is suppressed by injections of saline, and nicotine withdrawal is suppressed by smoking nicotine-free cigarettes (Butschky, Bailey, Henningfield, & Pickworth, 1995). Such effects are remarkably persistent and resistant to extinction. This is consistent with observations that organisms persist in the drug self-administration response long after the response ceases to deliver the drug (Caggiula et al., 2001). We believe this occurs because the self-administration ritual quells distress via learned associations. Consistent with this hypothesis, there is evidence that the self-administration ritual itself activates brain reward and incentive systems (Balfour, 2004). This hypothesis also accounts for the finding that drug replacement (e.g., nicotine patch and methadone) without the self-administration ritual only partially suppresses the drug withdrawal syndrome even with very high drug-replacement doses. The behavioral-withdrawal hypothesis suggests some novel predictions: For example, if the drug is administered without the self-administration ritual (e.g., via passive infusion), withdrawal will be less prolonged, persistent, and variable than it will be if the self-administration ritual is routinely reinforced. This explains the observation that the passive receipt of opiates by hospital patients tends not to lead to intense withdrawal or addiction: Such patients are withdrawn only from the drug, not from a highly ingrained self-administration ritual.

Viewing withdrawal as dysregulation helps to explain the apparently anomalous finding that withdrawal symptoms persist as long as they do: The addicted individual undergoes behavioral withdrawal each time he or she experiences spikes in negative affect or urges (regardless of the cause) and does not or cannot revert to drug use to cope. This perspective has implications for treatment. For instance, it suggests that pairing drug replacement with the self-administration ritual (e.g., using the nicotine patch and smoking nicotine-free cigarettes) will effectively quell withdrawal distress and promote successful cessation of drug use. In addition, it suggests that addicted individuals might be helped by practicing symptomatic regulation strategies well before they attempt to quit, in order to reduce the intense response conflict that occurs upon cessation.

SUMMARY

Modern theories of addiction motivation suggest that withdrawal is not a potent motivator of drug use and relapse. However, addicted individuals routinely attribute relapse to withdrawal distress. We believe that the motivational role of withdrawal is clear once withdrawal is conceptualized appropriately and accordingly analyzed. First, researchers should focus on a subset of withdrawal symptoms that possess motivational relevance: negative affect and urges. Second, when addicted individuals stop using drugs, they withdraw from both the drug molecule and from the self-administration ritual. Falling levels of the drug in the body certainly produce a rise-and-fall pattern in withdrawal symptoms. However, the absence of the drug self-administration ritual exacerbates negative affect and urges, making such symptoms especially prolonged, volatile, and intense. Research shows that when assessments focus on the motivationally relevant elements of withdrawal and capture the complex patterns of withdrawal over time, withdrawal is indeed an important influence on drug motivation and relapse. Therefore, according to the present model, withdrawal may be defined as response dys-regulation that occurs due to decreased levels of the drug in the body and discontinuation of the self-administration response.

Recommended Reading

Baker, T., Piper, M., McCarthy, D., Majeskie, M., & Fiore, M. (2004). (See References)
Curtin, J., McCarthy, D., Piper, M., & Baker, T. (2006). (See References)
Robinson, T., & Berridge, K. (1993). (See References)

Note

1. Address correspondence to Timothy B. Baker, Center for Tobacco Research and Intervention, University of Wisconsin School of Medicine and Public Health, 1930 Monroe St. Suite 200, Madison, WI 53711; e-mail: tbb@ctri.medicine.wisc.edu.

References

Baker, T., Piper, M., McCarthy, D., Majeskie, M., & Fiore, M. (2004). Addiction motivation reformulated: An affective processing model of negative reinforcement. *Psychological Review, 111*, 33–51.

Balfour, D. (2004). The neurobiology of tobacco dependence: A pre-clinical perspective on the role of dopamine projections to the nucleus. *Nicotine and Tobacco Research, 6*, 899–912.

Butschky, M., Bailey, D., Henningfield, J., & Pickworth, W. (1995). Smoking without nicotine delivery decreases withdrawal in 12-hour abstinent smokers. *Pharmacology Biochemistry and Behavior, 50*, 91–96.

Caggiula, A., Donny, E., White, A., Chaudhri, N., Booth, S., Gharib, M.A., Hoffman, A., Perkins, K., & Sved, A.F. (2001). Cue dependency of nicotine self-administration and smoking. *Pharmacology Biochemistry and Behavior, 70*, 515–530.

Curtin, J., McCarthy, D., Piper, M., & Baker, T. (2006). Implicit and explicit drug motivational processes: A model of boundary conditions. In R. Wiers & A. Stacy (Eds.), *Handbook of implicit cognition and addiction*. Thousand Oaks, CA: Sage Publications.

Frenois, F., Cador, M., Caille, S., Stinus, L., & LeMoine, C. (2002). Neural correlates of the motivational and somatic components of naloxone-precipitated morphine withdrawal. *European Journal of Neuroscience, 16*, 1377–1389.

Hogle, J., & Curtin, J. (in press). Sex differences in the affective consequences of smoking withdrawal. *Psychophysiology*.

McCarthy, D., Bolt, D., & Baker, T. (in press). The importance of how: A call for mechanistic research in tobacco dependence. In T. Treat, R. Bootzin, & T. Baker (Eds.), *Recent advances in theory and practice: Integrative perspectives in honor of Richard M. McFall*. New York: Erlbaum.

McCarthy, D., Piasecki, T., Fiore, M., & Baker, T. (in press). Life before and after quitting smoking: An electronic diary study. *Journal of Abnormal Psychology*.

Mucha, R. (1987). Is the motivational effect of opiate withdrawal reflected by common somatic indices of precipitated withdrawal? A place conditioning study in the rat. *Brain Research, 418*, 214–220.

Panksepp, J., Herman, B., Connor, R., Bishop, P., & Scott, J. (1978). The biology of social attachments: Opiates alleviate separation distress. *Biological Psychiatry, 13*, 607–618.

Piasecki, T., Niaura, R., Shadel, W., Abrams, D., Goldstein, M., Fiore, M., & Baker, T.B. (2000). Smoking withdrawal dynamics in unaided quitters. *Journal of Abnormal Psychology, 109*, 74–86.

Robinson, T., & Berridge, K. (1993). The neural basis of drug craving: An incentive-sensitization theory of addiction. *Brain Research Reviews, 18*, 247–291.

Sayette, M., West, J., Martin, C.S., Cohn, J., Perrott, M., & Hoebel, J. (2003). Effects of smoking opportunity on cue-elicited urge: A facial coding analysis. *Journal of Experimental and Clinical Psychopharmacology, 11*, 218–227.

The Neural Bases of Placebo Effects in Pain

Tor D. Wager[1]

Columbia University

Abstract

Placebo effects are beneficial effects of treatment caused not by the biological action of the treatment but by one's response to the treatment process itself. One possible mechanism of placebo treatments is that they create positive expectations, which change one's appraisal of the situation and may thereby shape sensory and emotional processing. Recent brain-imaging evidence suggests that placebo-induced expectations of analgesia increase activity in the prefrontal cortex in anticipation of pain and decrease the brain's response to painful stimulation. These findings suggest that placebo treatments can alter experience, not just alter what participants are willing to report about pain. To the extent that they involve neural systems mediating expectancy and appraisal, placebo effects in pain may share common circuitry with placebo effects in depression, Parkinson's disease, and other disorders.

Keywords

placebo; pain; expectancy; appraisal; fMRI

> If thou art pained by any external thing, it is not this that disturbs thee, but thy own judgment about it. And it is in thy power to wipe out this judgment now.
>
> —Marcus Aurelius Antoninus (2001, p. 44)

Belief in the healing power of positive expectations has existed since the beginning of recorded history. The power of expectation to make people feel better has been exploited by physicians and charlatans—sometimes to promote healing and other times for less altruistic reasons. The healing potential of expectations has formally been recognized in scientific literature as the *placebo effect*, a term that generally refers to beneficial effects of a treatment that cannot be ascribed to the physical action of the treatment itself. A patient in pain, for example, may report feeling less pain after an injection of saline (i.e., a placebo injection), if the patient believes that a painkiller was administered. Placebo effects have been reported in a cornucopia of ailments, including pain, depression, Parkinson's disease, alcoholism, irritable bowel syndrome, panic and anxiety disorders, and high blood pressure, and have been reported after sham surgeries for heart disease and arthritic knee pain. Recognition in the medical community of placebos' healing potential has led to the standard practice since the 1940s of using placebo control groups in clinical trials.

In spite of the volume and breadth of research involving placebos, most studies have focused on testing drug effects against a placebo baseline, not on testing whether placebo treatments themselves are effective. For example, suppose investigators test depressed patients over a 3-month period of treatment and find a 30% recovery rate in the placebo group. Many patients will spontaneously recover during this time, even with no treatment; thus, the 30% "placebo response rate" could be due either to placebo treatment or simply to the natural course of depression. Testing for placebo effects directly requires an additional no-treatment control group. Because such a group is not often included in clinical studies, we still understand very little about the scope of disorders that may respond to placebo treatments and the psychological mechanisms that underlie the placebo response.

This relative lack of knowledge has led some researchers to suggest that placebo treatment engages no active beneficial psychophysiological processes; rather, they suggest, placebo effects are simply statistical artifacts such as regression to the mean and spontaneous recovery or demand characteristics, the tendency to comply with experimenters' expectations (Hrobjartsson & Gotzsche, 2004). However, recent evidence using no-treatment controls has demonstrated that active placebo effects exist for at least some diseases. In pain, depression, and Parkinson's disease, placebo effects have been demonstrated both in behavioral outcomes and in disease-specific brain activity.

In this paper, I discuss placebo effects on pain, focusing on two questions related to the effects of verbal suggestions (i.e., the suggestion that you have been given a painkiller, in the earlier example). First, what aspects of the continuum from sensing a noxious stimulus to feeling and reporting pain are affected by this kind of placebo treatment: sensation, subjective pain experience, or demand characteristics? Drawing on evidence from behavioral and brain-imaging studies, I suggest that placebo treatment may most strongly impact the subjective experience of pain. I then turn to the issue of what psychological and brain mechanisms are engaged by placebo treatment. My view is that placebo treatment primarily affects expectancy and appraisal, two related processes crucial in determining subjective pain experience.

EFFECTS OF PLACEBO ON PAIN

Placebo treatments may affect several aspects of the pain sensation–experience–reporting continuum: sensory transmission and processing, appraisal and the generation of subjective pain, and the pain-reporting process (Fig. 1A). The issue of which aspects are affected is at the heart of the debate over whether placebo treatments have "real" effects.

Placebo Effects on Sensory Input

Ascending pain signals travel through the spinal cord to reach the thalamus and then the sensory-processing regions of the cerebral cortex (S1 and S2; Fig. 1B). I refer to these regions as the *sensory pain network*, as they appear to be specifically activated by physical pain and touch, but not by cognitive operations or negative emotions. Neurons both in the spinal cord and in the sensory network project to another set of regions, including the anterior insula, anterior cingulate cortex (ACC), and medio-dorsal thalamus. These regions constitute the *affective pain network*, as they are closely linked to the subjective feeling of pain (Craig, Chen, Bandy, & Reiman, 2000).

Changes in the sensory network or in the spinal cord itself would provide the strongest evidence for placebo effects on pain. According to the "gate control"

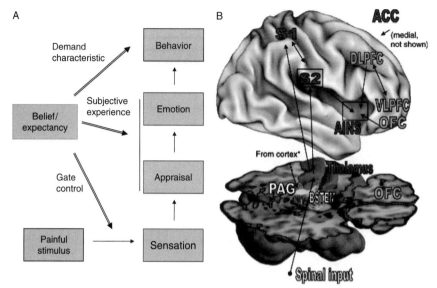

Fig. 1. (A) Routes by which expectancy, created by placebo treatments, may lead to changes in pain processing and (B) some important brain regions in the pain pathway. Pain begins when sensory signals from the spinal cord reach the brain via the thalamus and are sent to the primary (S1) and secondary somatosensory cortex (S2). These areas may be most important for the sensory aspects of pain, though the total pain experience may emerge from interactions among these and other regions, described below. From there, signals are sent to the anterior insula (AINS) and anterior cingulate (ACC), which are involved (along with regions in the limbic system) in the subjective experience and emotional quality of pain. These signals undergo an appraisal process, in which potential harm is assessed and corresponding emotions and behaviors are generated to tolerate, escape, or remove the source of pain. The appraisal and emotional components are central to what it means to "feel pain." Appraisals are generated through interactions among the orbitofrontal cortex (OFC), AINS, ACC, and other regions, and they may be maintained in the dorsolateral prefrontal cortex (DLPFC). Expectancies, in the generation of which the DLPFC, OFC, and ventrolateral prefrontal cortex (VLPFC) may play a role, may inhibit spinal input, alter the experience of pain directly, or affect behaviors and pain reporting directly. The periaqueductal gray (PAG), in the brainstem (BSTEM), can block ascending spinal signals if activated, and it receives input from many regions mentioned above, including the OFC, ACC, DLPFC, VLPFC, and amygdala. However, the PAG also modulates activity throughout the emotional and cognitive networks of the brain.

theory (Melzack & Wall, 1965), the brain can block pain by engaging opioid neurons in and near the midbrain periaqueductal gray (PAG; Fig. 1B), which then inhibit pain in the spinal cord. This is a standard explanation in medical textbooks for how placebos work.

Do placebos block pain in the spinal cord? This question has been difficult to test directly. However, indirect evidence indicates that placebo analgesia can be blocked by the opioid antagonist naloxone (Amanzio & Benedetti, 1999), suggesting that placebo treatment requires opioid systems in the PAG. Recent brain-imaging studies found that placebo treatment increased activity in the midbrain region surrounding the PAG (Wager et al., 2004) and in prefrontal regions that correlate with increases around the PAG (Petrovic, Kalso, Petersson, & Ingvar, 2002; Wager et al., 2004).

If placebo treatment engages opioid systems that block pain in the spinal cord, one might expect decreased pain responses in both sensory and affective pain networks. However, in our recent work (Wager et al., 2004), we found evidence that S2 activity actually increased with administration of a placebo. Real opiate analgesics also increase activity in S2, however, suggesting that the relationship between pain and activation may be more complex. Future studies are needed to test specifically for drug and placebo effects on the sensory network and the spinal cord.

Placebo Effects on Central Pain

If placebos reduce pain but not sensory pain inputs, why do opioid antagonists block placebo effects? An alternative explanation is that both opioids and placebos directly affect the brain processes that give rise to pain appraisal and experience. The PAG sends output not only to the spinal cord, but also directly to the affective pain network. Activity in this network increases with subjective pain, but also in response to a range of personally significant aversive events, such as losing in a game, experiencing negative emotions, or seeing someone else in pain. These situations involve negative appraisals that have personal significance (Lazarus, 1991). That subjective pain is much more than sensory experience is demonstrated by a number of phenomena—including wound-site-specific battlefield analgesia, phantom pain, neuropathic pain, stroke, and pain after removal of sensory nerves that carry pain-related signals (Melzack & Wall, 1965). Thus, it is likely that subjective pain is produced or heavily influenced by appraisals of valence (how bad does it feel?) represented at least partly within this network, and that placebo treatments most strongly influence the appraisal process (Fig. 1A). In our experiments, we found that placebo treatment decreased pain-evoked activity in the affective pain network, consistent with this hypothesis (Wager et al., 2004).

PLACEBO EFFECTS ON PAIN REPORTING ONLY

A final alternative explanation for placebo effects is that espoused by skeptics: that placebo treatment affects only demand characteristics (Hrobjartsson & Gotzsche, 2004; Fig. 1A). Finding changes in brain activity in pain-processing regions and during pain experience argues against this view (Lieberman et al., 2004; Petrovic et al., 2002; Wager et al., 2004). More studies with quantitative, non-self-report-based outcome measures, such as measures of brain activity and peripheral physiology, are needed to replicate and extend these findings.

PROCESSES ENGAGED BY PLACEBO TREATMENT

The evidence reviewed above suggests that placebo treatment engages active brain processes that dampen pain. The treatment may be nothing more than a verbal suggestion; so how do mere suggestions come to alter how the brain processes pain? Here I suggest that placebo treatment provides a context that shapes appraisal both of cues that signal upcoming pain and of pain itself, and thereby creates positive expectancies in the face of imminent pain (Kirsch, 1985).

According to this view, expectancies are moment-by-moment predictions of the nature and emotional value of upcoming events. They are created when cues that signal imminent pain are perceived. Expectancies are based on situational context, which includes prior experience with pain and drugs and beliefs about medical treatment (Kirsch, 1985). The information carried in expectancies may be integrated with incoming sensory input to shape subjective pain and emotion. For this integration to occur, expectancies must be maintained in the brain until the predicted sensory events occur.

Theories of context-based regulation of attention and memory provide some idea of how this process may work (Miller & Cohen, 2001). Research on attention has shown that expectancies about the nature and relevance of stimuli can shape perceptual processing, even enhancing neural representations of expected features before they appear. Placebo-induced expectancies may shape the perception and appraisal of somatosensory stimuli much in the same way that expectancy shapes visual, auditory, and tactile perceptions, in this case by reducing the feeling of pain. One factor that differentiates expectancies about pain from other sensory expectancies, however, is their affective component. Thus, placebo treatment may influence cognitive expectancies about whether stimuli are worthy of attention or affective expectancies about personal harm.

In neurobiological terms, pain perception begins with attitudes and previous experiences (including placebo-induced beliefs) stored in long-term-memory systems distributed across the cortex and hippocampus. When presented with cues signaling upcoming pain, relevant memories are recalled and used to generate expectancies about how bad the pain will be. This appraisal is likely to involve the orbitofrontal cortex (OFC), which is critical for representing and updating the emotional value of cues. Expectancies are likely to be maintained during anticipation of pain in the prefrontal cortex, particularly the dorsolateral and ventrolateral prefrontal cortices (DLPFC and VLPFC, respectively)—the same areas important for maintaining context information in working memory and biasing sensory processing (Miller & Cohen, 2001).

Recent brain-imaging studies provide preliminary evidence supporting this model. In our studies and in other pain- and emotion-regulation studies (e.g., Lorenz, Minoshima, & Casey, 2003), DLPFC activation is associated with effective pain regulation. We found that, during the anticipation of pain, ACC, OFC, and DLPFC activity was boosted by a placebo treatment. Participants with larger increases showed greater placebo-induced reductions in pain (Wager et al., 2004). Petrovic et al. (2002) also found that placebo treatment increased activation in the ACC and OFC, and Lieberman et al. (2004) found that activation of the right VLPFC and OFC correlated with pain relief in irritable bowel syndrome after placebo treatment.[2]

If expectations influence pain perception, then what is the difference between placebo-induced expectancy and simply expecting a less intense stimulus? Both reduce subjective pain. No studies have directly compared these two types of manipulations directly, but expectations about stimulus intensity also induce changes in pain processing in the insula that depend on the hippocampus

(Ploghaus et al., 2001). In psychological terms, the difference is that placebo expectancies involve more pervasive changes in the context surrounding pain. In brain activity, the difference is that placebo expectancy increases prefrontal activation, whereas the evidence to date does not suggest that expecting less pain has the same effect.

An additional kind of expectancy effect comes from expectancy theory in motivation science (Vroom, 1964), which emphasizes motivational components of expectancy, including the expected costs and benefits of strategic effort. Perhaps placebo treatment increases the desire for pain relief or the perception of control over pain, which in turn encourages use of explicit pain-regulation strategies such as directed attention. Desire for pain relief does not appear to predict the magnitude of placebo effects (Vase, Robinson, Verne, & Price, 2003). However, feelings of efficacy in controlling pain do appear to increase pain tolerance. Whether changes in self-efficacy mediate placebo effects is not known, so this possibility remains open. What are most needed for understanding the relationship between placebo treatment and motivation are direct assessments of attention allocation, motivation, self-efficacy, and strategy use during placebo and no-placebo conditions.

By suggesting that expectancy and appraisal are processes that may underlie many kinds of placebo effects, I am not suggesting that placebo treatments produce the same outcomes across diseases. Placebo effects in depression (but not pain or Parkinson's disease) have been found in the subgenual cingulate, an area in which metabolic changes have been linked to depressive symptoms. Placebo treatment in Parkinson's disease produces decreased firing of subthalamic neurons and decreased muscle rigidity in human patients (Benedetti et al., 2004). Both the neural and behavioral signs affected by the placebo are specific markers of disease severity in Parkinson's and are not likely to be outcomes shared by other kinds of placebo effects. In addition, motivation and appraisal are probably not the only mechanisms for placebo effects; conditioning procedures may produce significant and meaningful effects through a variety of other mechanisms.

BENEFITS OF STUDYING PLACEBOS, AND UNANSWERED QUESTIONS

There are many reasons for studying placebo effects, including the possibilities of interleaving effective placebo treatments with real drugs and reducing the costs of clinical trials by controlling expectations more precisely. But perhaps the most compelling argument is that placebo research can help us understand the mechanisms by which therapeutic agents have their effects. Whether a drug works to relieve depression, for example, is the easy question. The more difficult question is why it works. What part of the drug's effect is due to simple pharmacological action, and what part is due to expectancy and drug-expectancy interactions? Understanding how internal regulatory processes interact with external treatments is a key issue in both basic and applied research, and it is central to understanding how the mind regulates the body's physiological state.

However, realizing this goal will require concerted work on a number of fronts. First, the question of what neuro-cognitive processes placebo treatments affect must be asked separately in each domain—depression, Parkinson's, hypertension, anxiety disorders, cognitive performance, and social interactions, to name some. Are there common effects of expectancy that act across domains, or is the term "placebo response" just a rubric for a collection of separate processes? Is the appraisal and regulation of pain a similar internal process to the appraisal and regulation of negative emotion? Second, what are the psychological mediators for placebo effects—changes in attention, self-efficacy, anxiety, attitudes? And what are the neural correlates of these? Can placebo effects be explained in terms of some more well-defined mechanism?

At a broader level, future research must lay the foundations for bridges between psychological and neurobiological descriptions of placebo and other regulatory processes. The stronger these bridges, the more we will have objective biological measures for processes such as expectation, emotion, and pain that were previously knowable only through self-report.

Recommended Reading

Harrington, A., ed. (1999). *The placebo effect*. Cambridge, MA: Harvard University Press.
Kirsch, I. (1985). Response expectancy as a determinant of experience and behavior. *American Psychologist, 40*, 1189–1202.

Acknowledgments—Thanks to Ed Smith, Dagfinn Matre, Kevin Ochsner, Ralph Wager, Ethan Kross, and Hedy Kober for helpful comments, and to Bob Rose and the Mind Brain Body and Health initiative for their generous support.

Notes

1. Please address correspondence to Tor D. Wager, Department of Psychology, Columbia University, 1190 Amsterdam Ave., New York, NY 10027; e-mail: tor@psych.columbia.edu.

2. Importantly, brain increases in a placebo condition compared to a matched control are likely to reflect differences in the demand on retrieval, evaluation, and maintenance of context information. Thus, appraisals and expectancies are generated with or without a placebo, but the placebo treatment may increase demand on these processes, thus increasing activation.

References

Amanzio, M., & Benedetti, F. (1999). Neuropharmacological dissection of placebo analgesia: Expectation-activated opioid systems versus conditioning-activated specific subsystems. *Journal of Neuroscience, 19*, 484–494.
Antoninus, Marcus Aurelius (2001). *Meditations of Marcus Aurelius Antoninus* (G. Long, Trans.). Retrieved August 10, 2005 from http://www.netlibrary.com/Reader/
Benedetti, F., Colloca, L., Torre, E., Lanotte, M., Melcarne, A., Pesare, M., Bergamasco, B., & Lopiano, L. (2004). Placebo-responsive Parkinson patients show decreased activity in single neurons of subthalamic nucleus. *Nature Neuroscience, 7*, 587–588.
Craig, A.D., Chen, K., Bandy, D., & Reiman, E.M. (2000). Thermosensory activation of insular cortex. *Nature Neuroscience, 3*, 184–190.
Hrobjartsson, A., & Gotzsche, P.C. (2004). Is the placebo powerless? Update of a systematic review with 52 new randomized trials comparing placebo with no treatment. *Journal of Internal Medicine, 256*, 91–100.
Kirsch, I. (1985). Response expectancy as a determinant of experience and behavior. *American Psychologist, 40*, 1189–1202.

Lazarus, R.S. (1991). Cognition and motivation in emotion. *American Psychologist, 46*, 352–367.

Lieberman, M.D., Jarcho, J.M., Berman, S., Naliboff, B.D., Suyenobu, B.Y., Mandelkern, M., & Mayer, E.A. (2004). The neural correlates of placebo effects: A disruption account. *Neuroimage, 22*, 447–455.

Lorenz, J., Minoshima, S., & Casey, K.L. (2003). Keeping pain out of mind: The role of the dorsolateral prefrontal cortex in pain modulation. *Brain, 126*, 1079–1091.

Melzack, R., & Wall, P.D. (1965). Pain mechanisms: a new theory. *Science, 150*, 971–979.

Miller, E.K., & Cohen, J.D. (2001). An integrative theory of prefrontal cortex function. *Annual Review of Neuroscience, 24*, 167–202.

Petrovic, P., Kalso, E., Petersson, K.M., & Ingvar, M. (2002). Placebo and opioid analgesia—Imaging a shared neuronal network. *Science, 295*, 1737–1740.

Ploghaus, A., Narain, C., Beckmann, C.F., Clare, S., Bantick, S., & Wise, R., et al. (2001). Exacerbation of pain by anxiety is associated with activity in a hippocampal network. *Journal of Neuroscience, 21*, 9896–9903.

Vase, L., Robinson, E., Verne, G.N., & Price, D.D. (2003). The contributions of suggestion, desire, and expectation to placebo effects in irritable bowel syndrome patients: An empirical investigation. *Pain, 105*, 17–25.

Vroom, V.H. (1964). Work and motivation. New York: Wiley.

Wager, T.D., Rilling, J.K., Smith, E.E., Sokolik, A., Casey, K.L., Davidson, R.J., Kosslyn, S.M., Rose, R.M., & Cohen, J.D. (2004). Placebo-induced changes in fMRI in the anticipation and experience of pain. *Science, 303*, 1162–1167.

Section 4: Critical Thinking Questions

1. The review by Crombag and Robinson focuses on the influence of environment on sensitization of locomotor activity, design experiments using rats to determine whether environment also influences sensitization of incentive motivation and drug reward. Is it ethically possible to study sensitization to drugs in humans?

2. Do you think that individuals who are generally "hyper-responsive" to stress are more prone to progress from causal to compulsive drug use than individuals who are generally "hypo-responsive" to stress? What personality traits do you think might predispose individuals to drug addiction?

3. Given the evidence presented in the Resilience Section that hypothalamic-pituitary-adrenal axis function and stress responses can be shaped early in life, and the association between stress and addictive behavior presented in the current section, do you think that teaching stress coping skills in elementary and middle school would decrease the number of juveniles who experiment with, or become addicted to, illicit drugs?

4. Placebo treatment is effective in reducing symptoms in a large number health conditions including depression, Parkinson's disease and pain. Does the observation that an inert compound can reduce suffering suggest that some of the symptoms have psychological rather than physiological origins?

This article has been reprinted as it originally appeared in *Current Directions in Psychological Science*. Citation information for this article as originally published appears above.

Section 5: Health

Traditionally, the nervous system, endocrine system, and immune system were studied as independent entities. It was believed that the immune system defended its host from invading pathogens and rogue endogenous cells autonomously from the host's behavior or even environment. Variation in immune function reflected genetic propensities and historical encounters with pathogens. Since the 1970s, it has become increasingly accepted that vast and complex interactions among the nervous, endocrine, and immune systems are necessary to maintain health and well-being among individuals. The study of the interaction among these bodily components has been termed psychoneuroimmunology, and one of its founders, Robert Ader, provides the first article in this section on health. Behavioral influences on immune function have been demonstrated most convincingly by studies indicating that immunosuppression can be learned by using classical learning techniques. In one common variation, rodents are treated to a saccharin solution (in common with the bell for Pavlov's dog is the conditioned stimulus) prior to an injection with an immunosuppressant drug (in common with salivation in Pavlov's dog, the unconditioned stimulus). Animals receiving this pairing reduced antibody production in response to an antigen after re-exposure to the conditioned stimulus without the drug. That is, they learned to suppress their immune function. Stressors also can suppress immunity, and a number of stressful life events such as death of a spouse, long-term care-giving, academic examinations, and even happy events such as graduation, are associated with increased risks of the onset and severity of immune disorders and infectious diseases. Although the neural and endocrine correlates that putatively underlie the stress-evoked immunocompromise remain unspecified, this area is a particularly important part of biopsychology, and as Ader points out, many important research questions remain to be answered.

Biopsychology examines the intersection between biology and behavior. In the second article of this section, Neil Schneiderman describes the intersection of biology, behavior, and psychosocial factors in relation to health. Although the precise causative agents have not been identified, risk factors for chronic diseases such as coronary heart disease, cancer, and stroke, which kill the vast majority of people in developed countries, have been identified in these three domains. Behavioral risk factors include the so-called life-style factors such as smoking, high-fat diets, unsafe sexual practices, and high alcohol intake. Remarkably, behavioral risk factors contribute to over half of the deaths in the US, so understanding their contribution to chronic illnesses is critical. Psychosocial risk factors include perceived lack of control, hostility, and depression. Depression is the psychosocial risk factor most commonly associated with chronic diseases such as coronary heart disease, breast cancer, and AIDS. Societal risk factors include low socioeconomic status, membership in a racial or ethnic minority, and long-term exposure to occupational social stressors. In general, people with higher socioeconomic status have better disease outcomes, whereas individuals with lower socioeconomic status fare poorer in disease outcomes. Schneiderman points out that a better understanding is needed of how these various risk factors activate specific biological mechanisms that influence immune function and disease susceptibility, progression, and outcomes. Importantly, an appreciation of the pathways underlying behavioral variation and chronic disease susceptibility is necessary to duplicate the progress in eradicating and managing infectious diseases.

Although the evidence linking chronic stressors and depressive mood to susceptibility and severity of chronic disease continues, the mechanisms underlying these correlations remain unspecified. In the next article of this section, George Miller and Ekin Blackwell focus on inflammation as the mechanism linking chronic stress, depression, and coronary heart disease. Depressive symptoms occur along a continuum, ranging from low mood to clinical disorder, and clinical studies indicate that depressive symptoms after a heart attack are associated with a 3-fold increase in mortality within 5 years. Chronic stress both during adulthood and during childhood also contributes to coronary heart disease. Miller and Blackwell ask how depressive symptoms and chronic stressors "get under the skin" to influence disease. They hypothesize that chronic stressors activate the immune system in such a way that leads to persistent inflammation. The blood-born mediators of inflammation, interleukin (IL) 1β, tumor necrosis factor (TNF)α, and IL6 provoke the sickness responses that depress affect. These molecules also promote formation and growth of arteriosclerotic plaques in coronary and carotid arteries, leading to heart attacks and strokes, respectively. Miller and Blackwell identify future research questions, such as whether exposure to only major stressors (e.g., death of a spouse) promote proinflammatory responses leading to arteriosclerosis, or whether minor daily hassles, such as commuting in heavy traffic or having a demanding boss, also are sufficient to provoke health damaging responses. It will be important to identify interventions that might block the association among inflammation, chronic stress, depression, and heart disease.

Stressors that affect health may not be static across the year. In the wild, winter-stressors such as low temperatures and decreased food availability may compromise survival. Indeed, many health conditions including cardiovascular, infectious, and auto-immune disorders display significant seasonal fluctuations. The stress of coping with winter-evoked stressors compromises immune function, and Randy Nelson and Gregory Demas hypothesize that because winter stressors are predictable, individuals should shift energy from reproduction, growth, and other non-essential (to survival) activities during autumn to bolster immune function in *anticipation* of the onset of winter stressors. In common with reproductive function, individuals could anticipate winter conditions by using day length (photoperiod) information, which is encoded by the nightly duration of melatonin secretion. Nelson and Demas indicate that melatonin coordinates seasonal changes in immune function by acting both directly and indirectly to modulate stress hormones in response to perceived stressors.

Your grandmother likely extolled the virtues of sleep for your health and well-being. Recent studies have verified what your sensible grandmother already knew. Sleep has restorative and health-maintaining functions, and poor sleep is correlated with poor health outcomes. The final article in this section by Sarosh Motivala and Michael Irwin documents the important bidirectional relationship between sleep and immune function, and propose that poor sleep elevates pro-inflammatory cytokines, which as we learned in previous articles in this section, promotes coronary artery disease, stroke, and autoimmune diseases. Additionally, Motivala and Irwin suggest that sleep disturbances can be provoked by cytokines, setting up a potential positive feedback loop on poor health outcomes. Even brief periods of sleep deprivation can compromise immune function and negatively impact health. The importance of impaired sleep and immune dysregulation among clinical populations is reviewed. For example, chronic insomniacs display diminished natural-killer cell activities, and high cytokine levels. Another intriguing observation that suggests a link among depression, sleep, and immune function in health, is that ~90% of clinically-depressed patients report sleep difficulties, and the same immune dysfunctions as individuals with primary insomnia. The authors emphasize that future work must focus on cytokine antagonists as a pharmacological intervention, which might improve health, as well as sleep disorders.

Psychoneuroimmunology

Robert Ader[1]

Center for Psychoneuroimmunology Research, Department of Psychiatry, University of Rochester School of Medicine and Dentistry, Rochester, New York

Abstract

Psychoneuroimmunology is the study of the relationships among behavioral, neural and endocrine, and immune processes. Bidirectional pathways connect the brain and the immune system and provide the foundation for neural, endocrine, and behavioral effects on immunity. Examples of such effects are conditioned and stress-induced changes in immune function and in susceptibility to immunologically mediated diseases. These data indicate that researchers should no longer study the immune system as if it functioned independently of other systems in the body. Changes in immune function are hypothesized to mediate the effects of psychological factors on the development of some diseases, and research strategies for studying the clinical significance of behaviorally induced changes in immune function are suggested.

Keywords

conditioning; immunity; stress

Once upon a time, the immune system was considered an autonomous agency of defense. Research conducted over the past 25 years, however, has provided incontrovertible evidence that the immune system is influenced by the brain and that behavior, the nervous system, and the endocrine system are influenced by the immune system. Psychoneuroimmunology, a new hybrid subspecialty at the intersection of psychology, immunology, and the neurosciences, studies these interactions (Ader, 1981b).

The immune system's defense of the organism against foreign, "nonself" material (antigens) is carried out by white blood cells, primarily T and B lymphocytes, that respond in various ways to the presence of antigens and retain a "memory" of encounters with them. Different immune processes can be distinguished by the particular cells that mount the body's defense. Antibody-mediated immunity refers to the production of antibodies by B cells derived from bone marrow; cell-mediated immunity refers to the actions of a variety of T cells derived from the thymus gland. Typically, immune defenses involve interactions among T and B cells and other specialized white blood cells (e.g., macrophages) and substances (cytokines) secreted by activated T cells. Not all immunity is based on the body's recognition of a previously encountered antigen, however. Natural killer (NK) cells, implicated in protection against the spread of cancer cells and the recognition of and defense against viruses, are a type of lymphocyte capable of reacting against some antigens without having had prior experience with them. A readily accessible overview of immune system functions is provided at the following Web site: rex.nci.nih.gov/PATIENTS/INFO_TEACHER/bookshelf/NIH_immune.

BACKGROUND

Interactions between the brain and the immune system were first observed in the laboratory in the 1920s, when scientists found that immune reactions could be conditioned (Ader, 1981a). In the 1950s, there was a short-lived interest in the immunological effects of lesions and electrical stimulation of the brain. At the same time, research was initiated to study the effects of stressful life experiences on susceptibility to experimentally induced infectious diseases. Interest in this research was rejuvenated when, beginning in the 1970s, several independent lines of research provided verifiable evidence of interactions between the brain and the immune system.

We now know that the brain communicates with the immune system via the nervous system and neuroendocrine secretions from the pituitary. Lymphoid organs are innervated with nerve fibers that release a variety of chemical substances that influence immune responses. Lymphocytes bear receptors for a variety of hormones and are thereby responsive to these neural and endocrine signals. The best known of these signals are reflected in the anti-inflammatory and generally immunosuppressive effects of adrenocortical steroids (hormones released by the adrenal gland).

Lymphocytes activated by antigens are also capable of producing hormones and other chemical substances that the brain can detect. Thus, activation of the immune system is accompanied by changes in the nervous system and endocrine activity. Cytokines released by activated immune cells provide still another pathway through which the immune system communicates with the central nervous system (CNS). Although the precise site (or sites) at which cytokines act within the brain has not been identified, cytokines cause changes in the activity of the brain, in the endocrine system, and in behavior.

At the neural and endocrine levels, then, there is abundant evidence of interactions between the brain and the immune system. At the behavioral level, the most notable evidence of interactions between the CNS and immune system is the effects of conditioning and stressful life experiences on immune function. Another important line of research (not elaborated here) concerns the effects of immune processes on emotional states and other behaviors such as activity, sleep, and appetite.

BEHAVIORAL INFLUENCES ON IMMUNE FUNCTION

Pavlovian conditioning of alterations of immune function provides the most dramatic illustration of a functional relationship between the brain and the immune system. In a prototypical study using a paradigm referred to as taste-aversion conditioning, animals consumed a novel saccharin solution, the conditioned stimulus (CS), shortly before they were injected with an immunosuppressive drug, the unconditioned stimulus (UCS). When all animals were subsequently injected with antigen, conditioned animals that were reexposed to the CS alone showed an aversion to it and an attenuated antibody response compared with conditioned animals that were not reexposed to the CS and nonconditioned animals that were exposed to saccharin (Ader & Cohen, 1975).

Studies have since documented the acquisition and extinction of conditioned nonspecific responses such as NK cell activity and various antibody- and cell-mediated immune responses (Ader & Cohen, 2001). Conditioning is not limited to changes associated with taste-aversion learning, and there is no consistent relationship between conditioned changes in behavior and conditioned changes in immune responses. Also, conditioned immunosuppressive responses cannot be ascribed to stress-induced or conditioned elevations of adrenal hormones. More recently, the conditioned enhancement, as opposed to suppression, of immune responses has been observed using antigens rather than pharmacologic agents as UCSs.

Data on conditioning in humans are limited. The anticipatory (conditioned) nausea that frequently precedes cancer chemotherapy is associated with anticipatory suppression of the capacity of lymphocytes to respond to foreign stimuli, and multiple sclerosis patients being treated with an immunosuppressive drug show a conditioned decrease in total white blood cell count in response to a sham treatment. Healthy subjects show enhanced NK cell activity when reexposed to a distinctive flavor previously paired with injections of adrenaline. In another study, it was shown that repeated injections of saline (which do not elicit an immune response) could attenuate the response to a subsequent injection of antigen. Conversely, however, repeated injections of antigen may not precipitate a reaction to a subsequent injection of saline.

Psychosocial factors, including stressful life experiences, are capable of influencing the onset or severity of a variety of immune disorders and infectious diseases. Such factors are also capable of influencing immune function. The death of a spouse, other "losses" (e.g., divorce), and other chronic stressors (e.g., caregiving for a chronically ill person)—and even less traumatic events such as school examinations—elicit distress and associated declines in immune function, including a depressed response to a viral antigen.

Clinical depression tends to be associated with some immunologically mediated diseases, and this fact has focused attention on the immunological effects of depression. Depressed patients show a decline in several measures of immunity, elevated antibody levels to herpes viruses, and a diminished ability to mount a specific cell-mediated response to varicella zoster virus, which is responsible for shingles (Herbert & Cohen, 1993). In none of these instances, however, has it been demonstrated that changes in immune function specifically cause the health effects of depression or other affective responses to stress.

Evidence documenting stress-induced alterations in immunity comes mostly from animal research. Early life experiences such as disruption of an animal's interactions with its mother, the social environment, exposure to predators, odors emitted by stressed conspecifics, and physical restraint or other noxious conditions induce neuroendocrine changes and modulate both antibody- and cell-mediated immunity. In general, stress suppresses immune function, but the direction, magnitude, and duration of the effects depend on the antigen, the nature of the stressful experience, and the temporal relationship between the stressful experience and the encounter with antigen. The effects of stress also depend on a variety of host factors, such as species, age, and gender.

The neural and endocrine changes presumed to underlie the immunological effects of stressful life experiences have not been delineated. Any number of hormones or the patterning of hormonal responses could influence immunity. Elevated levels of adrenocortical steroids, the most common manifestation of the stress response, are generally immunosuppressive, and there are many stressor-induced changes in immune function that are mediated by adrenal hormones. However, many stress-induced changes in immunity are independent of adrenal activity.

The response to stressful life experiences involves complex interactions among behavior, the nervous system, the endocrine system, and immune response (Rabin, 1999). As a result, the literature on the immunological effects of stress has yielded some equivocal or seemingly inconsistent findings. It should not be surprising, though, that different stressors—commonly thought to elicit a common stress response—can have different effects on the same immune response. Also, one particular stressor can have different effects on different immune responses. Another source of variability may relate to the direct translation of procedures used in immunological research to behavioral studies. For example, a concentration of antigen that is optimal for the study of cellular processes or immunizations against disease may not be optimal for studies designed to investigate the psychobiological interactions that appear to influence immunoregulatory processes. Thus, for the latter purpose, we need studies in which antigen concentrations are at the lower levels to which individuals may be exposed in natural settings. Varying antigen dose would reduce the risk of masking the contribution of those biopsychosocial factors that influence health and illness in the real world.

If we are not always able to predict the direction, magnitude, or duration of the effects of stressful life experiences, it is clear nevertheless that stressful life experiences can influence immune functions; they can increase or decrease susceptibility to immunologically mediated diseases, permit an otherwise inconsequential exposure to some viruses to develop into clinical disease, or contribute to the reactivation of viral infections to which the individual was exposed in the past. Unfortunately, there are relatively few studies that have measured the relationship between susceptibility to a particular disease and those immune responses that are relevant to that disease.

BIOLOGICAL IMPACT OF BEHAVIORALLY INDUCED ALTERATIONS OF IMMUNE FUNCTION

The effects of conditioning and of stressful experiences on immune function have been referred to as "small." The changes in immune function have remained within normal limits, and it is argued, therefore, that the effects of behavior on immune function have no clinical significance. Although there may be reason to question the selective application of the criterion of effect size, a concern for the biological impact of behaviorally induced changes in immune function is quite legitimate. The association between stressful life experiences and susceptibility to disease and the association between stressful life events and changes in immune function do not establish a causal chain linking stress, immune function, and disease. Thus, a central question that remains to be addressed concerns the biological (clinical) significance of behaviorally induced changes in immunity.

There is little, if any, human research in which an altered resistance to disease has been shown to be a direct result of changes in immune function induced by stressful life experiences. Animal studies of experimentally induced or spontaneously occurring diseases, however, are being developed to address this issue. Stressful stimulation delays the production of virus-specific antibodies in mice infected with influenza and suppresses NK cell activity and the development of some T lymphocytes in animals inoculated with herpes simplex virus (HSV). Although physical restraint is ineffective in reactivating HSV infections, disruption of the social hierarchy within a colony of mice increases aggressive behavior, activates the HPA axis,[2] and results in reactivation of HSV in a significant proportion of infected animals. When the spread of a lung tumor is related to NK cell function, several different stressors can decrease NK cell activity and increase lung disease.

Inflammatory processes, an essential component in the healing of wounds, can be modulated by the sympathetic nervous system and HPA axis. It is not surprising, then, that experimentally produced wounds heal more slowly in caretakers of Alzheimer's patients than in control subjects and in students tested before an examination rather than during summer vacation. Mice restrained for several days before and after they are wounded show a diminished inflammatory response, an elevated level of adrenocortical steroids, and a dramatic delay in healing.

Additional work with animals will enable studies of the mechanisms through which stressful life experiences affect health and determine whether disease susceptibility can, as hypothesized, be influenced by behaviorally induced alterations in immune function.

The biological impact of conditioning was examined using mice that spontaneously develop a disease similar to systemic lupus erythematosus in which there is an overreactivity of the immune system. In this case, a suppression of immunological reactivity would be in the biological interests of these animals. CS presentations without active drug were provided on 50% of the pharmacotherapy trials on which animals were scheduled to receive immunosuppressive drug. By capitalizing on conditioned immunosuppressive responses, it was possible to delay the onset of lupus using a cumulative amount of drug that was not, by itself, sufficient to alter progression of the autoimmune disease. Similarly, resistance to experimentally induced arthritis was achieved by exposing animals to a CS previously paired with immunosuppressive treatments. Among mice previously conditioned by pairing a CS with an immunosuppressive drug, reexposure to the CS following transplantation of foreign tissues delayed the immunologically induced rejection of the tissues. There is one clinical case study of a child with lupus who was successfully treated using a conditioning protocol to reduce the total amount of immunosuppressive drug usually prescribed. Although the effects of conditioning have been described as small, conditioned immunological effects can have a profound biological impact on the development of disorders resulting from an overreactive immune system, some cancers, and the survival of tissue transplants.

The issue of clinical significance has occasioned a lot of misplaced breast-beating and apologias in the name of scientific conservatism. Except, perhaps, for extreme and rare circumstances, the notion that a conditioned stimulus or psychosocial conditions could, by themselves, perturb the immune system to an extent that exceeds normal boundaries and leads to overt disease is somewhat simplistic from either an immunological or a behavioral perspective. Given the complexity of the cellular interactions within the immune system and the interactions between the immune and nervous systems, a behaviorally induced deviation from baseline that did not exceed the normal boundaries would seem to be the only response that could reasonably be expected. As far as susceptibility to a particular disease is concerned, however, it would not be unreasonable to theorize that changes capable of altering immune responses relevant to disease could have clinical consequences when interacting with environmental pathogens or when superimposed upon existing pathology or an immune system compromised by host factors such as age or external influences such as immunosuppressive drugs of abuse. The potential importance of psychoneuroimmunological interactions, then, requires that we adopt research strategies that capitalize on individual differences; high-risk populations (e.g., the very young or old, people whose immune systems are compromised, those with genetic predispositions to particular diseases, those with existing disease); systematic variation of the magnitude of the antigen; and the measurement of responses that are demonstrably relevant to particular diseases.

CONCLUSIONS

Psychoneuroimmunology is an interdisciplinary field that has developed and now prospers by ignoring the arbitrary and illusory boundaries of the biomedical sciences. As a result of the integrative research conducted in recent years, a paradigm shift is occurring; researchers can no longer study immunoregulatory processes as the independent activity of an autonomous immune system. These processes take place within a neuroendocrine environment that is sensitive to the individual's perception of and adaptive responses to events occurring in the external world.

Research predicated on the hypothesis that there is a single, integrated defense system could change the way we define and study certain diseases. Theoretically, it is likely that behavioral, neural, and endocrine interventions are relevant in the treatment of some immune system-related diseases (e.g., arthritis) and that immune system activity may contribute to the understanding and treatment of behavioral, neural, and endocrine disorders (e.g., depression or even schizophrenia).

We cannot yet detail the mechanisms mediating the effects of conditioning or stressful life experiences on immune responses, and further studies are needed. However, we do know that neural and endocrine changes are associated with changes in behavior and that there is a network of connections between the brain and the immune system. The existence of these bidirectional pathways reinforces the hypothesis that changes in the immune system constitute an important mechanism through which psychosocial factors could influence health and disease.

Recommended Reading

Ader, R. (1995). Historical perspectives on psychoneuroimmunology. In H. Friedman, T.W. Klein, & A.L. Friedman (Eds.), *Psychoneuroimmunology, stress and infection* (pp. 1–21). Boca Raton, FL: CRC Press.
Ader, R., Madden, K., Felten, D., Bellinger, D.L., & Schiffer, R.B. (1996). Psychoneuroimmunology: Interactions between the brain and the immune system. In B.S. Fogel,

R.B. Schiffer, & S.M. Rao (Eds.), *Neuropsychiatry* (pp. 193–221). Philadelphia: Williams & Wilkins.

Glaser, R., & Kiecolt-Glaser, J.K. (Eds.). (1994). *Handbook of human stress and immunity.* New York: Academic Press.

Schedlowski, M., & Tewes, U. (Eds.). (1999). *Psychoneuroimmunology: An interdisciplinary introduction.* New York: Kluwer Academic/Plenum.

Acknowledgments—Preparation of this article was supported by a Research Scientist Award (K05 MH06318) from the National Institute of Mental Health.

Notes

1. Address correspondence to Robert Ader, Department of Psychiatry, University of Rochester Medical Center, Rochester, NY 14642.

2. This term comes from the structures involved in the secretion of so-called stress hormones. During a stress response, the brain's hypothalamus (H) releases a chemical that affects the pituitary gland (P). The pituitary then secretes a hormone that causes the adrenal glands (A) to release corticosteroids (cortisol in humans, corticosterone in rodents) into the bloodstream.

References

Ader, R. (1981a). A historical account of conditioned immunobiologic responses. In R. Ader (Ed.), *Psychoneuroimmunology* (pp. 321–354). New York: Academic Press.

Ader, R. (Ed.). (1981b). *Psychoneuroimmunology.* New York: Academic Press.

Ader, R., & Cohen, N. (1975). Behaviorally conditioned immunosuppression. *Psychosomatic Medicine, 37,* 333–340.

Ader, R., & Cohen, N. (2001). Conditioning and immunity. In R. Ader, D.L. Felten, & N. Cohen (Eds.), *Psychoneuroimmunology* (3rd ed., Vol. 2, pp. 3–34). New York: Academic Press.

Herbert, T.B., & Cohen, S. (1993). Depression and immunity: A meta-analytic review. *Psychological Bulletin, 113,* 472–486.

Rabin, B.S. (1999). *Stress, immune function, and health.* New York: Wiley-Liss.

This article has been reprinted as it originally appeared in *Current Directions in Psychological Science*. Citation information for this article as originally published appears above.

Psychosocial, Behavioral, and Biological Aspects of Chronic Diseases

Neil Schneiderman[1]

Department of Psychology and Behavioral Medicine Research Center, University of Miami

Abstract

Behavioral, psychosocial, and societal risk factors have been associated with several chronic diseases. Biological processes closely linked to lifestyle, stress, and psychological status appear to mediate the associations. Lifestyle and psychosocial interventions have been developed to prevent and manage chronic diseases. Field and laboratory studies help to specify causal pathways connecting lifestyle and psychosocial variables to disease processes. However, large-scale randomized clinical trials are required to determine whether interventions lower rates of illness and death.

Keywords

chronic disease; lifestyle; physiology; stress

Improvements in public health (e.g., through better hygiene, nutrition, and immunization) and clinical medicine (e.g., antibiotics) during the first half of the 20th century increased longevity by decreasing the incidence and prevalence of infectious diseases. As infectious diseases declined as the leading cause of death, they were supplanted by chronic diseases such as coronary heart disease (CHD), cancer, and stroke (Schneiderman & Speers, 2001). When scientists were unable to identify single causes for these diseases, they turned to probabilistic models based on the presence of risk factors. During the second half of the 20th century, many risk factors, including psychosocial and lifestyle variables, were identified. This progress, in turn, stimulated research examining behavioral and biological pathways of disease, as well as psychosocial and lifestyle interventions to decrease rates of illness and death due to chronic disease.

BEHAVIORAL, PSYCHOSOCIAL, AND SOCIETAL RISK FACTORS

Behavioral, psychosocial, and societal risk factors have been implicated in the development and progression of chronic diseases. Behavioral, or so-called lifestyle, risk factors include cigarette smoking, lack of exercise, faulty diet, excessive alcohol use, high-risk sex, and shared use of needles for injecting recreational drugs. Psychosocial risk factors include hostility and depression. Societal risk factors include low educational or job status, being a member of an ethnic or racial minority, or being subjected to chronic occupational social stressors.

Behavioral Risk Factors

More than half of all deaths in the United States are linked to behavioral risk factors (McGinnis & Foege, 1993). Cigarette smoking is the major preventable cause of illness and death. The combination of physical inactivity and unhealthy dietary patterns, including excess caloric intake, is the second leading factor contributing to mortality, after tobacco. Long-term excessive use of alcohol increases risk of cardiovascular disease and stroke, as well as some cancers, chronic liver disease, and poor pregnancy outcomes. HIV, the virus that causes AIDS, is transmitted primarily through sexual contact or the sharing of drug paraphernalia. Other, more common, sexually transmitted infections (e.g., human papilloma virus, chlamydia) have been associated with poor health outcomes, including cancer.

Psychosocial Risk Factors

Several large-scale epidemiological studies have established that depressed affect is associated with an increased incidence of mortality from all causes combined, as well as specifically from CHD and cancer (Williams & Schneiderman, 2002). Depression has also been related to an increased rate of death in patients with established CHD, breast cancer, and HIV-AIDS, as well as to faster disease progression to AIDS in HIV-infected individuals. Faster progression to AIDS has also been associated with stressful life events, excessive use of denial as a coping mechanism, and low satisfaction with social support (Leserman et al., 2000). Several epidemiological studies have also documented that high propensities for hostility and anger as stable personality characteristics are associated with increased incidence of CHD and rate of death in the general population (Williams & Schneiderman, 2002).

Societal Risk Factors

Social variables, including education, income, occupation, social cohesion, ethnicity, and race, have been related to health and illness. The effects of these variables on increased rates of illness and death are related both to behaviors (e.g., smoking) that influence bodily systems and to psychological-physiological interactions (e.g., stress responses) mediated by the brain. Because the relationships between social variables and disease processes are complex, detailed examination of the social context is required if societal contributions to health and illness are to be understood.

Socioeconomic position (SEP), defined by education, income, occupation, or a combination of these variables, has been linked to health outcomes in epidemiological studies carried out in many countries (Marmot, 2003). The basic finding is that across multiple measures of health outcome, individuals having the highest SEP fare best, whereas those having the lowest SEP fare worst. A striking feature of the association between SEP and poor health outcomes is that it is graded and continuous—it is not confined to people living in poverty or with poor access to health care. Thus, other factors are also involved. Although there is also an inverse relation between SEP and prevalence of behaviors that pose health risks, statistical adjustment for behavioral and biological factors attenuate, but do not eliminate, the adverse health effects associated with low SEP.

Epidemiological studies have shown that the gradient relating SEP and health outcomes can be related to occupational status. Individuals in executive positions have better health outcomes than white-collar workers, who in turn fare better than blue-collar workers. Examination of some of the factors involved indicates that job strain is related to health outcomes. Other factors, such as gender, may complicate the issue. For example, marital stress, but not work stress, appears to predict poor prognosis in working-age women with CHD, whereas for men, it is work stress, but not marital stress, that is associated with poor prognosis (Orth-Gomér et al., 2000). Another variable that appears to influence the relation between SEP and health outcomes is race. In the United States, African American men and women have a lower life expectancy than Whites at every income level (Anderson, Sorlie, Backlund, Johnson, & Kaplan, 1997). This has led investigators to examine the variables responsible. Although there does not appear to be a clear explanation for the finding, contextual factors, such as racism, de facto segregation, and lack of community investment in human capital, have been implicated.

PATHWAYS OF DISEASE

Exact causal pathways linking behavioral, psychological, and societal variables to chronic disease have not yet been mapped, but plausible biological pathways have been identified. These pathways to disease involve lifestyle, stress, and psychological status. Given current information about the effects of multiple risk factors on disease, it appears that some of the segments along these paths are shared.

Pathways Linking Lifestyle and Disease

An example of a pathway linking lifestyle and disease involves diet and CHD (Schneiderman & Skyler, 1996). The hormone insulin controls the absorption of sugar by the body. This sugar is necessary to maintain a balance between the body's metabolic needs and energy expenditure. If more calories are consumed than are needed to maintain the balance, the excess sugar is stored as fat, which becomes available as an energy source during periods of fasting or physical exertion. The temporary storage of fats has an important adaptive significance, but long-term storage of large amounts of fat can be harmful to health. Studies have documented important connections relating dietary patterns and psychological stress to insulin metabolism and sympathetic nervous system (SNS) activity, which in turn are related to lipid profiles and development of CHD.

Stress can play an indirect role in the pathway between lifestyle and disease when it leads to diet changes that result in obesity. Stress can also promote CHD more directly by activating the SNS, thereby increasing the circulation of fats in the absence of physical exertion. This, in turn, can lead to these fats becoming deposited in the coronary arteries, causing atherosclerosis, which is the anatomical substrate of the disease process underlying CHD. The interaction of psychological stress and diet in the development of CHD has been studied under experimental conditions in cynomolgus monkeys (Kaplan & Manuck, 2003). Briefly, Kaplan and Manuck found that coronary atherosclerosis is significantly enhanced by a high-fat diet, together with a stressful living environment that promotes excess SNS activation.

Pathways Linking Stress and Disease

Humans, as well as other animals, respond to threat with a number of biological adjustments. In response to threat, the SNS releases epinephrine and norepinephrine, while the adrenal cortex, which is part of the adrenal gland, releases cortisol. In threatening environments involving the fight-or-flight response, these stress hormones have transitory adaptive and protective effects, including maximizing the possibilities for muscular exertion. If the threat is too persistent, however, the long-term effects of SNS and adrenal activation may damage health. Adverse effects of persistent stress on health are particularly common in humans, whose high capacity for symbolic thought may elicit chronic stress responses to a broad range of adverse living and working conditions. The relation between psychosocial stressors and chronic disease is complex and is affected, for example, by a person's biological vulnerability (i.e., genetics, constitutional factors) and learned patterns of coping.

HIV provides an example of the role of stress in disease progression, as elevated levels of cortisol have been related to changes in immune function that favor HIV replication and decrease protection against foreign pathogens. Indeed, chronically high levels of cortisol are associated with faster progression of HIV to AIDS (Leserman et al., 2000). More generally, stress-induced modulation of the immune system has been linked to the expression of inflammatory, infectious, and autoimmune diseases. The role of the endocrine and immune systems in mediating the link between psychosocial stressors and chronic diseases is currently an active area of investigation.

Pathways Linking Psychological Status and Disease

There is strong epidemiological evidence that psychological variables such as depression are associated with disease outcomes for CHD, cancer, and HIV-AIDS. One pathway to poor CHD outcome in depressed individuals, for example, involves poor lifestyle habits, such as smoking and excessive use of alcohol. An alternative pathway may involve physiological changes associated with depression, such as increased cortisol production, or an increased tendency for blood to clot.

Another point of view, expressed by Appels, Bar, Bar, Bruggeman, and de Bates (2000), is that exhaustion or fatigue, masking as depression, may be a symptom of subclinical heart disease involving inflammation of the coronary arteries that supply blood to heart muscle. Inflammation is also associated with heart attacks, referred to as myocardial infarctions. Proinflammatory substances (cytokines) are released from damaged arteries and heart muscle and make their way to the brain, producing "sickness behavior." Sickness behavior refers to subjective feelings of fatigue, weakness, malaise, and listlessness, which can be accompanied by changes in appetite and weight, altered sleep patterns, diminished interest in one's surroundings, and difficulties in concentration. It was once thought that these symptoms were caused by infection, but it now seems that they can be caused in the absence of infection by the body's own inflammatory response to damaged coronary arteries or to heart attack. It thus appears that psychosocial and biobehavioral factors not only contribute to chronic diseases, but also can themselves be influenced by disease processes.

LIFESTYLE AND PSYCHOSOCIAL INTERVENTIONS

Lifestyle and psychosocial interventions have been developed to lower the risk that healthy individuals will contract chronic diseases such as HIV-AIDS and CHD (primary prevention), as well as to improve health outcomes among patients who already have these diseases (secondary prevention). Traditionally, two strategies have been used to prevent and treat chronic diseases. One of these is a clinical approach that is aimed at people who already have disease or are at high risk. The second strategy is a public-health approach that is aimed at prevention in the general population. Although special interests have advocated each strategy to the exclusion of the other, comprehensive prevention of chronic disease often requires both approaches.

Lifestyle Interventions

Cigarette smoking is the major preventable cause of chronic illness (e.g., cancer, CHD) in the United States. Although highly addictive, and still a major health problem, cigarette smoking declined dramatically during the second half of the 20th century because of a multilevel approach to the problem. At the individual level, aimed at people at high risk, smoking-cessation programs helped smokers quit. Educational programs offered through the schools provided interventions at an organizational level. And at the community and societal levels, increases in cigarette taxes and bans on smoking in restaurants, workplaces, and public buildings and conveyances were aimed at reducing smoking in the general population.

As previously noted, the combination of physical inactivity and unhealthy dietary patterns, including excessive caloric intake, is the second leading factor contributing to mortality in the United States, after tobacco (McGinnis & Foege, 1993). Recently, a large randomized clinical trial examining behavioral and pharmacological strategies for preventing Type 2 diabetes in people at high risk provided evidence for the efficacy of a behavioral intervention (Diabetes Prevention Program Research Group, 2002). The intervention included one-on-one counseling about diet, exercise, and behavior-modification techniques. Although medication also reduced risk of developing diabetes, it was not as effective as the behavioral intervention. The lifestyle intervention was effective in both men and women across racial and ethnic groups. Although this clinical intervention in a high-risk group proved to be successful, community and societal interventions, facilitating improved diet and increased exercise in the general population, could prove useful in the prevention of Type 2 diabetes and CHD.

Psychosocial Interventions

Psychosocial interventions, such as cognitive-behavioral stress management, have been shown to have a positive effect on the quality of life of patients with chronic disease (Schneiderman, Antoni, Saab, & Ironson, 2001). Such interventions have been shown to decrease negative mood (e.g., depression), improve perceived social support, facilitate problem-focused coping, and change interpretations of experience, as well as decrease SNS arousal and the release of cortisol from the adrenal gland. Psychosocial interventions also appear to help chronic-pain patients, not only reducing their distress and perceived pain, but also increasing their physical activity and ability to return to work, and decreasing their use of medication and overuse of the health care system (Morley, Eccleston, & Williams, 1999). There is also some evidence that psychosocial interventions can have a positive influence on a number of biological variables (e.g., some immune measures), disease progression (e.g., increased survival in melanoma patients), and cardiac mortality (Schneiderman et al., 2001).

Clinical trials have reported both positive and null results for psychosocial treatment of patients following heart attack (Schneiderman et al., 2001). Several meta-analyses (i.e., statistical analyses combining the results of multiple studies) of such interventions have reported significant decreases in heart attack recurrence and death after myocardial infarction. The largest randomized clinical trial reporting positive results was the Recurrent Coronary Prevention Project (Friedman et al., 1986), whereas the most recent study reporting null results was the Enhancing Recovery in Coronary Heart Disease trial (ENRICHD, 2003). Psychosocial interventions related to cancer have also had mixed results.

CONCLUSIONS

Epidemiological studies have established important associations between lifestyle factors (e.g., diet, exercise) and disease (e.g., Type 2 diabetes). To the extent that scientists have developed effective strategies for changing health behaviors, lifestyle interventions have proven useful in preventing chronic disease (Diabetes Prevention Program Research Group, 2002). Sustained success for such interventions will likely depend on effective coordination of behavioral strategies at the individual, organizational, and societal levels.

Epidemiological studies have also established robust associations between psychosocial factors (e.g., depression, hostility) and disease (e.g., CHD, HIV-AIDS). Development of effective psychosocial interventions may depend on identifying and intervening in pathways linking psychosocial variables with disease processes. Thus, for example, studies with HIV-infected people have shown that psychosocial interventions that increase social support and decrease depressed mood can cause decreases in SNS activity and lower cortisol levels, changes that in turn can influence immune status and disease progression (Schneiderman et al., 2001).

Thus far, randomized clinical trials have reported both positive and null results for the effects of psychosocial treatment on the incidence and progression of chronic disease. Paradoxical results in randomized clinical trials are not unusual and often stimulate fine research. The null findings in ENRICHD (2003) have led to provocative secondary analyses. These analyses, although exploratory, suggest that future randomized clinical trials on CHD patients might profitably be tailored to particular subgroups of patients and utilize group therapy.

In conclusion, it appears that lifestyle and psychosocial variables are associated with disease outcomes, influence disease processes, and play an important role in the prevention and management of chronic diseases.

Recommended Reading

Institute of Medicine. (2001). *Health and behavior*. Washington, DC: National Academy Press.

Schneiderman, N., & Antoni, M. (2003). Learning to cope with HIV/AIDS. In F. Kessel, P.L. Rosenfield, & N.B. Anderson (Eds.), *Expanding the boundaries of health and social science* (pp. 316–347). New York: Oxford University Press.

Smith, T.W., & Ruiz, J.M. (2002). Psychosocial influence on the development and course of coronary heart disease: Current status and implication for research and practice. *Journal of Consulting and Clinical Psychology, 70,* 548–568.

Note

1. Address correspondence to Neil Schneiderman, Department of Psychology, University of Miami, P.O. Box 248185, Coral Gables, FL 33124-0751; e-mail: nschneid@miami.edu.

References

Anderson, R.T., Sorlie, P., Backlund, E., Johnson, N., & Kaplan, G.A. (1997). Mortality effects of community socioeconomic status. *Epidemiology, 8,* 42–47.

Appels, A., Bar, F.W., Bar, J., Bruggeman, C., & de Bates, M. (2000). Inflammation, depressive symptomatology and coronary artery disease. *Psychosomatic Medicine, 62,* 601–605.

Diabetes Prevention Program Research Group. (2002). Reduction in the incidence of Type 2 diabetes with lifestyle intervention and metformin. *New England Journal of Medicine, 346,* 393–403.

ENRICHD. (2003). Effects of treating depression and low perceived social support on clinical events after myocardial infarction: The Enhancing Recovery in Coronary Heart Disease patients (ENRICHD) randomized trial. *Journal of the American Medical Association, 289,* 3106–3116.

Friedman, M., Thoresen, C.E., Gill, J.J., Ulmer, D., Powell, L.H., Price, V.A., Brown, B., Thompson, L., Rabin, D.D., Breall, W.S., Bourg, E., Levy, R., & Dixon, T. (1986). Alteration of type A behavior and its effect on cardiac recurrences in post myocardial infarction patients: Summary results of the recurrent coronary prevention project. *American Heart Journal, 112,* 653–665.

Kaplan, J.R., & Manuck, S.B. (2003). Status, stress, and heart disease: A monkey's tale. In F. Kessel, P.L. Rosenfield, & N.B. Anderson (Eds.), *Expanding the boundaries of health and social science* (pp. 68–91). New York: Oxford University Press.

Leserman, J., Petitto, J. M., Golden, R.N., Gaynes, B.N., Gu, H., Perkins, D.O., Silva, S.G., Folds, J.D., & Evans, D.L. (2000). Impact of stressful life events, depression, social support, coping, and cortisol on progression to AIDS. *American Journal of Psychiatry, 157,* 1221–1228.

Marmot, M. (2003). Social resources and health. In F. Kessel, P.L. Rosenfield, & N.B. Anderson (Eds.), *Expanding the boundaries of health and social science* (pp. 259–285). New York: Oxford University Press.

McGinnis, J.M., & Foege, W.H. (1993). Actual causes of death in the United States. *Journal of the American Medical Association, 270,* 2207–2212.

Morley, S., Eccleston, C., & Williams, A. (1999). Systematic review and meta-analysis of randomized controlled trials of cognitive behavior therapy and behavior therapy for chronic pain in adults, excluding headache. *Pain, 80,* 1–13.

Orth-Gomér, K., Wamala, S.P., Horsten, M., Schenck-Gustafsson, K., Schneiderman, N., & Mittleman, M.A. (2000). Marital stress worsens prognosis in women with coronary heart disease. *Journal of the American Medical Association, 284,* 3008–3014.

Schneiderman, N., Antoni, M.H., Saab, P.G., & Ironson, G. (2001). Health psychology: Psychosocial and biobehavioral aspects of chronic disease management. *Annual Review of Psychology, 52,* 555–580.

Schneiderman, N., & Skyler, J.S. (1996). Insulin metabolism, sympathetic nervous system regulation, and coronary heart disease prevention. In K. Orth-Gomér & N. Schneiderman (Eds.),

Behavioral medicine approaches to cardiovascular disease prevention (pp. 105–134). Mahwah, NJ: Erlbaum.

Schneiderman, N., & Speers, M.A. (2001). Behavioral science, social science, and public health in the 21st century. In N. Schneiderman, M.A. Speers, J.M. Silva, H. Tomes, & J.H. Gentry (Eds.), *Integrating behavioral and social sciences with public health* (pp. 3–30). Washington, DC: American Psychological Association.

Williams, R.B., & Schneiderman, N. (2002). Resolved: Psychosocial interventions can improve clinical outcomes in organic disease (pro). *Psychosomatic Medicine, 64*, 552–557.

This article has been reprinted as it originally appeared in *Current Directions in Psychological Science*. Citation information for this article as originally published appears above.

Turning Up the Heat: Inflammation as a Mechanism Linking Chronic Stress, Depression, and Heart Disease

Gregory E. Miller[1] and Ekin Blackwell
Department of Psychology, University of British Columbia

Abstract

Mounting evidence indicates that chronic stressors and depressive symptoms contribute to morbidity and mortality from cardiac disease. However, little is known about the underlying mechanisms responsible for these effects or about why depressive symptoms and cardiac disease co-occur so frequently. In this article we outline a novel model that seeks to address these issues. It asserts that chronic stressors activate the immune system in a way that leads to persistent inflammation. With long-term exposure to the products of inflammation, people develop symptoms of depression and experience progression of atherosclerosis, the pathologic condition that underlies cardiac disease.

Keywords

stress; depression; inflammation; atherosclerosis

Though people have long believed that certain thoughts and feelings are toxic for their health, only in the past 30 years has convincing evidence accumulated to support this view. This research indicates that while not all negative thoughts and feelings are bad for health, specific cognitive and emotional processes do contribute to the development and progression of medical illness. In this article we focus on two of the best-studied culprits, chronic stressors and depressive symptoms, and how they "get under the skin" to influence disease. We focus on coronary heart disease (CHD), the leading cause of mortality in developed countries and the context in which mind–body connections are best documented.

STRESSORS, DEPRESSION, AND CHD RISK

Chronic stressors come in different packages, ranging from troubled marriages to difficult workplaces. What they have in common is the tendency to be appraised as threatening and unmanageable. They can involve situations in which the troubling stimulus persists over a long time (an abusive boss), as well as situations in which the event is brief but the threat persists longer (a sexual assault). Research indicates that exposure to chronic stress generally increases vulnerability to CHD. In a study of 12,000 healthy males followed over 9 years, those facing chronic difficulties at work or home were 30% more likely to die of CHD (Matthews & Gump, 2002). Another project measured adverse childhood experiences in 17,000 adults and found a dose–response relationship with CHD incidence. Those who reported a variety of adverse experiences such as neglect, domestic violence, and parental criminal behavior were 3.1 times more likely to develop CHD (Dong et al., 2004).

Depression can take the form of a low mood or a clinical syndrome. In both cases it typically involves sadness and anhedonia, which may be accompanied by disturbances in eating, sleeping, and cognition. Depression is common in CHD. About 20% of patients meet criteria for a clinical diagnosis, and even more have symptoms below the diagnostic threshold. These symptoms diminish quality of life and contribute to poorer medical outcomes. For example, in a study of 900 patients interviewed in the hospital following a heart attack, high levels of depressive symptoms were associated with a threefold increase in cardiac mortality over 5 years (Lesperance, Frasure-Smith, Talajic, & Bourassa, 2002). There is also evidence that in healthy young adults, depressive symptoms can accelerate the development of CHD. For example, in a 27-year study of middle-aged adults, those with high levels of depressive symptoms at baseline were 1.7 times more likely to have a fatal heart attack (Barefoot & Schroll, 1996).

Although these findings provide compelling evidence of mind–body connections in CHD, they also raise challenging questions that researchers are just starting to address. One has to do with the underlying mechanisms linking mind and body. How can nebulous patterns of thinking and feeling "get inside the body" in a way that alters disease trajectories? A second question has to do with the high rate of comorbidity between depression and CHD. There are other serious medical conditions, such as cancer, for which the rates of depression are much lower (Dew, 1998). Why is it especially common in cardiac patients? Another question researchers struggle with concerns theoretical integration. Though most studies have focused on chronic stress or depressive symptoms, these states are likely to be closely related and to influence disease through similar pathways. So an important challenge involves conceptually integrating literatures that have evolved separately and determining where the "action" really is.

AN INTEGRATIVE CONCEPTUAL FRAMEWORK

We have developed a conceptual framework to begin answering these questions (Fig. 1). It begins with the notion that chronic stressors activate the immune system in a way that leads to persistent inflammation. This refers to a molecular and cellular cascade the body uses to eliminate infections and resolve injuries. The model suggests that with long-term exposure to the products of inflammation, people develop symptoms of depression and experience accelerated CHD progression. This occurs because the signaling molecules deployed to orchestrate inflammation—pro-inflammatory cytokines—elicit adaptations in the brain that are manifested as symptoms of depression. These molecules also promote growth of plaques in blood vessels and stimulate processes that lead those plaques to rupture. In doing so, they bring about heart attacks. The model goes on to assert that the excessive inflammation is responsible for bidirectional connections between depression and atherosclerosis. That is, cytokines are viewed as a mechanism through which depression fosters CHD progression, and at the same time as the reason cardiac patients experience high rates of affective difficulties. It should be noted that although chronic stress is depicted as the model's starting point, a person could enter the cascade as a result of depressive symptoms or coronary disease; chronic stress is sufficient, but not necessary, to initiate the model's processes.

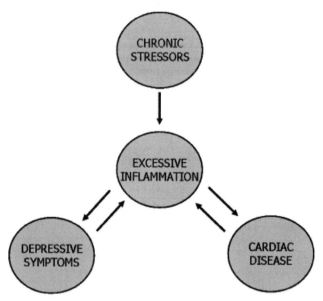

Fig. 1. Model of how inflammatory processes mediate the relations among chronic stressors, depressive symptoms, and cardiac disease. Stressors activate the immune system in a way that leads to persistent inflammation. With long-term exposure to the molecular products of inflammation, people are expected develop symptoms of depression and experience progression of cardiac disease. Excessive inflammation is also viewed as responsible for the bidirectional relationship between depression and atherosclerosis. (Some pathways in the model are excluded for the sake of brevity and simplicity—for example, the likely bidirectional relationship between chronic stressors and depressive symptoms.)

WHAT IS INFLAMMATION?

When the immune system detects invading microbes like viruses or bacteria, it launches an inflammatory response, which causes white blood cells to accumulate at the site of infection. These cells attempt to eliminate the pathogen, rid the body of cells that have been infected with it, and repair any tissue damage that it has caused. This entire process is orchestrated by inflammatory cytokines, which are signaling molecules secreted by white blood cells. The most critical cytokines are interleukin-1β, interleukin-6 (IL-6), and tumor necrosis factor-α, and they have wide-ranging functions that include directing cells toward infections, signaling them to divide, and activating their killing mechanisms. Because these molecules are released when the immune system is active, researchers use their presence as a rough index of the magnitude of inflammation in the body. This is also done by measuring C-reactive protein (CRP), a molecule produced by the liver in response to IL-6.

DOES CHRONIC STRESS TRIGGER INFLAMMATION?

What evidence is there to support the idea that chronic stressors activate the immune system in a way that promotes inflammation? Over the past few years a number of studies have found that among persons facing serious chronic stressors, concentrations of inflammatory molecules such as IL-6 and CRP are significantly elevated (Segerstrom & Miller, 2004). One project followed older adults caring for a relative with dementia. Caregiving is a potent chronic stressor that presents challenges in nearly every domain of life, and it does so at a time of life when coping resources are often waning. Over a 6-year follow-up, caregivers displayed marked increases in IL-6 and did so at a rate that was four times more rapid than controls (Kiecolt-Glaser et al., 2003). This pattern of findings was initially puzzling to researchers, because chronic stressors were believed to suppress immune functions. But it is now clear that the immune system responds to any given stressor in a complex fashion; some of its functions are activated at the same time as others are disabled (Segerstrom & Miller, 2004).

Researchers are now seeking to understand the mechanisms through which chronic stressors bring about inflammation. Some evidence indicates that chronic stressors "prime" the immune system to respond to challenges in an especially aggressive fashion. Another hypothesis is that chronic stressors interfere with the immune system's capacity to shut down after a challenge has been minimized. One signal the body uses to do this is cortisol; at high levels, this hormone dampens the release of cytokines. However, chronic stressors interfere with this process. In parents whose children were being treated for cancer, for example, cortisol's ability to suppress IL-6 production was markedly diminished (Miller, Cohen, & Ritchey, 2002). This suggests that chronic stressors "take the brakes off" inflammation. Another intriguing possibility derives from animal research showing that stressors like social isolation can bring about inflammation in the brain (Maier, Watkins, & Nance, 2001). This process has been shown, in turn, to activate inflammation in the periphery. So, in humans, chronic stressors may trigger a cytokine cascade that starts in the brain and then makes its way to other areas of the body.

DEPRESSION AND INFLAMMATION

Can inflammation bring about depression? To answer this question, researchers have exposed rodents to bacterial products that trigger inflammation and shown that the animals develop symptoms resembling depression—symptoms known as "sickness behaviors." These include declines in food intake, motor activity, grooming behavior, and social exploration, as well as a lack of interest in hedonic activities such as sex (Yirmiya, 1996). It has been difficult to examine this process directly in humans, because they cannot safely be exposed to inflammatory substances. However, researchers have been able to address this question indirectly in cancer patients, who are administered cytokines with the hope that they will boost immune functions. About 50% of patients treated with cytokines develop symptoms, such as dysphoria, anhedonia, fatigue, anorexia, and cognitive impairment, that are consistent with a diagnosis of major depression (Musselman et al., 2001). The extent of these symptoms is directly related to the dose of cytokine therapy, and prophylactic treatment with antidepressant medications can often prevent them from arising. Although these findings suggest that inflammation brings about adaptations that resemble depression, further research is necessary to determine whether these conditions are one and the same or merely "look-alikes." It may also be the case that sickness behavior underlies some cases of depression—like those that arise in CHD and other inflammatory conditions—but is not responsible for affective difficulties more generally.

Researchers are still attempting to understand how and why sickness behaviors emerge. They may be an evolved strategy to maximize the chances of survival after infection (Maier & Watkins, 1998). When infected, an organism's survival depends on its capacity to mount a vigorous defense and to avoid contact with pathogens and predators that might capitalize on its vulnerability. Organisms must initiate a febrile response, which interferes with pathogens' capacity to reproduce, and mobilize their immune systems to fight. These responses, however, pose significant metabolic demands. By spending more time sleeping and withdrawing from activities, the organism conserves energy and avoids contact with pathogens and predators. When viewed from this perspective, the "depressive" symptoms that arise following inflammation are behavioral adaptations that evolved to maximize the chances of survival during infection.

And can depression provoke inflammation? Cross-sectional studies indicate that among patients suffering from clinical depression, concentrations of CRP and IL-6 are increased by 40% to 50% (Miller, Stetler, Carney, Freedland, & Banks, 2002). These effects do not seem to be limited to clinical depression; similar patterns are found in patients with depressive symptoms, even when they are not severe enough to warrant a diagnosis. But it is difficult to rigorously evaluate whether depression provokes inflammation, because humans cannot be randomly assigned to experience affective difficulties. To overcome this difficulty, researchers have studied patients before and after treatment and have shown that cytokine volumes decrease after depressive symptoms have been ameliorated. These findings suggest that depression operates causally. How it does so remains unclear. Depressive symptoms could prime the immune system to respond aggressively to challenges; alternatively, they could initiate a cytokine cascade in the brain that spreads elsewhere. They also could foster maladaptive behaviors that themselves activate inflammatory processes. The best data to date are consistent with the latter hypothesis; much of the inflammation in depression is attributable to excess weight and sleeping disturbances (Miller, Stetler, et al., 2002; Motivala & Irwin, in press).

INFLAMMATION CONTRIBUTES TO CHD

CHD begins when infections and injuries damage the arteries supplying the heart, causing an influx of white blood cells that are seeking to repair the lesion. These cells accumulate in the vessel wall, where they become engorged with cholesterol, and eventually contribute to formation of plaque. Much later in the disease process, these cells help to destabilize the plaque. When this occurs, the plaque can rupture, and its remnants can block blood flow in the vessel. This process deprives the heart of nutrients, and results in death of cardiac tissues, an outcome known as myocardial infarction, or heart attack. Because inflammation is centrally involved in the progression of CHD, studies have examined whether the presence of inflammatory molecules forecasts disease. This work shows that high levels of such molecules, particularly CRP and IL-6, confer risk for later CHD morbidity and mortality (Libby, 2002).

WHERE DO WE GO FROM HERE?

While several of the model's basic predictions have been confirmed, more work needs to be done before its overall utility can be evaluated. The first step in the process should entail testing the model's mediational hypotheses. Do stressful experiences foster depressive symptoms and cardiac disease by triggering inflammation? Does inflammation operate as a bidirectional pathway linking depression and atherosclerosis? To answer these questions, researchers will need to conduct multiwave prospective investigations assessing constructs frequently. If the model's predictions turn out to be accurate, it will become important to further differentiate its constructs so that their most toxic elements are revealed. Must stressors be severe, like caregiving, to bring about inflammation? Or can more day-to-day concerns such as deadlines and traffic elicit the same processes? There are also nagging questions about the depression construct. Do the symptoms of depression have a unique capacity to initiate the cascades depicted in the model, or is their effect attributable to a broader cluster of negative emotions that also includes anger and anxiety (Suls & Bunde, 2005)? For the model to be maximally valuable as a research tool, the next wave of studies will have to distill these constructs. Fortunately, there are some good leads to guide this work. For example, an intriguing program of research indicates that when stressors elicit feelings of shame, they are especially potent triggers of inflammation and have a special capacity to bring about depressive episodes (Dickerson, Gruenewald, & Kemeny, 2004; Kendler, Hettema, Butera, Gardner, & Prescott, 2003). As time goes on it will also become important to incorporate additional mechanisms linking the model's constructs. Research has already identified a number of candidate pathways. In focusing our discussion on inflammation, we do not mean to imply that these pathways are unimportant; we simply view inflammation as the best candidate for pulling together the disparate literatures we have discussed. Of course, for the model to be complete, these other pathways must be integrated. To the extent that the next wave of studies can meet these challenges, researchers will be able to develop convincing mechanistic explanations for the age-old belief that the mind and body are connected.

Recommended Reading

Irwin, M.R. (2002). Psychoneuroimmunology of depression: Clinical implications. *Brain, Behavior and Immunity, 16*, 1–16.

Kop, W.J. (1999). Chronic and acute psychological risk factors for clinical manifestations of coronary artery disease. *Psychosomatic Medicine, 61*, 476–487.

Maier, S.F., & Watkins, L.R. (1998). (See References)

Acknowledgments—The authors thank Dr. Edith Chen for helpful feedback on this manuscript, and the Michael Smith Foundation for Health Research and the Heart and Stroke Foundation of Canada for supporting this work.

Note

1. Address correspondence to Dr. Gregory Miller, Department of Psychology, University of British Columbia, 2136 West Mall Avenue, Vancouver BC V6T 1Z4 Canada; e-mail: gemiller@psych.ubc.ca.

References

Barefoot, J.C., & Schroll, M. (1996). Symptoms of depression, acute myocardial infarction, and total mortality in a community sample. *Circulation, 93,* 1976–1980.

Dew, M.A. (1998). Psychiatric disorder in the context of physical illness. In B.P. Dohrenwend (Ed.), *Adversity, stress, and psychopathology* (pp. 177–218). New York: Oxford University Press.

Dickerson, S.S., Gruenewald, T.L., & Kemeny, M.E. (2004). When the social self is threatened: Shame, physiology, and health. *Journal of Personality, 72,* 1191–1216.

Dong, M., Giles, W.H., Felitti, V.J., Dube, S.R., Williams, J.E., Chapman, D.P., & Anda, R.F. (2004). Insights into causal pathways for ischemic heart disease: Adverse childhood experiences study. *Circulation, 110,* 1761–1766.

Kendler, K.S., Hettema, J.M., Butera, F., Gardner, C.O., & Prescott, C.A. (2003). Life event dimensions of loss, humiliation, entrapment, and danger in the prediction of onsets of major depression and generalized anxiety. *Archives of General Psychiatry, 60,* 789–796.

Kiecolt-Glaser, J.K., Preacher, K.J., MacCallum, R.C., Atkinson, C., Malarkey, W.B., & Glaser, R. (2003). Chronic stress and age-related increases in the proinflammatory cytokine IL-6. *Proceedings of the National Academy of Sciences, U.S.A., 100,* 9090–9095.

Lesperance, F., Frasure-Smith, N., Talajic, M., & Bourassa, M.G. (2002). Five-year risk of cardiac mortality in relation to initial severity and one-year changes in depression symptoms after myocardial infarction. *Circulation, 105,* 1049–1053.

Libby, P. (2002). Atherosclerosis: The new view. *Scientific American, 286,* 46–55.

Maier, S.F., & Watkins, L.R. (1998). Cytokines for psychologists: Implications of bidirectional immune-to-brain communication for understanding behavior, mood, and cognition. *Psychological Review, 105,* 83–107.

Maier, S.F., Watkins, L.R., & Nance, D.M. (2001). Multiple routes of action of IL-1 on the nervous system. In R. Ader, D. Felten, & N. Cohen (Eds.), *Psychoneuroimmunology* (3rd ed., pp. 563–579). New York: Academic Press.

Matthews, K., & Gump, B.B. (2002). Chronic work stress and marital dissolution increase risk of posttrial mortality in men from the Multiple Risk Factor Intervention Trial. *Archives of Internal Medicine, 162,* 309–315.

Miller, G.E., Cohen, S., & Ritchey, A.K. (2002). Chronic psychological stress and the regulation of pro-inflammatory cytokines: A glucocorticoid resistance model. *Health Psychology, 21,* 531–541.

Miller, G.E., Stetler, C.A., Carney, R.M., Freedland, K.E., & Banks, W.A. (2002). Clinical depression and inflammatory risk markers for coronary heart disease. *The American Journal of Cardiology, 90,* 1279–1283.

Motivala, S.J., & Irwin, M.R. (in press). Sleep and immunity: Cytokine pathways linking sleep and health outcomes. *Current Directions in Psychological Science.*

Musselman, D.L., Lawson, D.H., Gumnick, J.F., Manatunga, A.K., Penna, S., Goodkin, R.S., Greiner, K., Nemeroff, C.B., & Miller, A.H. (2001). Paroxetine for the prevention of depression induced by high-dose interferon alfa. *New England Journal of Medicine, 344,* 961–966.

Segerstrom, S.C., & Miller, G.E. (2004). Psychological stress and the immune system: A meta analytic study of 30 years of inquiry. *Psychological Bulletin, 130,* 601–630.

Suls, J., & Bunde, J. (2005). Anger, anxiety, and depression as risk factors for cardiovascular disease: The problems and implications of overlapping affective dispositions. *Psychological Bulletin, 131,* 260–300.

Yirmiya, R. (1996). Endotoxin produces a depressive-like episode in rats. *Brain Research, 711,* 163–174.

This article has been reprinted as it originally appeared in *Current Directions in Psychological Science*. Citation information for this article as originally published appears above.

Seasonal Patterns of Stress, Disease, and Sickness Responses

Randy J. Nelson[1]
Departments of Psychology and Neuroscience, Ohio State University, Columbus

Gregory E. Demas
Department of Biology, Indiana University, Bloomington

Abstract

The combined challenge of low food availability and low temperatures can make winter difficult for survival, and nearly impossible for breeding. Traditionally, studies of seasonality have focused on reproductive adaptations and largely ignored adaptations associated with survival. We propose shifting the focus from reproduction to immune function, a proxy for survival, and hypothesize that evolved physiological and behavioral mechanisms enable individuals to anticipate recurrent seasonal stressors and enhance immune function in advance of their occurrence. These seasonal adaptations, which have an important influence on seasonal patterns of survival, are reviewed here. We then discuss studies suggesting that photoperiod (day length) and photoperiod-dependent melatonin secretion influence immune function. Our working hypothesis is that short day lengths reroute energy from reproduction and growth to bolster immune function during winter. The net effect of these photoperiod-mediated adjustments is enhanced immune function and increased survival.

Keywords

allostasis; illness; stressors; annual cycles; sickness behavior

And as for sickness: Are we not almost tempted to ask whether we could get along without it?

—Nietzsche (1887/1974, p. iv)

In the preface to the second edition of *The Gay Science*, published in 1887, Nietzsche (1887/1974) wrote about the "contradictions" between winter and summer, as well as between sickness and health. Nietzsche emphasized that these apparent contradictions are nonetheless held together in the experience of the body. Over evolutionary time, the experiences of recurrent summers and winters have provoked the evolution of adaptations that allow modern-day individuals to cope with the seasonally fluctuating environments in which they live. Coping with stressors, however, requires energy, and because energy is finite, competing functions within the body must be curtailed as stressors increase. A primary means by which individuals cope with seasonal stressors is by shifting energy allocations from less critical functions to those most important for immediate survival. This re-allocation of energy allows individuals to adapt to environmental stressors and maximize survival and reproductive success.

Confrontation with a stressor, an agent that disturbs the body's equilibrium, or homeostasis, triggers a stress response in which an individual releases hormones, such as adrenaline or cortisol, from the adrenal glands. These hormones work in the short term to restore homeostasis, often by shunting resources from nonessential activities to functions necessary for survival. However, if the stressors persist, chronic exposure to the so-called stress hormones may cause problems within several biological systems, including the digestive, cardiovascular, reproductive, metabolic, and nervous systems. Over time, organisms have evolved adaptations that attenuate the stress response during the winter, when energy shortages limit the ability to cope. Chronic exposure to stressors, however, can still leave energy levels low, and because immunity entails high energy costs, it might be compromised. Enhancing immune function in anticipation of seasonally recurring winter stressors could improve the likelihood of survival, but this would be possible only if other energy-demanding activities (e.g., reproduction and growth) are curtailed. Indeed, by monitoring the annual cycle of changing day lengths, organisms can determine the time of year and use this information to switch between winter and summer adaptations.

The cycle of breeding seasons is probably the most salient annual cycle among animals. Generally, breeding is limited in nontropical climates, so that offspring are produced during spring or summer, when food is most abundant and other environmental conditions are optimal for survival. In contrast, when resources are limited, energy is shunted into survival mechanisms. Pathogens introduce a complication into this evolutionary dance between reproductive success and survival, because energy is required to cope with them. The varying availability of energy over the course of the year means that the consequences of pathogenic infection also vary seasonally (Nelson, Demas, Klein, & Kriegsfeld, 2002). Consequently, the seasonal adaptations that have evolved (e.g., inhibition of reproductive functions and behavior) allow trade-offs in whether energy is invested in boosting immune function, fighting disease, or coping with other stressors.

Our working hypothesis is that during winter, animals shift their energy expenditure from reproduction and growth to survival. Immune function can serve as a proxy for measuring this shift. Thus, we hypothesize that by attending to day length (photoperiod), animals anticipate the onset of winter stressors and bolster their immune function. Although immune function is in fact compromised by the chronic stressors of winter, we hypothesize that it would be compromised even further without this photoperiodic bolstering.

SEASONAL PATTERNS OF DISEASE AND SICKNESS RESPONSES

Many human and nonhuman diseases show strong seasonal patterns (Nelson et al., 2002; see Table 1). Often these patterns reflect the life history of the pathogen. In many cases, however, seasonal changes in the host or in the interactions between host and pathogen underlie seasonal patterns in disease. Changes in social behavior may also contribute to seasonal patterns of disease. For example, individuals of many species suspend territorial behaviors during winter and huddle in groups to conserve heat and humidity. These overwintering groups may contain multiple

Table 1. *Seasonal patterns of infectious diseases in humans in the northern hemisphere*

Disease	Peak occurrence
Diphtheria	Winter
HIV	Summer
Influenza	Winter
Legionnaire's disease	Summer
Malaria	Winter
Measles	Summer
Parainfluenza virus	Fall
Pneumococcal disease	Winter
Polio	Summer
Rotavirus	Winter
Rubella	Spring
Tuberculosis	Winter

species that normally do not associate during the breeding season. Close proximity increases the potential for pathogens to be shared both within a species and across species. Indeed, many novel influenza variants begin in Asia when the virus "jumps" from swine or fowl as farmers bring their animals indoors for the winter. The incidence of severe acute respiratory syndrome (SARS) may have a seasonal pattern that reflects the vernal interaction between humans and civet cats (the putative native pool of the virus that causes SARS).

One of the greatest challenges that an animal faces on a daily basis is avoiding and overcoming pathogenic infections. Animals have co-evolved with pathogens; therefore, it is reasonable to expect that animals have evolved appropriate responses to fight infection. Indeed, not only have complex cascades of molecular and cellular responses evolved to defend against invading pathogens, but behavioral adaptations are also important for this purpose. Acute exposure to bacteria or other harmful stimuli triggers a highly stereotyped set of responses called the acute phase response (APR). APR includes physiological changes such as fever, increased sleep, alterations in circulating ions (such as decreased iron) and protein synthesis, and elevated numbers of white blood cells circulating in the blood (Berczi, 1993). Behavioral changes resulting from infection and APR include reduced food and water intake, activity, exploration, and social and sexual interactions, and are collectively called *sickness behaviors* (Hart, 1988). Rather than nonspecific manifestations of illness, these behaviors are organized, adaptive strategies that are critical to the host's survival (Dantzer, 2001). Individuals that do not express sickness behaviors survive less well than those that do.

Energy shortages during winter should make it difficult for individuals to display prolonged energy-demanding symptoms such as fever or anorexia. The notion that the expression of sickness behaviors is constrained by energy availability was tested in a recent study by measuring these symptoms in infected Siberian hamsters (Bilbo, Drazen, Quan, He, & Nelson, 2002). The duration of fever and anorexia was, in fact, reduced in hamsters housed under simulated winter photoperiods, relative to hamsters maintained under long-day-length conditions. In addition, the animals in the short-day condition had an attenuated response to lipopolysaccharide (LPS; a complex sugar that is present on the cell wall of certain bacteria and to which the immune system responds). Thus, short days can attenuate the symptoms of infection, presumably to optimize energy expenditure and survival outcome. In addition, short-day animals decreased their intake of dietary iron, a nutrient vital to bacterial replication.

ENERGY AND THE IMMUNE RESPONSE

Mounting an immune response takes considerable energy (reviewed in Lochmiller & Deerenberg, 2000; Nelson et al., 2002). Many diseases (including cancer, AIDS, diabetes mellitus, and arthritis), as well as trauma, can substantially increase energy expenditures in humans, and often result in cachexia (wasting). Fever requires an increase in resting metabolic rate of about 10% for every increase of 1 °C in body temperature. During disease states, abnormal protein metabolism, the breakdown of fatty acids, and the production of humoral and inflammatory mediators (the components of the immune system that fight pathogens) all increase energy expenditure. In addition, mice injected with a novel antigen consume more oxygen (an indication of increased energy expenditure) than noninjected animals (Demas, Chefer, Talan, & Nelson, 1997).

Insufficient food intake, starvation, or malnutrition generally decreases immunity (reviewed in Nelson et al., 2002). A recent study demonstrated that immune responses are diminished in bumblebees during starvation, and energy is instead allocated to cardiac and brain metabolism, processes vital for immediate survival. Mortality rates increase among bees that are infected and mount an immune response during starvation (Moret & Schmid-Hempel, 2000). Similarly, Siberian hamsters in the lab reduce antibody production during short day lengths when the availability of food is reduced to the point that their body mass is significantly decreased (Drazen, Bilu, Bilbo, & Nelson, 2001).

Experimentally reducing body fat via surgical removal is an effective way to mimic the decreases in body fat seen in lab animals housed under short-day conditions. We recently examined the effects of partial surgical removal of body fat on antibody production in two seasonally breeding rodent species, prairie voles and Siberian hamsters (Demas, Drazen, & Nelson, 2003). In general, removal of body fat reduced antigen-induced antibody production in the short term in both species. Several weeks later, however, the hamsters who underwent this treatment had compensatory increases in their remaining fat tissues compared with control hamsters, and their antibody levels no longer differed from those of control hamsters. Voles, in contrast, never displayed compensatory increases in body fat, and their immune function remained depressed. Thus, reductions in energy stores in the form of body fat correlate with reduced immunity. Collectively, these results support the idea that immunity is energetically expensive.

MELATONIN AND PHOTOPERIODIC CHANGES IN IMMUNE FUNCTION

Ultimately, seasonal breeding patterns are driven by the availability of food and water. However, animals need to forecast the onset of environmental changes well in advance in order to initiate appropriate seasonal adaptations. The autumnal collapse of the reproductive system in seasonally breeding animals, for example, requires several weeks to accomplish; it would not prove useful for this response to be directly initiated by low temperatures or limited food, as energy savings would not be realized for several weeks. Seasonally breeding animals have evolved the ability to detect and respond to environmental cues that accurately signal, in advance, the arrival or departure of particular seasons; of these cues, the most reliable are changes in photoperiod. With only two pieces of information, the current day length and whether day length is increasing or decreasing, animals can precisely determine the time of year.

Substantial research demonstrates that changes in day length induce not only changes in reproduction, but also changes in immunity (reviewed in Nelson et al., 2002). Furthermore, these photoperiod-induced changes in immune function appear to be adaptive responses. For example, deer mice housed in short, "winterlike" day lengths for 8 weeks display increased antibody responses compared with animals housed in long, "summerlike" days (Fig. 1). In addition, low temperatures reduced antibody levels in long-day deer mice, but this effect was blocked by moving deer mice to short days (Fig. 1). Thus, short-day conditions not only increase immunity, but also counteract the reductions in antibodies seen in response to other environmental stressors (e.g., low temperatures), preventing the immune system from falling below baseline levels.

Another recent test of this hypothesis was conducted in a study on toxic shock and survival after challenge with LPS (Prendergast, Hotchkiss, Bilbo, Kinsey, & Nelson, 2003). Short days significantly improved survival of hamsters treated with high doses of LPS, which mimicked a severe infection. Immune system cells obtained from short-day hamsters produced significantly lower amounts of specific

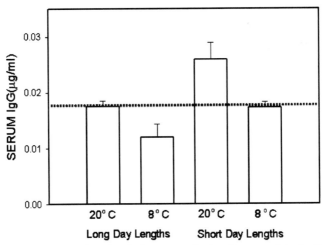

Fig. 1. Effects of day length on level of serum antibodies (Immunoglobulin G, or IgG) in deer mice maintained at low (8 °C) and normal (20 °C) room temperatures. Baseline immune function (i.e., function of animals housed in long-day conditions and at room temperature) is indicated by the horizontal dotted line. Redrawn after Demas and Nelson (1996).

cytokines (chemical messengers of the immune system) than similar cells obtained from long-day hamsters. Excessive cytokine production can lead to toxic shock (physiological reactions that include blood vessel damage, low blood pressure, and respiratory problems), so one explanation of these results is that diminished cytokine responses to LPS in short-day animals may reduce their mortality from toxic shock and provide several additional days for recovery (Prendergast et al., 2003).

Because melatonin, a hormone from the pineal gland, is a biological signal of day length and is a well-established modulator of immunity, we propose that it plays a pivotal role in seasonal adjustments of immunity. The synthesis and secretion of melatonin occurs exclusively at night, and is inhibited directly by light. Melatonin serves as the biological signal for day length because the duration of its release is proportional to the duration of the night. Animals experience longer durations of melatonin when daylight hours are few than when the day is long and use this information to determine time of year.

The role of melatonin in modulating immunity is well established for many species, including humans (reviewed in Guerrero & Reiter, 1992; Nelson et al., 2002). Melatonin receptors have been identified on cells of the immune system, such as lymphocytes, and treating immune cells of rodents with melatonin increases the rate at which they divide and produce new cells (Drazen et al., 2001). Enhancement of immune function in mice appears to be mediated directly via one of the specific types (MT-2) of melatonin receptors on lymphocytes (Drazen et al., 2001). Melatonin also stimulates the production of opioids directly from certain immune cells, and this effect may play a role in the immunoenhancing effects of melatonin, as well as modulate the effects of stressors on immune function during the winter (reviewed in Nelson et al., 2002).

Melatonin has been investigated therapeutically (e.g., for the treatment of infection), and has been implicated as an antitumor agent (reviewed in Nelson et al., 2002). Furthermore, some reports suggest that melatonin has antioxidant properties and may slow damage caused during aging (Reiter, 1993). Melatonin may also counteract the suppression of immune function that can follow drug treatments or accompany viral disease (reviewed in Nelson et al., 2002). Melatonin should not be considered a miracle drug, but it does have immunomodulatory effects that may have clinical relevance. Careful clinical research is necessary to delineate the benefits and costs of melatonin treatment.

CONCLUSIONS

Both the incidence of and responses to stressors vary on a seasonal basis. Furthermore, it is well established that stress can impair immune function and increase susceptibility to disease. We hypothesize that a seasonal bolstering of immune function has evolved as an adaptive mechanism to counter the immune suppression that is induced by seasonal stress; these changes in immunity appear to be constrained by seasonal fluctuations in energy availability. This hypothesis provides a means for resolving the apparent discrepancy between field studies reporting immunosuppression during the winter and laboratory investigations reporting that immunity is enhanced under short-day conditions. Experimental manipulations of energy availability alter immune function in the expected direction: Low energy availability limits immune responses. The environmental regulation of seasonal changes in immunity is mediated primarily by day length, which also plays a central role in mediating the development of other seasonally appropriate adaptations (e.g., in reproduction and metabolism).

Thus far, research suggests that melatonin coordinates photoperiodic changes in immune function. Whether the immunoenhancing effects of melatonin are unique to seasonally breeding rodents or generalize to humans is an important empirical question that requires further study. Although physiological responses are important mediators of seasonal, photoperiodic changes in immune function, behavioral alterations may play an equally critical role in mediating seasonal strategies of coping with stress and thus coping with infection. There are many gaps in current knowledge, but we believe research on the interplay between the behavioral and physiological mechanisms underlying seasonality of immune function will likely provide important insights into the role of the environment and stressors in influencing health and well-being. Ongoing studies of the physiological mechanisms underlying sickness behavior will continue to provide novel and important clinically relevant information. And as for sickness, perhaps people cannot do without it, but an integrative approach to the study of the mechanisms underlying responses to it may provide better tools with which to control it.

Recommended Reading

Bilbo, S.D., Dhabhar, F.S., Viswanathan, K., Saul, A., Yellon, S.M., & Nelson, R.J. (2002). Short day lengths augment stress-induced leukocyte trafficking and stress-induced enhancement of skin immune function. *Proceedings of the National Academy of Sciences, USA, 99*, 4067–4072.

Demas, G.E. (2004). The energetics of immunity: A neuroendocrine link between energy balance and immune function. *Hormones and Behavior, 43*, 75–80.

Konsman, J.P., Parnet, P., & Dantzer, R. (2002). Cytokine-induced sickness behaviour: Mechanisms and implications. *Trends in Neurosciences, 25*, 154–159.

Nelson, R.J., Demas, G.E., Klein, S.L., & Kriegsfeld, L.J. (2002). (See References)

Yellon, S.M., & Tran, L.T. (2002). Photoperiod, reproduction, and immunity in select strains of inbred mice. *Journal of Biological Rhythms, 17*, 65–75.

Acknowledgments—This work was supported by National Science Foundation Grant IBN 04-16897 and National Institutes of Health Grants MH057535 and MH066144.

Note

1. Address correspondence to Randy J. Nelson, Department of Psychology, Townshend Hall, The Ohio State University, Columbus, OH 43210; e-mail: rnelson@osu.edu.

References

Berczi, I. (1993). Neuroendocrine defence in endotoxin shock (a review). *Acta Microbiology Hungary, 40*, 265–302.

Bilbo, S.D., Drazen, D.L., Quan, N., He, L., & Nelson, R.J. (2002). Short day lengths attenuate the symptoms of infection in Siberian hamsters. *Proceedings of the Royal Society of London B, 269*, 447–454.

Dantzer, R. (2001). Cytokine-induced sickness behavior: Where do we stand? *Brain, Behavior and Immunity, 15*, 7–24.

Demas, G.E., Chefer, V., Talan, M., & Nelson, R.J. (1997). Metabolic costs of mounting an antigen-stimulated antibody response in adult and aged C57BL/6J mice. *American Journal of Physiology, 273*, R1631–R1637.

Demas, G.E., Drazen, D.L., & Nelson, R.J. (2003). Reductions in total body fat decrease humoral immunity. *Proceedings of the Royal Society of London B, 270*, 905–911.

Demas, G.E., & Nelson, R.J. (1996). Photoperiod and temperature interact to affect immune parameters in male deer mice (*Peromyscus maniculatus*). *Journal of Biological Rhythms, 11*, 95–103.

Drazen, D.L., Bilu, D., Bilbo, S.D., & Nelson, R.J. (2001). Melatonin enhancement of splenocyte proliferation is attenuated by luzindole, a melatonin receptor antagonist. *American Journal of Physiology, 280*, R1476–R1482.

Guerrero, J.M., & Reiter, R.J. (1992). A brief survey of pineal gland-immune system interrelationships. *Endocrine Research, 18*, 91–113.

Hart, B.L. (1988). Biological basis of the behavior of sick animals. *Neuroscience and Biobehavioral Reviews, 12*, 123–137.

Lochmiller, R.L., & Deerenberg, C. (2000). Trade-offs in evolutionary immunology: Just what is the cost of immunity? *Oikos, 88*, 87–98.

Moret, Y., & Schmid-Hempel, P. (2000). Survival for immunity: The price of immune system activation for bumblebee workers. *Science, 290*, 1166–1168.

Nelson, R.J., Demas, G.E., Klein, S.L., & Kriegsfeld, L.J. (2002). *Seasonal patterns of stress, immune function, and disease*. New York: Cambridge University Press.

Nietzsche, F.W. (1974). *The gay science; with a prelude in rhymes and an appendix of songs* (W. Kaufmann, Trans.). New York: Vintage Books. (Original work published 1887)

Prendergast, B.J., Hotchkiss, A.K., Bilbo, S.D., Kinsey, S.G., & Nelson, R.J. (2003). Photoperiodic adjustments in immune function protect Siberian hamsters from lethal endotoxemia. *Journal of Biological Rhythms, 18*, 51–62.

Reiter, R.J. (1993). Interactions of the pineal hormone melatonin with oxygen-centered free radicals: A brief review. *Brazilian Journal of Medical and Biological Research, 26*, 1141–1155.

This article has been reprinted as it originally appeared in *Current Directions in Psychological Science*. Citation information for this article as originally published appears above.

Sleep and Immunity: Cytokine Pathways Linking Sleep and Health Outcomes

Sarosh J. Motivala[1] and Michael R. Irwin
Cousins Center for Psychoneuroimmunology, University of California, Los Angeles

Abstract

The functions of sleep are enigmatic but are beginning to be delineated. Sleep has been long thought to be important for health, and poor sleep is prospectively associated with worsened health outcomes. Yet the mechanisms accounting for this are only partially understood. In this review, we suggest that the immune system plays a role in the relationship between sleep and health and that sleep processes and immunity show bidirectional interactions, as evidenced in both animal and human studies. Immunological signaling molecules, termed cytokines, are important in coordinating brain–immune system communication, and particular cytokines such as tumor necrosis factor, interleukin-1, and interleukin-6 play a crucial role in sleep regulation. Elevated levels of these cytokines are also associated with a number of chronic diseases and may provide a pathway linking poor sleep with health outcomes.

Keywords

sleep; immunity; cytokines

For about 8 hours a day, humans engage in a behavior whose functions are still somewhat ambiguous: sleep. This nightly behavior is clearly important for health. Poor sleep has been shown to be predictive of all-cause mortality, and sleep disorders such as insomnia have health consequences including higher numbers of missed work days and increased health-care utilization (Bryant, Trinder, & Curtis, 2004). This review describes the bidirectional relationship between sleep and immunity and explores how this relationship plays a role in linking poor sleep with subsequent deleterious health outcomes. We posit that poor sleep stimulates increased expression of immune-signaling molecules called cytokines; these molecules promote inflammatory processes associated with a range of health consequences including cardiovascular disease progression and exacerbation of autoimmune disorders such as rheumatoid arthritis. Cytokines also affect sleep, suggesting a pathway through which elevated levels of cytokines involved in inflammation can dys-regulate sleep.

OVERVIEW OF SLEEP

Sleep behavior is coordinated through the central nervous system (CNS) and can be measured via polysomnogram (PSG) recordings, comprising electroencephalogram, electromyogram, and electrooculogram—which measure brain activity, muscle tone, and eye movements, respectively. Respiration, heart rate, and body temperature are also often measured. Through PSG, one can assess measures of sleep continuity, including total sleep time, sleep latency, and sleep

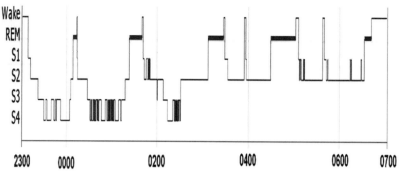

Fig. 1. The progression of sleep stages across a single night in a healthy male adult, with clock time represented on the horizontal axis, 11 p.m. (2300) to 7 a.m. (0700). REM = rapid eye movement sleep; S1–S4 represent sleep stages one through four. The figure demonstrates the repeated cycling of sleep stages through the course of a night's sleep.

efficiency. Sleep latency is defined as the amount of time it takes to fall asleep, and sleep efficiency is the percentage of total sleep time divided by total time in bed. PSG also measures sleep architecture by characterizing sleep stages one through four, which make up non-rapid-eye-movement (NREM) sleep, and rapid-eye-movement (REM) sleep. Stages three and four are also termed slow-wave sleep and are the deepest sleep. In contrast, during REM sleep, brain activity appears similar to the waking state and is characterized by periodic eye movements and partial muscle paralysis. Healthy humans enter NREM sleep from wakefulness and transition to REM sleep. The sleeping person cycles through these stages repeatedly through the night as shown in Figure 1.

OVERVIEW OF THE IMMUNE SYSTEM

The immune system exerts a broad repertoire of defenses against external challenge and abnormal internal cells (i.e., tumors) and can be divided into nonspecific and specific branches. Nonspecific immunity involves innate, generalized responses to pathogens, whereas specific immunity refers to acquired, specialized responses. Nonspecific immune cells such as natural killer cells kill virally infected cells without needing prior exposure to the virus. In contrast, T and B cells, the primary effector cells of specific immunity, typically require activation to attack a specific target; they attack by secreting antibodies (B cell) or by killing cells of the body that harbor a virus (T cell).

Cytokines are signaling molecules that coordinate these nonspecific and specific immune responses. There are numerous cytokines, and some are involved in cross-talk between the immune system and the brain, which ultimately regulates the course of immune response via the release of neuroendocrine substances and through autonomic signaling. The CNS also launches integrated behavioral responses to fight infection. Collectively termed *sickness behaviors*, these changes include decreased appetite, social withdrawal, fever, increased fatigue, and changes in sleep. Sickness behaviors are an adaptive response to infection that occur across numerous species (Kelley et al., 2003).

Cytokines, most notably interleukin-1 (IL-1), tumor necrosis factor (TNF), and IL-6, are involved in sleep–wake regulation (Opp, 2005), and these same cytokines also stimulate inflammatory responses. Elevated circulating levels of these molecules promote atherosclerotic plaque development by initiating a cascade of proinflammatory processes including activating immune cells, and stimulating recruitment and infiltration of these cells to sites of sclerotic plaque (Libby, 2002). In certain auto-immune inflammatory disorders such as rheumatoid arthritis, these same cytokines play a major role in increasing inflammation and exacerbating pain and tenderness in the joints.

DIURNAL VARIATION OF IMMUNE SYSTEM FUNCTIONING: ROLE OF SLEEP

The immune system shows a dynamic variation over the course of a normal sleep–wake cycle due to a combination of circadian and sleep-related factors. Immune cells peak early at night and then progressively decrease to a nadir in the morning, likely due to increased adhesion to blood vessel walls and/or migration into lymphoid tissue (Redwine, Dang, & Irwin, 2004). Circulating levels of cytokines such as IL-1, IL-6, and TNF reach peak levels during the nocturnal period (Born, Lange, Hansen, Molle, & Fehm, 1997; Redwine, Hauger, Gillin, & Irwin, 2000). These immunologic changes are similar to those of growth hormone, whose levels peak close in time to sleep onset at night, but are in contrast with those of the hormone cortisol whose levels are at their nadir before sleep and peak between 7 and 9 a.m.

Why these dynamic variations in the immune system occur is subject to debate. It is conceivable that the quiescent period of sleep serves to reallocate energy resources from functions related to wakefulness to processes that, for example, facilitate and promote immune responses to latent infectious challenge. With the nocturnal movement of immune cells out of the circulatory system and possibly into the lymph nodes, naive T and B cells get their first exposure to foreign antigens and an adaptive immune response is initiated. Such responses that involve immune-cell division and differentiation require metabolic resources, and this need can be supported efficiently during sleep. Extended periods of wakefulness have dramatic consequences on the body's ability to resist the challenge of pathogens.

SLEEP DEPRIVATION: EFFECTS ON IMMUNITY

In animals that undergo prolonged sleep deprivation, a progressive infiltration and growth of lethal bacteria from the gastrointestinal tract into normally aseptic organs occurs. Despite these encroachments, the immune system of a sleep-deprived animal is unable to mount an appropriate response, ultimately resulting in the animal's death within 3 weeks (Everson & Toth, 2000). In humans, viral response studies show that even brief periods of sleep deprivation can affect immunity. Four hours of sleep per night for 4 nights before inoculation with influenza virus produced poorer antibody response as compared to subjects who had regular sleep across the same period (Spiegel, Sheridan, & Van Cauter, 2002). Even brief sleep deprivation (4–8 hours) is associated with robust declines in natural-killer-cell activity (Irwin et al., 1996), although extended sleep deprivation is associated with increased activity (Dinges et al., 1994). These functional immune responses are coordinated by cytokines, which are also affected by sleep. Experimental sleep deprivation is associated with subsequent increases in circulating levels of IL-6 and TNF, and these increases may be particularly pronounced in sleep-impaired populations (Irwin et al., 2004).

IMPAIRED SLEEP AND IMMUNITY IN CLINICAL POPULATIONS

In order to examine the clinical importance of sleep–cytokine interactions, scientists have studied vulnerable populations with sleep impairments and/or altered immunity. The health consequences of sleep–cytokine dysregulation may be most relevant for these individuals (as schematically illustrated in Fig. 2). Studies with sleep-disordered populations, such as those with insomnia, major depression, and alcohol dependence have been consistent with findings from experimental sleep-deprivation studies.

Chronic primary insomnia is characterized by poor sleep continuity with resulting impairment in daytime functioning, and it is not driven by the presence of an underlying current psychiatric or medical disorder. Immunologically, patients with such insomnia have impaired natural-killer-cell activity (Irwin, Clark, Kennedy, Gillen, & Ziegler, 2003), similar to the changes induced by partial sleep deprivation, and elevated levels of IL-6 both during the day and at night, which correlate with poorer self-reported sleep quality. Large-scale studies suggest that sleep complaints (similar to insomnia) predict cardiovascular disease, raising the possibility that increases of inflammatory cytokine activity in insomnia may be a relevant mechanism.

Sleep difficulties are highly prevalent in major depression, with as many as 90% of patients reporting sleep complaints that typically involve difficulty falling asleep,

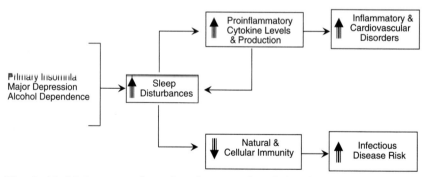

Fig. 2. Model depicting relationships between clinical disorders, sleep disturbance, immunity, and health outcomes. This model is not intended to be comprehensive but, instead, to illustrate possible immunologic pathways linking sleep impairments to health outcomes. Sleep loss can lead to increased expression of proinflammatory cytokines and, conversely, in clinical studies, nighttime levels of inflammatory cytokines are associated with poorer sleep. Increased proinflammatory cytokine levels may lead to inflammatory and cardiovascular disorders; and by lowering immunity, impaired sleep increases the risk for infectious disease.

frequent waking during the night, and early morning waking. In addition, depressed individuals have decreased natural-killer-cell activity, as well as elevated circulating levels of IL-6 (Motivala, Sarfatti, Olmos, & Irwin, 2005). In depressed patients, lower natural-killer-cell activity correlates with greater severity of insomnia symptoms, lower total sleep time, and poorer sleep continuity (Irwin, Lacher, & Caldwell, 1992). Furthermore, higher levels of nocturnal plasma IL-6 is a better predictor of longer sleep latency time than depression status (Motivala et al., 2005). These findings suggest that sleep-related inflammatory mechanisms may be important in explaining the increased risk of cardiovascular disease seen in depressed patients.

Lastly, alcohol-dependent patients have marked loss of slow-wave sleep and poor sleep continuity even during abstinence (from weeks to months), suggesting that these impairments are not solely driven by acute alcohol consumption. In addition, insomnia is considered a risk factor for relapse in this population. Alcoholic subjects have lower natural-killer-cell activity and higher nocturnal circulating levels of inflammatory cytokines as compared to controls (Redwine, Dang, Hall, & Irwin, 2003; Fig. 2). One night of partial sleep deprivation is associated with increased IL-6 and TNF levels in alcoholics, suggesting that disturbances in homeostatic sleep processes may mediate increases of proinflammatory cytokines in these patients (Irwin et al., 2004). Diminished natural-killer-cell activity and/or abnormal cytokine expression in alcoholics are thought to contribute to increased susceptibility to infectious diseases, including an increase in the incidence of tuberculosis, hepatitis C, and possibly HIV infection, although the clinical significance of the magnitude of immune alterations is not known (Redwine et al., 2003).

These clinical findings are part of a broader body of research showing that experimental sleep loss and poor sleep have an impact on the immune system. However, it would be simplistic to assume that sleep–immune interactions are unidirectional. Sleep processes affect cytokine expression, but cytokine expression can also modulate sleep, as described in the following section.

EFFECTS OF INFECTION AND CYTOKINES ON SLEEP

There is a large body of research demonstrating that administration of infectious agents can modulate sleep via inflammatory cytokine expression (Opp, 2005). In experimental studies, the effects of administration of an infectious agent can vary, depending on the dose administered, the timing of the administration, and the aspect of sleep examined (architecture, continuity). When an infectious agent such as lipopolysaccharide (LPS), a molecular fragment from the cell wall of bacteria such as salmonella or E. coli, is injected into mice or rabbits, it initially increases and then decreases NREM sleep and decreases REM sleep. In humans, LPS injection can fragment sleep, evidenced by longer awake times through the night (Mullington et al., 2000). Rhinovirus (i.e., the cause of the common cold) administration also fragments sleep in humans, decreasing sleep efficiency by 5% and decreasing total sleep time (Bryant et al., 2004).

The mechanism by which infectious agents affect sleep is likely via cytokine expression. Both animal and human studies have shown that administration of cytokine into the CNS directly affects sleep and that the nature of the effects depends on the cytokine administered and its dose and timing (Opp, 2005). In animals, administration of inflammatory cytokines produces changes in sleep that are similar to those found with administration of infectious agents—namely, increased NREM sleep and decreased REM sleep. In addition, IL-6 administration promotes sleep fragmentation in animals. In humans, naturalistic studies indicate that higher circulating IL-6 prior to sleep onset—but not later at night—correlates with poorer sleep latency, corroborating animal studies suggesting that IL-6 might mediate disturbances in sleep continuity (Irwin et al., 2004). IL-6 administration in humans impairs slow wave sleep in the first half of the night and results in greater fatigue during the day (Spath-Schwalbe et al., 1998).

CYTOKINE–SLEEP RELATIONSHIPS IN PATIENTS WITH INFLAMMATORY DISORDERS

In diseases characterized by increased inflammatory cytokine expression, sleep disturbances and insomnia are prominent. For example, in rheumatoid arthritis, elevations of IL-1, TNF, and IL-6 are implicated in promoting inflammation, joint pain, and destruction of cartilage and bone. Current treatment includes medications that specifically block the effects of these cytokines. In conjunction with overexpression of inflammatory cytokines, over 50% of these patients also report chronic difficulties sleeping that persist through periods of disease/pain quiescence. Even when pain is successfully treated by nonsteroidal anti-inflammatory drugs, which do not alter the central behavioral (e.g., sleep) effects of cytokines, PSG sleep fragmentation persists. No study to date has examined the impact of cytokine antagonists on cytokine levels and sleep, but one recent study showed that administration of a TNF antagonist improved sleep efficiency and total sleep time. These effects on sleep were unrelated to joint pain, which did not change over the course of the experimental trial (Zamarron, Maceiras, Mera, & Gomez-Reino, 2004). Unfortunately, cytokines were not measured, nor was it a double blind study, but these data do suggest that cytokine antagonist administration studies offer a promising paradigm to study relationships between cytokines and sleep. Overall, administration studies of infectious agents, cytokines, and cytokine antagonists show that cytokines modulate aspects of sleep architecture and continuity.

FUTURE DIRECTIONS FOR SLEEP AND IMMUNITY RESEARCH

Recent work is documenting bidirectional relationships between sleep and cytokines, and the clinical implications of these relationships are only now being explored. Perhaps the most fruitful findings will be obtained by continuing to study clinical populations with poor sleep and dysregulated inflammatory processes (e.g., patients with rheumatoid arthritis). Administration of inflammatory cytokine antagonists would test whether sleep improves and whether this improvement is associated with subsequent lessening of disease severity. Conversely, behavioral trials with sleep-impaired patients, such as those with insomnia, could test whether treatment-related improvements in sleep reduce levels of inflammatory cytokines such as TNF and IL-6. Such studies would not only test the underlying mechanisms regulating sleep and immunity but also would offer novel approaches to treating poor sleep, with implications for health in such vulnerable persons.

Recommended Reading

Bryant, P.A., Trinder, J., & Curtis, N. (2004). (See References)

Irwin, M. (2002). Effects of sleep and sleep loss on immunity and cytokines. *Brain, Behavior and Immunity, 16*, 503–512.

Opp, M.R. (2005). (See References)

Watkins, L.R., & Maier, S.F. (1999). Implications of immune-to-brain communication for sickness and pain. *Proceedings of the National Academy of Sciences, U.S.A., 96*, 7710–7713.

Acknowledgments—This work was supported in part by Grants AA13239, MH55253, T32-MH18399, AG18367, AT00255, AR/AG41867, and National Institutes of Health Grant M01 RR00827.

Note

1. Address correspondence to Sarosh J. Motivala, Cousins Center for Psychoneuroimmunology, UCLA Semel Institute for Neuroscience and Human Behavior, 300 UCLA Medical Plaza, Room 3153, Los Angeles, CA 90095; e-mail: smotivala@mednet.ucla.edu.

References

Born, J., Lange, T., Hansen, K., Molle, M., & Fehm, H.L. (1997). Effects of sleep and circadian rhythm on human circulating immune cells. *Journal of Immunology, 158*, 4454–4464.

Bryant, P.A., Trinder, J., & Curtis, N. (2004). Sick and tired: Does sleep have a vital role in the immune system? *Nature Reviews Immunology, 4*, 457–467.

Dinges, D.F., Douglas, S.D., Zaugg, L., Campbell, D.E., McMann, J.M., Whitehouse, W.G., Orne, E.C., Kapoor, S.C., Icaza, E., & Orne, M.T. (1994). Leukocytosis and natural killer cell function parallel neurobehavioral fatigue induced by 64 hours of sleep deprivation. *Journal of Clinical Investigation, 93*, 1930–1939.

Everson, C.A., & Toth, L.A. (2000). Systemic bacterial invasion induced by sleep deprivation. *American Journal of Physiology–Regulatory, Integrative and Comparative Physiology, 278*, R905–R916.

Irwin, M., Clark, C., Kennedy, B., Gillin, J.C., & Ziegler, M. (2003). Nocturnal catecholamines and immune function in insomniacs, depressed patients, and control subjects. *Brain, Behavior, and Immunity, 17*, 365–372.

Irwin, M., Lacher, U., & Caldwell, C. (1992). Depression and reduced natural killer cytotoxicity: A longitudinal study of depressed patients and control subjects. *Psychological Medicine, 22*, 1045–1050.

Irwin, M., McClintick, J., Costlow, C., Fortner, M., White, J., & Gillin, J.C. (1996). Partial night sleep deprivation reduces natural killer and cellular immune responses in humans. *Federation of American Societies for Experimental Biology Journal, 10*, 643–653.

Irwin, M., Rinetti, G., Redwine, L., Motivala, S., Dang, J., & Ehlers, C. (2004). Nocturnal proinflammatory cytokine-associated sleep disturbances in abstinent African American alcoholics. *Brain, Behavior, and Immunity, 18*, 349–360.

Kelley, K.W., Bluthe, R.-M., Dantzer, R., Zhou, J.-H., Shen, W.-H., Johnson, R.W., & Broussard, S.R. (2003). Cytokine-induced sickness behavior. *Brain, Behavior, and Immunity, 17*(Suppl. 1), 112.

Libby, P. (2002). Inflammation in atherosclerosis. *Nature, 420*, 868–874.

Motivala, S.J., Sarfatti, A., Olmos, L., & Irwin, M.R. (2005). Inflammatory markers and sleep disturbance in major depression. *Psychosomatic Medicine, 67*, 187–194.

Mullington, J., Korth, C., Hermann, D.M., Orth, A., Galanos, C., Holsboer, F., & Pollmächer, T. (2000). Dose-dependent effects of endotoxin on human sleep. *American Journal of Physiology–Regulatory, Integrative and Comparative Physiology, 278*, R947–R955.

Opp, M.R. (2005). Cytokines and sleep. *Sleep Medicine Review, 9*, 355–364.

Redwine, L., Dang, J., Hall, M., & Irwin, M. (2003). Disordered sleep, nocturnal cytokines, and immunity in alcoholics. *Psychosomatic Medicine, 65*, 75–85.

Redwine, L., Dang, J., & Irwin, M. (2004). Cellular adhesion molecule expression, nocturnal sleep, and partial night sleep deprivation. *Brain, Behavior, and Immunity, 18*, 333–340.

Redwine, L., Hauger, R.L., Gillin, J.C., & Irwin, M. (2000). Effects of sleep and sleep deprivation on interleukin-6, growth hormone, cortisol, and melatonin levels in humans. *Journal of Clinical Endocrinology and Metabolism, 85*, 3597–3603.

Spath-Schwalbe, E., Hansen, K., Schmidt, F., Schrezenmeier, H., Marshall, L., Burger, K., Fehm, H.L., & Born, J. (1998). Acute effects of recombinant human interleukin-6 on endocrine and central nervous sleep functions in healthy men. *Journal of Clinical Endocrinology and Metabolism, 83*, 1573–1579.

Spiegel, K., Sheridan, J.F., & Van Cauter, E. (2002). Effect of sleep deprivation on response to immunization. *JAMA: The Journal of the American Medical Association, 288*, 1471–1472.

Zamarron, C., Maceiras, F., Mera, A., & Gomez-Reino, J.J. (2004). Effect of the first infliximab infusion on sleep and alertness in patients with active rheumatoid arthritis. *Annals of Rheumatic Disorders, 63*, 88–90.

Section 5: Critical Thinking Questions

1. Most elementary school children have streptococcus bacteria in their mouths and throats, but only a few develop strep throat. Based on the article by Ader, what accounts for such individual differences in susceptibility to disease? Koch's third postulate of the "germ theory" of disease stated that the cultured microorganism should cause disease when introduced into a healthy organism. Does the germ theory of disease need to be modified in view of psychoneuroimmunology?

2. Before pathogens were identified as the causes of infectious diseases, associations between disease and behavioral, psychosocial, and societal risk factors were known. Discuss the associations among psychosocial, behavioral, and behavioral risk factors in heart disease and cancer. Discuss the value of such correlations if pathogens are identified that ultimately cause cancer or heart disease.

3. Based on the article by Miller and Blackwell, would you predict that individuals who take anti-inflammatory drugs would display more, less, or the same rate of depression? Discuss your answer in relation to pro-inflammatory cytokines and their role in aggression.

4. Some new sleep medications work by stimulating melatonin receptors. Given what you read in the Nelson and Demas article about the effects of melatonin on immune function, what sorts of potential side-effects would you predict? How would you design an experiment to dissect the effects of host versus the effects of pathogen in seasonal changes in disease?

5. Based on the Motivala and Irwin article, do you suspect that a mutation would be observed in mice or humans that prevented sleep? Why or why not? If poor sleep leads to increased cytokine production, and a bidirectional relationship exists between sleep and immunity, then what would you predict sleep architecture would resemble in mutant mice lacking interleukin (IL) 1β, IL6, and tumor necrosis factor (TNF)?

This article has been reprinted as it originally appeared in *Current Directions in Psychological Science*. Citation information for this article as originally published appears above.